PATHFINDERS OF THE WEST

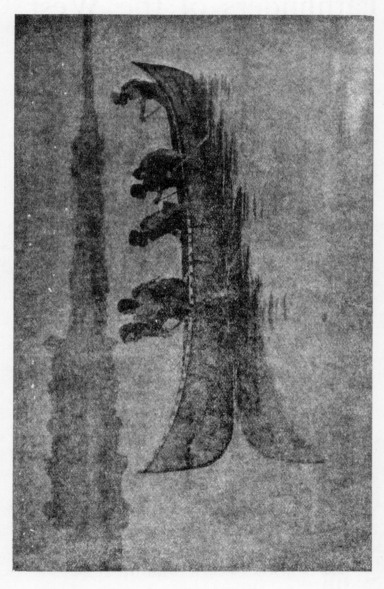

Frontispiece.

Stealing from the Fort by Night.

Pathfinders of the West

BEING

*THE THRILLING STORY OF THE ADVENTURES
OF THE MEN WHO DISCOVERED
THE GREAT NORTHWEST*

RADISSON, LA VÉRENDRYE, LEWIS
AND CLARK

BY

AGNES CHRISTINA LAUT

*ILLUSTRATIONS BY
REMINGTON, GOODWIN, MARCHAND
AND OTHERS*

Essay Index Reprint Series

BOOKS FOR LIBRARIES PRESS
FREEPORT, NEW YORK

First Published 1904
Reprinted 1969

STANDARD BOOK NUMBER:
8369-1220-9

LIBRARY OF CONGRESS CATALOG CARD NUMBER:
74-90651

PRINTED IN THE UNITED STATES OF AMERICA

WILDWOOD PLACE, WASSAIC, N.Y.
August 15, 1904.

DEAR MR. SULTE:

A few years ago, when I was a resident of the Far West and tried to trace the paths of early explorers, I found that all authorities — first, second, and third rate — alike referred to one source of information for their facts. The name in the tell-tale footnote was invariably your own.

While I assume *all* responsibility for upsetting the apple cart of established opinions by this book, will you permit me to dedicate it to you as a slight token of esteem to the greatest living French-Canadian historian, from whom we have all borrowed and to whom few of us have rendered the tribute due?

Faithfully,

AGNES C. LAUT.

MR. BENJAMIN SULTE,
PRESIDENT ROYAL SOCIETY,
OTTAWA, CANADA.

THE GREAT NORTHWEST

I love thee, O thou great, wild, rugged land
Of fenceless field and snowy mountain height,
Uprearing crests all starry-diademed
Above the silver clouds ! A sea of light
Swims o'er thy prairies, shimmering to the sight
A rolling world of glossy yellow wheat
That runs before the wind in billows bright
As waves beneath the beat of unseen feet,
And ripples far as eye can see — as far and fleet !

Here's chances for every man ! The hands that work
Become the hands that rule ! Thy harvests yield
Only to him who toils ; and hands that shirk
Must empty go ! And here the hands that wield
The sceptre work ! O glorious golden field !
O bounteous, plenteous land of poet's dream !
O'er thy broad plain the cloudless sun ne'er wheeled
But some dull heart was brightened by its gleam
To seize on hope and realize life's highest dream !

Thy roaring tempests sweep from out the north —
Ten thousand cohorts on the wind's wild mane —
No hand can check thy frost-steeds bursting forth
To gambol madly on the storm-swept plain !
Thy hissing snow-drifts wreathe their serpent train,
With stormy laughter shrieks the joy of might —
Or lifts, or falls, or wails upon the wane —

Thy tempests sweep their stormy trail of white
Across the deepening drifts — and man must die, or fight!

Yes, man must sink or fight, be strong or die!
That is thy law, O great, free, strenuous West!
The weak thou wilt make strong till he defy
Thy buffetings ; but spacious prairie breast
Will never nourish weakling as its guest!
He must grow strong or die!   Thou givest all
An equal chance — to work, to do their best —
Free land, free hand — thy son must work or fall
Grow strong or die!   That message shrieks the storm-wind's
    call!

And so I love thee, great, free, rugged land
Of cloudless summer days, with west-wind croon,
And prairie flowers all dewy-diademed,
And twilights long, with blood-red, low-hung moon
And mountain peaks that glisten white each noon
Through purple haze that veils the western sky —
And well I know the meadow-lark's far rune
As up and down he lilts and circles high
And sings sheer joy — be strong, be free ; be strong or die!

Foreword

THE question will at once occur why no mention is made of Marquette and Jolliet and La Salle in a work on the pathfinders of the West. The simple answer is — they were *not* pathfinders. Contrary to the notions imbibed at school, and repeated in all histories of the West, Marquette, Jolliet, and La Salle did *not* discover the vast region beyond the Great Lakes. Twelve years before these explorers had thought of visiting the land which the French hunter designated as the *Pays d'en Haut*, the West had already been discovered by the most intrepid *voyageurs* that France produced, — men whose wide-ranging explorations exceeded the achievements of Cartier and Champlain and La Salle put together.

It naturally rouses resentment to find that names revered for more than two centuries as the first explorers of the Great Northwest must give place to a name almost unknown. It seems impossible that at this late date history should have to be rewritten. Such is the fact *if we would have our history true.* Not Marquette, Jolliet, and La Salle discovered the West, but two poor adventurers, who sacrificed all earthly possessions to the enthusiasm for discovery,

and incurred such bitter hostility from the governments of France and England that their names have
been hounded to infamy.   These were Sieur Pierre
Esprit Radisson and Sieur Médard Chouart Groseillers, fur traders of Three Rivers, Quebec.[1]

The explanation of the long oblivion obscuring the
fame of these two men is very simple.   Radisson and
Groseillers defied, first New France, then Old France,
and lastly England.   While on friendly terms with
the church, they did not make their explorations sub-
servient to the propagation of the faith.   In consequence, they were ignored by both Church and State.
The *Jesuit Relations* repeatedly refer to two young
Frenchmen who went beyond Lake Michigan to a
" Forked River " (the Mississippi), among the Sioux
and other Indian tribes that used coal for fire because
wood did not grow large enough on the prairie.   Contemporaneous documents mention the exploits of the
young Frenchmen.   The State Papers of the Marine
Department, Paris, contain numerous references to
Radisson and Groseillers.   But, then, the *Jesuit Relations* were not accessible to scholars, let alone the
general public, until the middle of the last century,
when a limited edition was reprinted of the Cramoisy
copies published at the time the priests sent their
letters home to France.   The contemporaneous writ-

___

[1] I of course refer to the West as *beyond* the Great Lakes ; for Nicolet, in 1634,
and two nameless Frenchmen — servants of Jean de Lauzon — in 1654, had been
beyond the Sault.

ings of Marie de l'Incarnation, the Abbé Belmont, and Dollier de Casson were not known outside the circle of French savants until still later; and it is only within recent years that the Archives of Paris have been searched for historical data. Meantime, the historians of France and England, animated by the hostility of their respective governments, either slurred over the discoveries of Radisson and Groseillers entirely, or blackened their memories without the slightest regard to truth. It would, in fact, take a large volume to contradict and disprove half the lies written of these two men. Instead of consulting contemporaneous documents, — which would have entailed both cost and labor, — modern writers have, unfortunately, been satisfied to serve up a rehash of the detractions written by the old historians. In 1885 came a discovery that punished such slovenly methods by practically wiping out the work of the pseudo-historians. There was found in the British Museum, the Bodleian Library, and Hudson's Bay House, London, unmistakably authentic record of Radisson's voyages, written by himself. The Prince Society of Boston printed two hundred and fifty copies of the collected journals. The Canadian Archives published the journals of the two last voyages. Francis Parkman was too conscientious to ignore the importance of the find; but his history of the West was already written. He made what reparation he could to Radisson's memory by appending a footnote to subsequent edi-

tions of two of his books, stating that Radisson and
Groseillers' travels took them to the "Forked River"
before 1660. Some ten other lines are all that Mr.
Parkman relates of Radisson; and the data for these
brief references have evidently been drawn from Radisson's enemies, for the explorer is called "a renegade." It is necessary to state this, because some
writers, whose zeal for criticism was much greater
than their qualifications, wanted to know why any one
should attempt to write Radisson's life when Parkman
had already done so.

Radisson's life reads more like a second Robinson
Crusoe than sober history. For that reason I have
put the corroborative evidence in footnotes, rather
than cumber the movement of the main theme. I
am sorry to have loaded the opening parts with so
many notes; but Radisson's voyages change the relative positions of the other explorers so radically that
proofs must be given. The footnotes are for the
student and may be omitted by the general reader.
The study of Radisson arose from using his later
exploits on Hudson Bay as the subject of the novel,
Heralds of Empire. On the publication of that book,
several letters came from the Western states asking how far I thought Radisson had gone beyond
Lake Superior before he went to Hudson Bay.
Having in mind — I am sorry to say — mainly the
early records of Radisson's enemies, I at first answered that I thought it very difficult to identify the

discoverer's itinerary beyond the Great Lakes. So
many letters continued to come on the subject that
I began to investigate contemporaneous documents.
The path followed by the explorer west of the Great
Lakes — as given by Radisson himself — is here written. Full corroboration of all that Radisson relates
is to be found — as already stated — in chronicles
written at the period of his life and in the State
Papers. Copies of these I have in my possession.
Samples of the papers bearing on Radisson's times,
copied from the Marine Archives, will be found in
the Appendix. One must either accept the explorer's
word as conclusive, — even when he relates his own
trickery, — or in rejecting his journal also reject as
fictions the *Jesuit Relations*, the *Marine Archives*,
Dollier de Casson, *Marie de l'Incarnation*, and the
Abbé Belmont, which record the same events as Radisson. In no case has reliance been placed on second-
hand chronicles. Oldmixon and Charlevoix must
both have written from hearsay; therefore, though
quoted in the footnotes, they are not given as conclusive proof. The only means of identifying Radisson's
routes are (1) by his descriptions of the countries,
(2) his notes of the Indian tribes; so that personal
knowledge of the territory is absolutely essential in
following Radisson's narrative. All the regions traversed by Radisson — the Ottawa, the St. Lawrence,
the Great Lakes, Labrador, and the Great Northwest
— I have visited, some of them many times, except

the shores of Hudson Bay, and of that region I have some hundreds of photographs.

Material for the accounts of the other pathfinders of the West has been drawn directly from the different explorers' journals.

For historical matter I wish to express my indebtedness to Dr. N. E. Dionne of the Parliamentary Library, Quebec, whose splendid sketch of Radisson and Groseillers, read before the Royal Society of Canada, does much to redeem the memory of the discoverers from ignominy ; to Dr. George Bryce of Winnipeg, whose investigation of Hudson's Bay Archives adds a new chapter to Radisson's life ; to Mr. Benjamin Sulte of Ottawa, whose destructive criticism of inaccuracies in old and modern records has done so much to stop people writing history out of their heads and to put research on an honest basis ; and to M. Edouard Richard for scholarly advice relating to the Marine Archives, which he has exploited so thoroughly. For transcripts and archives now out of print, thanks are due Mr. L. P. Sylvain of the Parliamentary Library, Ottawa, the officials of the Archives Department, Ottawa, Mr. F. C. Wurtele of Quebec, Professor Andrew Baird of Winnipeg, Mr. Alfred Matthews of the Prince Society, Boston, the Hon. Jacob V. Brower and Mr. Warren Upham of St. Paul. Mr. Lawrence J. Burpee of Ottawa was so good as to give me a reading of his exhaustive notes on La Vérendrye and of data found on the Radisson

FOREWORD xv

family. To Mrs. Fred Paget of Ottawa, the daughter
of a Hudson's Bay Company officer, and to Mr. and
Mrs. C. C. Farr of the Northern Ottawa, I am indebted for interesting facts on life in the fur posts.
Miss Talbot of Winnipeg obtained from retired officers
of the Hudson's Bay Company a most complete set
of photographs relating to the fur trade. To her
and to those officers who loaned old heirlooms to be
photographed, I beg to express my cordial appreciation. And the thanks of all who write on the North
are permanently due Mr. C. C. Chipman, Chief Commissioner of the Hudson's Bay Company, for unfail-
ing courtesy in extending information.

Wildwood Place,
Wassaic, N.Y.

Just as this volume was going to the printer, I received a copy of the very valuable
Minnesota *Memoir*, Vol. VI, compiled by the Hon. J. V. Brower of St. Paul,
to whom my thanks are due for this excellent contribution to Western annals. It may
be said that the authors of this volume have done more than any other writers to vindi-
cate Radisson and Groseillers as explorers of the West. The very differences of opinion
over the regions visited establish the fact that Radisson *did* explore parts of Minnesota.
I have purposely avoided trying to say *what* parts of Minnesota he exploited, because,
it seems to me, the controversy is futile. Radisson's memory has been the subject of
controversy from the time of his life. The controversy — first between the governments of France and England, subsequently between the French and English historians
— has eclipsed the real achievements of Radisson. To me it seems non-essential as to
whether Radisson camped on an island in the Mississippi, or only visited the region
of that island. The fact remains that he discovered the Great Northwest, meaning by
that the region west of the Mississippi. The same dispute has obscured his explorations
of Hudson Bay, French writers maintaining that he went overland to the North
and put his feet in the waters of the bay, the English writers insisting that he only
crossed over the watershed toward Hudson Bay. Again, the fact remains that he did

what others had failed to do — discovered an overland route to the bay. I am sorry
that Radisson is accused in this *Memoir* of intentionally falsifying his relations in two
respects ; (1) in adding a fanciful year to the 1658–1660 voyage ; (2) in saying that
he had voyaged down the Mississippi to Mexico.   (1) Internal evidence plainly shows
that Radisson's first four voyages were written twenty years afterward, when he was in
London, and not while on the voyage across the Atlantic with Cartwright, the Boston
commissioner.   It is the most natural thing in the world that Radisson, who had so
often been to the wilds, should have mixed his dates.   Every slip as to dates is so easily
checked by contemporaneous records — which, themselves, need to be checked — that
it seems too bad to accuse Radisson of wilfully lying in the matter.   When Radisson
lied it was to avoid bloodshed, and not to exalt himself.   If he had had glorification of
self in mind, he would not have set down his own faults so unblushingly ; for instance,
where he deceives M. Colbert of Paris.   (2) Radisson does not try to give the impression that he went to Mexico.   The sense of the context is that he met an Indian tribe
— Illinois, Mandans, Omahas, or some other — who lived next to another tribe who
told *of* the Spaniards.   I feel almost sure that the scholarly Mr. Benjamin Sulte is
right in his letter to me when he suggests that Radisson's manuscript has been mixed
by transposition of pages or paragraphs, rather than that Radisson himself was confused
in his account.   At the same time every one of the contributors to the Minnesota
Memoir deserves the thanks of all who love *true* history.

ADDENDUM

Since the above foreword was written, the contents of this volume have appeared
serially in four New York magazines.   The context of the book was slightly abridged
in these articles, so that a very vital distinction — namely, the difference between what
is given as in dispute, and what is given as incontrovertible fact — was lost ; but what
was my amusement to receive letters from all parts of the West all but challenging me to
a duel.   One wants to know " how a reputable author dare " suggest that Radisson's
voyages be taken as authentic.   There is no " dare " about it.   It is a fact.   For any
" reputable " historian to suggest — as two recently have — that Radisson's voyages are
a fabrication, is to stamp that historian as a pretender who has not investigated a single
record contemporaneous with Radisson's life.   One cannot consult documents contemporaneous with his life and not learn instantly that he was a very live fact of the most
troublesome kind the governments of France and England ever had to accept.   That
is why it impresses me as a presumption that is almost comical for any modern writer to
condescend to say that he "accepts" or "rejects" this or that part of Radisson's
record.   If he " rejects " Radisson, he also rejects the *Marine Archives* of Paris, and
the *Jesuit Relations*, which are the recognized sources of our early history.

Another correspondent furiously denounces Radisson as a liar because he mixes his dates of the 1660 trip. It would be just as reasonable to call La Salle a liar because there are discrepancies in the dates of his exploits, as to call Radisson a liar for the slips in his dates. When the mistakes can be checked from internal evidence, one is hardly justified in charging falsification.

A third correspondent is troubled by the reference to the Mascoutin Indians being *beyond* the Mississippi. State documents establish this fact. I am not responsible for it ; and Radisson could not circle west-northwest from the Mascoutins to the great encampments of the Sioux without going far west of the Mississippi. Even if the Jesuits make a slip in referring to the Sioux's use of some kind of coal for fire because there was no wood on the prairie, and really mean turf or buffalo refuse, — which I have seen the Sioux use for fire, — the fact is that only the tribes far west of the Mississippi habitually used such substitutes for wood.

My Wisconsin correspondents I have offended by saying that Radisson went beyond the Wisconsin ; my Minnesota friends, by saying that he went beyond Minnesota ; and my Manitoba co-workers of past days, by suggesting that he ever went beyond Manitoba. The fact remains that when we try to identify Radisson's voyages, we must take his own account of his journeyings ; and that account establishes him as the Discoverer of the Northwest.

For those who know, I surely do not need to state that there is no picture of Radisson extant ; and that some of the studies of his life are just as genuine (?) as alleged old prints of his likeness.

CONTENTS

PART ONE

PIERRE ESPRIT RADISSON

ADVENTURES OF THE FIRST WHITE MAN TO EXPLORE THE
WEST, THE NORTHWEST, AND THE NORTH

CHAPTER I

RADISSON'S FIRST VOYAGE

PAGE

The Boy Radisson is captured by the Iroquois and carried to
the Mohawk Valley — In League with Another Captive,
he slays their Guards and escapes — He is overtaken in
Sight of Home — Tortured and adopted in the Tribe,
he visits Orange, where the Dutch offer to ransom him —
His Escape   3

CHAPTER II

RADISSON'S SECOND VOYAGE

Radisson returns to Quebec, where he joins the Jesuits to go to
the Iroquois Mission — He witnesses the Massacre of the
Hurons among the Thousand Islands — Besieged by the
Iroquois, they pass the Winter as Prisoners of War —
Conspiracy to massacre the French foiled by Radisson .   43

CONTENTS

CHAPTER III

RADISSON'S THIRD VOYAGE

PAGE

The Discovery of the Great Northwest — Radisson and his
Brother-in-law, Groseillers, visit what are now Wisconsin,
Minnesota, Dakota, and the Canadian Northwest — Radis-
son's Prophecy on first beholding the West — Twelve
Years before Marquette and Jolliet, Radisson sees the
Mississippi — The Terrible Remains of Dollard's Fight
seen on the Way down the Ottawa — Why Radisson's
Explorations have been ignored   68

CHAPTER IV

RADISSON'S FOURTH VOYAGE

The Success of the Explorers arouses Envy — It becomes known
that they have heard of the Famous Sea of the North —
When they ask Permission to resume their Explorations,
the French Governor refuses except on Condition of
receiving Half the Profits — In Defiance, the Explorers
steal off at Midnight — They return with a Fortune and
are driven from New France   101

CHAPTER V

RADISSON RENOUNCES ALLEGIANCE TO TWO CROWNS

Rival Traders thwart the Plans of the Discoverers — Entangled
in Lawsuits, the Two French Explorers go to England —
The Organization of the Hudson's Bay Fur Company —
Radisson the Storm-centre of International Intrigue — Boston Merchants in the Struggle to capture the Fur Trade .   132

CHAPTER VI

RADISSON GIVES UP A CAREER IN THE NAVY FOR THE FUR TRADE

PAGE

Though opposed by the Monopolists of Quebec, he secures Ships for a Voyage to Hudson Bay — Here he encounters a Pirate Ship from Boston and an English Ship of the Hudson's Bay Company — How he plays his Cards to win against Both Rivals 150

CHAPTER VII

THE LAST VOYAGE OF RADISSON TO HUDSON BAY

France refuses to restore the Confiscated Furs and Radisson tries to redeem his Fortune — Reëngaged by England, he captures back Fort Nelson, but comes to Want in his Old Age — His Character 178

PART TWO

THE SEARCH FOR THE WESTERN SEA, BEING AN ACCOUNT OF THE DISCOVERY OF THE ROCKY MOUNTAINS, THE MISSOURI UPLANDS, AND THE VALLEY OF THE SASKATCHEWAN

CHAPTER VIII

THE SEARCH FOR THE WESTERN SEA

M. de la Vérendrye continues the Exploration of the Great Northwest by establishing a Chain of Fur Posts across the Continent — Privations of the Explorers and the Massacre of Twenty Followers — His Sons visit the Mandans and discover the Rockies — The Valley of the Saskatchewan is next explored, but Jealousy thwarts the Explorer, and he dies in Poverty 193

PART THREE

SEARCH FOR THE NORTHWEST PASSAGE LEADS SAMUEL HEARNE
TO THE ARCTIC CIRCLE AND ATHABASCA REGION

CHAPTER IX
SAMUEL HEARNE

PAGE

The Adventures of Hearne in his Search for the Coppermine
River and Northwest Passage — Hilarious Life of Wassail
led by Governor Norton — The Massacre of the Eskimo by
Hearne's Indians North of the Arctic Circle — Discovery
of the Athabasca Country — Hearne becomes Resident
Governor of the Hudson's Bay Company, but is captured by
the French — Death of Norton and Suicide of Matonabbee   241

PART FOUR

FIRST ACROSS THE ROCKIES — HOW MACKENZIE CROSSED THE
NORTHERN ROCKIES AND LEWIS AND CLARK WERE FIRST
TO CROSS FROM MISSOURI TO COLUMBIA

CHAPTER X
FIRST ACROSS THE ROCKIES

How Mackenzie found the Great River named after him and
then pushed across the Mountains to the Pacific, forever
settling the Question of a Northwest Passage   .   .   275

CHAPTER XI
LEWIS AND CLARK

The First White Men to ascend the Missouri to its Sources and
descend the Columbia to the Pacific — Exciting Adventures
on the Cañons of the Missouri, the Discovery of the Great
Falls and the Yellowstone — Lewis' Escape from Hostiles   307

APPENDIX   335

INDEX   369

ILLUSTRATIONS

Stealing from the Fort by Night . . . . *Frontispiece*

PAGE

Map of the Great Fur Country . . . *Facing* 1
Three Rivers in 1757 5
Map of the Iroquois Country in the Days of Radisson . . 14
Albany from an Old Print 32
The Battery, New York, in Radisson's Time . . . 37
Fort Amsterdam, from an ancient engraving executed in Holland 41
One of the Earliest Maps of the Great Lakes . *Facing* 43
Paddling past Hostiles 50
Jogues, the Jesuit Missionary, who was tortured by the Mohawks 56
Château de Ramezay, Montreal 61
A Cree Brave, with the Wampum String . . . 70
An Old-time Buffalo Hunt on the Plains among the Sioux *Facing* 81
Father Marquette, from an old painting discovered in Montreal 83
Voyageurs running the Rapids of the Ottawa River . . 95
Montreal in 1760 . . . . . . *Facing* 101
Château St. Louis, Quebec, 1669 108
A Parley on the Plains . . . . . *Facing* 120
Martello Tower of Refuge in Time of Indian Wars — Three
    Rivers 134
Skin for Skin, Coat of Arms and Motto, Hudson's Bay Company 151
Hudson's Bay Company Coins, made of Lead melted from Tea-
    chests at York Factory 163
Hudson Bay Dog Trains laden with Furs arriving at Lower
    Fort Garry, Red River 187

PAGE

Indians and Hunters spurring to the Fight   .   .   *Facing* 194
Fights at the Foothills of the Rockies, between Crows and
    Snakes . . . .   *Facing* 196
Each Man landed with Pack on his Back and trotted away over
    Portages 199
A Cree Indian of the Minnesota Borderlands   .   .   . 200
A Group of Cree Indians   207
The Soldiers marched out from Mount Royal for the Western
    Sea . . . .   *Facing* 212
Traders' Boats running the Rapids of the Athabasca River   . 217
The Ragged Sky-line of the Mountains   220
Hungry Hall, 1870 223
A Monarch of the Plains   228
Fur Traders towed down the Saskatchewan in the Summer of
    1900 231
Tepees dotted the Valley 236
An Eskimo Belle 242
Samuel Hearne 248
Eskimo using Double-bladed Paddle   250
Eskimo Family, taken by Light of Midnight Sun .   *Facing* 258
Fort Garry, Winnipeg, a Century Ago   262
Plan of Fort Prince of Wales, from Robson's drawing, 1733–
    1747 266
Fort Prince of Wales 270
Beaver Coin of the Hudson's Bay Company   .   .   . 271
Alexander Mackenzie 276
Eskimo trading his Pipe, carved from Walrus Tusk, for the
    Value of Three Beaver Skins   278
Quill and Beadwork on Buckskin   281
Fort William, Headquarters Northwest Company, Lake Superior 283
Running a Rapid on Mackenzie River   .   .   *Facing* 286
Slave Lake Indians 290
Good Hope, Mackenzie River, Hudson's Bay Company Fort . 301

ILLUSTRATIONS

	PAGE
The Mouth of the Mackenzie by the Light of the Midnight Sun	306
Captain Meriwether Lewis	309
Captain William Clark	310
Tracking up Stream	314
Typical Mountain Trapper	316
The Discovery of the Great Falls . . . *Facing*	317
Fighting a Grizzly . . . . . . *Facing*	319
Packer carrying Goods across Portage	320
Spying on Enemy's Fort	322
Indian Camp at Foothills of Rockies	324
On Guard . . . . *Facing*	328
Indians of the Up-country or Pays d'en Haut . . .	330

PART I

PIERRE ESPRIT RADISSON

ADVENTURES OF THE FIRST WHITE MAN TO
EXPLORE THE WEST, THE NORTHWEST, AND
THE NORTH

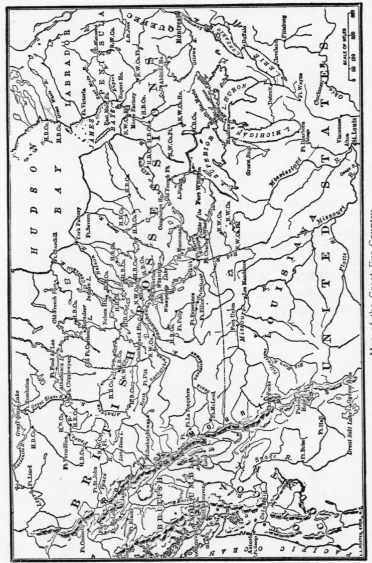

Map of the Great Fur Country.

Pathfinders of the West

CHAPTER I

1651–1653

RADISSON'S FIRST VOYAGE

The Boy Radisson is captured by the Iroquois and carried to the Mohawk Valley — In League with Another Captive, he slays their Guards and escapes — He is overtaken in Sight of Home — Tortured and adopted in the Tribe, he visits Orange, where the Dutch offer to ransom him — His Escape

EARLY one morning in the spring of 1652 three young men left the little stockaded fort of Three Rivers, on the north bank of the St. Lawrence, for a day's hunting in the marshes of Lake St. Peter. On one side were the forested hills, purple with the mists of rising vapor and still streaked with white patches of snow where the dense woods shut out the sunlight. On the other lay the silver expanse of the St. Lawrence, more like a lake than a river, with mile on mile southwestward of rush-grown marshes, where plover and curlew and duck and wild geese flocked to their favorite feeding-grounds three hundred years ago just

3

as they do to-day.   Northeastward, the three mouths of the St. Maurice poured their spring flood into the St. Lawrence.

The hunters were very young.   Only hunters rash with the courage of untried youth would have left the shelter of the fort walls when all the world knew that the Iroquois had been lying in ambush round the little settlement of Three Rivers day and night for the preceding year.   Not a week passed but some settler working on the outskirts of Three Rivers was set upon and left dead in his fields by marauding Iroquois. The tortures suffered by Jogues, the great Jesuit missionary who had been captured by the Iroquois a few years before, were still fresh in the memory of every man, woman, and child in New France.   It was from Three Rivers that Piescaret, the famous Algonquin chief who could outrun a deer, had set out against the Iroquois, turning his snowshoes back to front, so that the track seemed to lead north when he was really going south, and then, having thrown his pursuers off the trail, coming back on his own footsteps, slipping up stealthily on the Iroquois that were following the false scent, and tomahawking the laggards.[1]   It was from Three Rivers that the Mohawks had captured the Algonquin girl who escaped by slipping off the thongs that bound her.   Stepping over the prostrate

[1] Benjamin Sulte in *Chronique Trifluvienne.*

forms of her sleeping guards, such a fury of revenge possessed her that she seized an axe and brained the nearest sleeper, then eluded her pursuers by first hiding in a hollow tree and afterward diving under the débris of a beaver dam.

These things were known to every inhabitant of Three Rivers. Farmers had flocked into the little

Three Rivers in 1757.

fort and could venture back to their fields only when armed with a musket.[1] Yet the three young hunters rashly left the shelter of the fort walls and took the

---

[1] It was in August of this same year, 1652, that the governor of Three Rivers was slain by the Iroquois. Parkman gives this date, 1653; Garneau, 1651; L'Abbé Tanguay, 1651; Dollier de Casson, 1651; Belmont, 1653. Sulte gives the name of the governor Duplessis-Kerbodot, not Bochart, as given in Parkman.

very dangerous path that led between the forests and the water. One of the young men was barely in his seventeenth year.[1] This was Pierre Esprit Radisson, from St. Malo, the town of the famous Cartier. Young Radisson had only come to New France the year before, and therefore could not realize the dangers of Indian warfare. Like boys the world over, the three went along, boasting how they would fight if the Indians came. One skirted the forest, on the watch for Iroquois, the others kept to the water, on the look-out for game. About a mile from Three Rivers they encountered a herdsman who warned them to keep out from the foot of the hills. Things that looked like a multitude of heads had risen out of the earth back there, he said, pointing to the forests. That set the young hunters loading their pistols and priming muskets. It must also have chilled their zest; for, shooting some ducks, one of the young men presently declared that he had had enough — he was going back. With that daring which was to prove both the lodestar and the curse of his life, young

[1] Dr. Bryce has unearthed the fact that in a petition to the House of Commons, 1698, Radisson sets down his age as sixty-two. This gives the year of his birth as 1636. On the other hand, Sulte has record of a Pierre Radisson registered at Quebec in 1681, aged fifty-one, which would make him slightly older, if it is the same Radisson. Mr. Sulte's explanation is as follows : Sébastien Hayet of St. Malo married Madeline Hénault. Their daughter Marguerite married Chouart, known as Groseillers. Madeline Hénault then married Pierre Esprit Radisson of Paris, whose children were Pierre, our hero, and two daughters.

Radisson laughed to scorn the sudden change of mind. Thereupon the first hunter was joined by the second, and the two went off in high dudgeon. With a laugh, Pierre Radisson marched along alone, foreshadowing his after life, — a type of every pathfinder facing the dangers of the unknown with dauntless scorn, an immortal type of the world-hero.

Shooting at every pace and hilarious over his luck, Radisson had wandered some nine miles from the fort, when he came to a stream too deep to ford and realized that he already had more game than he could possibly carry. Hiding in hollow trees what he could not bring back, he began trudging toward Three Rivers with a string of geese, ducks, and odd teal over his shoulders. Wading swollen brooks and scrambling over windfalls, he retraced his way without pause till he caught sight of the town chapel glimmering in the sunlight against the darkening horizon above the river. He was almost back where his comrades had left him; so he sat down to rest. The cowherd had driven his cattle back to Three Rivers.[1] The river came lapping through the rushes. There was a clacking of wild-fowl flocking down to

[1] A despatch from M. Talon in 1666 shows there were 461 families in Three Rivers. State papers from the Minister to M. Frontenac in 1674 show there were only 6705 French in all the colony. Averaging five a family, there must have been 2000 people at Three Rivers. Fear of the Iroquois must have driven the country people inside the fort, so that the population enrolled was larger than the real population of Three Rivers. Sulte gives the normal population of Three Rivers in 1654 as 38 married couples, 13 bachelors, 38 boys, 26 girls — in all not 200.

their marsh nests; perhaps a crane flopped through
the reeds; but Radisson, who had laughed the ner-
vous fears of the others to scorn, suddenly gave a
start at the lonely sounds of twilight. Then he
noticed that his pistols were water-soaked. Emptying the charges, he at once reloaded, and with characteristic daring crept softly back to reconnoitre the
woods. Dodging from tree to tree, he peered up
and down the river. Great flocks of ducks were
swimming on the water. That reassured him, for
the bird is more alert to alarm than man. The fort
was almost within call. Radisson determined to have
a shot at such easy quarry; but as he crept through
the grass toward the game, he almost stumbled over
what rooted him to the spot with horror. Just as
they had fallen, naked and scalped, with bullet and
hatchet wounds all over their bodies, lay his comrades
of the morning, dead among the rushes. Radisson
was too far out to get back to the woods. Stooping,
he tried to grope to the hiding of the rushes. As
he bent, half a hundred heads rose from the grasses,
peering which way he might go. They were behind,
before, on all sides — his only hope was a dash for
the cane-grown river, where he might hide by diving
and wading, till darkness gave a chance for a rush to
the fort. Slipping bullet and shot in his musket as
he ran, and ramming down the paper, hoping against

hope that he had not been seen, he dashed through the brushwood. A score of guns crashed from the forest.[1] Before he realized the penalty that the Iroquois might exact for such an act, he had fired back ; but they were upon him. He was thrown down and disarmed. When he came giddily to his senses, he found himself being dragged back to the woods, where the Iroquois flaunted the fresh scalps of his dead friends. Half drawn, half driven, he was taken to the shore. Here, a flotilla of canoes lay concealed where he had been hunting wild-fowl but a few hours before. Fires were kindled, and the crotched sticks driven in the ground to boil the kettle for the evening meal. The young Frenchman was searched, stripped, and tied round the waist with a rope, the Indians yelling and howling like so many wolves all the while till a pause was given their jubilation by the alarm of a scout that the French and Algonquins were coming. In a trice, the fire was out and covered. A score of young braves set off to reconnoitre. Fifty remained at the boats ; but if Radisson hoped for a rescue, he was doomed to disappointment. The warriors returned. Seventy Iroquois gathered round a second fire for the night. The one predominating pas-

---

[1] At first flush, this seems a slip in *Radisson's Relation*. Where did the Mohawks get their guns ? *New York Colonial Documents* show that between 1640 and 1650 the Dutch at Fort Orange had supplied the Mohawks alone with four hundred guns.

sion of the savage nature is bravery. Lying in
ambush, they had heard this French youth laugh
at his comrades' fears. In defiance of danger, they
had seen him go hunting alone. After he had heard
an alarm, he had daringly come out to shoot at the
ducks. And, then, boy as he was, when attacked
he had instantly fired back at numerous enough
enemies to have intimidated a score of grown men.
There is not the slightest doubt it was Radisson's
bravery that now saved him from the fate of his
companions.

His clothes were returned. While the evening meal
was boiling, young warriors dressed and combed the
Frenchman's hair after the manner of braves. They
daubed his cheeks with war-paint; and when they
saw that their rancid meats turned him faint, they
boiled meat in clean water and gave him meal
browned on burning sand.[1] He did not struggle
to escape, so he was now untied. That night he
slept between two warriors under a common blanket,
through which he counted the stars. For fifty years
his home was to be under the stars. It is typically
Radisson when he could add : " I slept a sound

---

[1] One of many instances of Radisson's accuracy in detail. All tribes have a
trick of browning food on hot stones or sand that has been taken from fire. The
Assiniboines gained their name from this practice : they were the users of " boiling
stones."

sleep; for they wakened me upon the breaking of the day." In the morning they embarked in thirty-seven canoes, two Indians in each boat, with Radisson tied to the cross-bar of one, the scalps lying at his feet. Spreading out on the river, they beat their paddles on the gunwales of the canoes, shot off guns, and uttered the shrill war-cry — " Ah-oh ! Ah-oh ! Ah-oh !" [1] Lest this were not sufficient defiance to the penned-up fort on the river bank, the chief stood up in his canoe, signalled silence, and gave three shouts. At once the whole company answered till the hills rang; and out swung the fleet of canoes with more shouting and singing and firing of guns, each paddle-stroke sounding the death knell to the young Frenchman's hopes.

By sunset they were among the islands at the mouth of the Richelieu, where muskrats scuttled through the rushes and wild-fowl clouded the air. The south shore of Lake St. Peter was heavily forested; the north, shallow. The lake was flooded with spring thaw, and the Mohawks could scarcely find camping-ground among the islands. The young prisoner was deathly sick from the rank food that he

---

[1] I have asked both natives and old fur-traders what combination of sounds in English most closely resembles the Indian war-cry, and they have all given the words that I have quoted. One daughter of a chief factor, who went through a six weeks' siege by hostiles in her father's fort, gave a still more graphic description. She said : " If you can imagine the snarls of a pack of furiously vicious dogs saying ' ah-oh ' with a whoop, you have it ; and you will not forget it ! "

had eaten and heart-sick from the widening distance
between himself and Three Rivers. Still, they treated
him kindly, saying, "Chagon! Chagon!—Be merry!
Cheer up!" The fourth day up the Richelieu, he was
embarked without being fastened to the cross-bar, and
he was given a paddle. Fresh to the work, Radisson
made a labor of his oar. The Iroquois took the
paddle and taught him how to give the light, deft,
feather strokes of the Indian canoeman. On the
river they met another band of warriors, and the
prisoner was compelled to show himself a trophy
of victory and to sing songs for his captors. That
evening the united bands kindled an enormous camp-
fire and with the scalps of the dead flaunting from
spear heads danced the scalp dance, reënacting in
pantomime all the episodes of the massacre to the
monotonous chant-chant of a recitative relating the
foray. At the next camping-ground, Radisson's hair
was shaved in front and decorated on top with the
war-crest of a brave. Having translated the white
man into a savage, they brought him one of the tin
looking-glasses used by Indians to signal in the sun.
"I, viewing myself all in a pickle," relates Radisson,
"smeared with red and black, covered with such a
top, . . . could not but fall in love with myself, if
I had not had better instructions to shun the sin of
pride."

Radisson saw that apparent compliance with the Mohawks might win him a chance to escape; so he was the first to arise in the morning, wakening the others and urging them that it was time to break camp. The stolid Indians were not to be moved by an audacious white boy. Watching the young prisoner, the keepers lay still, feigning sleep. Radisson rose. They made no protest. He wandered casually down to the water side. One can guess that the half-closed eyelids of his guards opened a trifle: was the mouse trying to get away from the cat? To the Indians' amusement, instead of trying to escape, Radisson picked up a spear and practised tossing it, till a Mohawk became so interested that he jumped up and taught the young Frenchman the proper throws. That day the Indians gave him the present of a hunting-knife. North of Lake Champlain, the river became so turbulent that they were forced to land and make a *portage*. Instead of lagging, as captives frequently did from very fear as they approached nearer and nearer what was almost certain to mean death-torture in the Iroquois villages — Radisson hurried over the rocks, helping the older warriors to carry their packs. At night he was the first to cut wood for the camp fire.

About a week from the time they had left Lake St. Peter, they entered Lake Champlain. On the shores of the former had been enacted the most hideous of all Indian customs — the scalp dance. On the shores of the latter was performed one of the most redeeming rites of Indian warfare. Round a small pool of water a coppice of branches was interlaced. Into the water were thrown hot stones till the enclosure was steaming. Here each warrior took a sweat-bath of purification to prepare for reunion with his family. Invoking the spirits as they

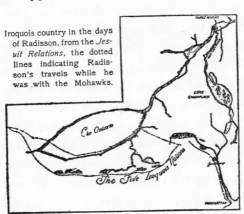

Iroquois country in the days of Radisson, from the *Jesuit Relations*, the dotted lines indicating Radisson's travels while he was with the Mohawks.

bathed, the warriors emerged washed — as they thought — of all blood-guilt.[1]

In the night shots sounded through the heavy silence of the forest, and the Mohawks embarked in alarm, compelling their white prisoner to lie flat in the bottom of the canoe. In the morning when he awak-

[1] This practice was a binding law on many tribes. Catlin relates it of the Mandans, and Hearne of the Chipewyans. The latter considered it a crime to kiss wives and children after a massacre without the bath of purification. Could one know where and when that universal custom of washing blood-guilt arose, one mystery of existence would be unlocked.

ened, he found the entire band hidden among the
rushes of the lake.   They spent several days on Lake
Champlain, then glided past wooded mountains down
a calm river to Lake George, where canoes were abandoned and the warriors struck westward through dense
forests to the country of the Iroquois.   Two days from
the lake slave women met the returning braves, and
in Radisson's words, " loaded themselves like mules
with baggage."   On this woodland march Radisson
won golden opinions for himself by two acts : struck
by an insolent young brave, he thrashed the culprit
soundly ; seeing an old man staggering under too
heavy a load, the white youth took the burden on his
own shoulders.

The return of the warriors to their villages was always
celebrated as a triumph.   The tribe marched out to
meet them, singing, firing guns, shouting a welcome,
dancing as the Israelites danced of old when victors
returned from battle.   Men, women, and children lined
up on each side armed with clubs and whips to scourge
the captives.   Well for Radisson that he had won the
warriors' favor ; for when the time came for him to
run the gantlet of Iroquois *diableries*, instead of being
slowly led, with trussed arms and shackled feet, he was
stripped free and signalled to run so fast that his tormentors could not hit him.   Shrieks of laughter from
the women, shouts of applause from the men, always

greeted the racer who reached the end of the line un-scathed. A captive Huron woman, who had been adopted by the tribe, caught the white boy as he dashed free of a single blow clear through the lines of tormentors. Leading him to her cabin, she fed and clothed him. Presently a band of braves marched up, demanded the surrender of Radisson, and took him to the Council Lodge of the Iroquois for judgment.

Old men sat solemnly round a central fire, smoking their calumets in silence. Radisson was ordered to sit down. A coal of fire was put in the bowl of the great Council Pipe and passed reverently round the assemblage. Then the old Huron woman entered, gesticulating and pleading for the youth's life. The men smoked on silently with deep, guttural "ho-ho's," meaning "yes, yes, we are pleased." The woman was granted permission to adopt Radisson as a son. Radisson had won his end. Diplomacy and courage had saved his life. It now remained to await an opportunity for escape.

Radisson bent all his energies to become a great hunter. He was given firearms, and daily hunted with the family of his adoption. It so happened that the family had lost a son in the wars, whose name had signified the same as Radisson's — that is, "a stone"; so the Pierre of Three Rivers became the Orimha of the Mohawks. The Iroquois husband of the woman who had befriended him gave such a feast to the Mohawk braves as befitted the prestige of a warrior who had slain nineteen enemies with his own hand. Three hundred young Mohawks sat down to a collation of moose nose and beaver tails and bears' paws, served by slaves. To this banquet Radisson was led, decked out in colored blankets with garnished leggings and such a wealth of wampum strings hanging from wrists, neck, hair, and waist that he could scarcely walk. Wampum means more to the Indian than money to the white man. It represents not only wealth but social standing, and its value may be compared to the white man's estimate of pink pearls. Diamond-cutters seldom spend more than two weeks in polishing a good stone. An Indian would spend thirty days in perfecting a single bit of shell into fine wampum. Radisson's friends had ornamented him for the feast in order to win the respect of the Mohawks for the French boy. Striking his hatchet through a kettle of sagamite to signify thus would he break peace to all Radisson's foes, the old Iroquois warrior made a speech to the assembled guests. The guests clapped their hands and shouted, " Chagon, Orimha!—Be merry, Pierre!" The Frenchman had been formally adopted as a Mohawk.

The forests were now painted in all the glories of autumn. All the creatures of the woodlands shook off

c

the drowsy laziness of summer and came down from
the uplands seeking haunts for winter retreat.   Moose
and deer were on the move.   Beaver came splashing
down-stream to plaster up their wattled homes before
frost.   Bear and lynx and marten, all were restless as
the autumn winds instinct with coming storm.   This
is the season when the Indian sets out to hunt and
fight.   Furnished with clothing, food, and firearms,
Radisson left the Mohawk Valley with three hunters.
By the middle of August, the rind of the birch is in
perfect condition for peeling.   The first thing the
hunters did was to slit off the bark of a thick-girthed
birch and with cedar linings make themselves a skiff.
Then they prepared to lay up a store of meat for the
winter's war-raids.   Before ice forms a skim across the
still pools, nibbled chips betray where a beaver colony
is at work ; so the hunters began setting beaver traps.
One night as they were returning to their wigwam,
there came through the leafy darkness the weird sound
of a man singing.   It was a solitary Algonquin captive,
who called out that he had been on the track of a
bear since daybreak.   He probably belonged to some
well-known Iroquois, for he was welcomed to the
camp-fire.   The sight of a face from Three Rivers
roused the Algonquin's memories of his northern
home.   In the noise of the crackling fire, he succeeded
in telling Radisson, without being overheard by the

Iroquois, that he had been a captive for two years and longed to escape.

"Do you love the French?" the Algonquin asked Radisson.

"Do you love the Algonquin?" returned Radisson, knowing they were watched.

"As I do my own nation." Then leaning across to Radisson, "Brother — white man! — Let us escape! The Three Rivers — it is not far off! Will you live like a Huron in bondage, or have your liberty with the French?" Then, lowering his voice, "Let us kill all three this night when they are asleep!"

From such a way of escape, the French youth held back. The Algonquin continued to urge him. By this time, Radisson must have heard from returning Iroquois warriors that they had slain the governor of Three Rivers, Duplessis-Kerbodot, and eleven other Frenchmen, among whom was the husband of Radisson's eldest sister, Marguerite.[1]

While Radisson was still hesitating, the suspicious Iroquois demanded what so much whispering was about; but the alert Algonquin promptly quieted their fears by trumping up some hunting story.

[1] I have throughout followed Mr. Sulte's correction of the name of this governor. The mistake followed by Parkman, Tanguay, and others — it seems — was first made in 1820, and has been faithfully copied since. Elsewhere will be found Mr. Sulte's complete elucidation of the hopeless dark in which all writers have involved Radisson's family.

Wearied from their day's hunt, the three Mohawks slept heavily round the camp-fire. They had not the least suspicion of danger, for they had stacked their arms carelessly against the trees of the forest. Terrified lest the Algonquin should attempt to carry out his threat, Radisson pretended to be asleep. Rising noiselessly, the Algonquin sat down by the fire. The Mohawks slept on. The Algonquin gave Radisson a push. The French boy looked up to see the Algonquin studying the postures of the sleeping forms. The dying fire glimmered like a blotch of blood under the trees. Stepping stealthy as a cat over the sleeping men, the Indian took possession of their firearms. Drawn by a kind of horror, Radisson had risen. The Algonquin thrust one of the tomahawks into the French lad's hands and pointed without a word at the three sleeping Mohawks. Then the Indian began the black work. The Mohawk nearest the fire never knew that he had been struck, and died without a sound. Radisson tried to imitate the relentless Algonquin, but, unnerved with horror, he bungled the blow and lost hold of the hatchet just as it struck the Mohawk's head. The Iroquois sprang up with a shout that awakened the third man, but the Algonquin was ready. Radisson's blow proved fatal. The victim reeled back dead, and the third man was already despatched by the Algonquin.

Radisson was free.   It was a black deed that freed him, but not half so black as the deeds perpetrated in civilized wars for less cause ; and for that deed Radisson was to pay swift retribution.

Taking the scalps as trophies to attest his word, the Algonquin threw the bodies into the river.   He seized all the belongings of the dead men but one gun and then launched out with Radisson on the river.   The French youth was conscience-stricken.   " I was sorry to have been in such an encounter," he writes, " but it was too late to repent."   Under cover of the night mist and shore foliage, they slipped away with the current. At first dawn streak, while the mist still hid them, they landed, carried their canoe to a sequestered spot in the dense forest, and lay hidden under the upturned skiff all that day, tormented by swarms of mosquitoes and flies, but not daring to move from concealment. At nightfall, they again launched down-stream, keeping always in the shadows of the shore till mist and darkness shrouded them, then sheering off for mid-current, where they paddled for dear life.   Where camp-fires glimmered on the banks, they glided past with motionless paddles.   Across Lake Champlain, across the Richelieu, over long *portages* where every shadow took the shape of an ambushed Iroquois, for fourteen nights they travelled, when at last with many windings and false alarms they swept out on the wide surface of Lake St. Peter in the St. Lawrence.

Within a day's journey of Three Rivers, they were really in greater danger than they had been in the forests of Lake Champlain. Iroquois had infested that part of the St. Lawrence for more than a year. The forest of the south shore, the rush-grown marshes, the wooded islands, all afforded impenetrable hiding. It was four in the morning when they reached Lake St. Peter. Concealing their canoe, they withdrew to the woods, cooked their breakfast, covered the fire, and lay down to sleep. In a couple of hours the Algonquin impatiently wakened Radisson and urged him to cross the lake to the north shore on the Three Rivers side. Radisson warned the Indian that the Iroquois were ever lurking about Three Rivers. The Indian would not wait till sunset. " Let us go," he said. " We are past fear. Let us shake off the yoke of these whelps that have killed so many French and black robes (priests). . . . If you come not now that we are so near, I leave you, and will tell the governor you were afraid to come."

Radisson's judgment was overruled by the impatient Indian. They pushed their skiff out from the rushes. The water lay calm as a sea of silver. They paddled directly across to get into hiding on the north shore. Halfway across Radisson, who was at the bow, called out that he saw shadows on the water ahead. The Indian stood up and declared that the shadow was the reflection of a flying bird. Barely had they gone a boat length when the shadows multiplied. They were the reflections of Iroquois ambushed among the rushes. Heading the canoe back for the south shore, they raced for their lives. The Iroquois pursued in their own boats. About a mile from the shore, the strength of the fugitives fagged. Knowing that the Iroquois were gaining fast, Radisson threw out the loathsome scalps that the Algonquin had persisted in carrying. By that strange fatality which seems to follow crime, instead of sinking, the hairy scalps floated on the surface of the water back to the pursuing Iroquois. Shouts of rage broke from the warriors. Radisson's skiff was so near the south shore that he could see the pebbled bottom of the lake; but the water was too deep to wade and too clear for a dive, and there was no driftwood to afford hiding. Then a crash of musketry from the Iroquois knocked the bottom out of the canoe. The Algonquin fell dead with two bullet wounds in his head and the canoe gradually filled, settled, and sank, with the young Frenchman clinging to the cross-bar mute as stone. Just as it disappeared under water, Radisson was seized, and the dead Algonquin was thrown into the Mohawk boats.

Radisson alone remained to pay the penalty of a

double crime; and he might well have prayed for the boat to sink. The victors shouted their triumph. Hurrying ashore, they kindled a great fire. They tore the heart from the dead Algonquin, transfixed the head on a pike, and cast the mutilated body into the flames for those cannibal rites in which savages thought they gained courage by eating the flesh of their enemies. Radisson was rifled of clothes and arms, trussed at the elbows, roped round the waist, and driven with blows back to the canoes. There were other captives among the Mohawks. As the canoes emerged from the islands, Radisson counted one hundred and fifty Iroquois warriors, with two French captives, one white woman, and seventeen Hurons. Flaunting from the canoe prows were the scalps of eleven Algonquins. The victors fired off their muskets and shouted defiance until the valley rang. As the seventy-five canoes turned up the Richelieu River for the country of the Iroquois, hope died in the captive Hurons and there mingled with the chant of the Mohawks' war-songs, the low monotonous dirge of the prisoners: —

> " If I die, I die valiant !
> I go without fear
> To that land where brave men
> Have gone long before me —
> If I die, I die valiant.''

Twelve miles up the Richelieu, the Iroquois landed to

camp. The prisoners were pegged out on the sand, elbows trussed to knees, each captive tied to a post. In this fashion they lay every night of encampment, tortured by sand-flies that they were powerless to drive off. At the entrance to the Mohawk village, a yoke was fastened to the captives' necks by placing pairs of saplings one on each side down the line of prisoners. By the rope round the waist of the foremost prisoner, they were led slowly between the lines of tormentors. The captives were ordered to sing. If one refused or showed fear, a Mohawk struck off a finger with a hatchet, or tore the prisoners' nails out, or thrust red-hot irons into the muscles of the bound arms.[1] As Radisson appeared, he was recognized with shouts of rage by the friends of the murdered Mohawks. Men, women, and children armed with rods and skull-crackers — leather bags loaded with stones — rushed on the slowly moving file of prisoners.

"They began to cry from both sides," says Radisson ; "we marching one after another, environed with

---

[1] If there were not corroborative testimony, one might suspect the excited French lad of gross exaggeration in his account of Iroquois tortures ; but the Jesuits more than confirm the worst that Radisson relates.   Bad as these torments were, they were equalled by the deeds of white troops from civilized cities in the nineteenth century. A band of Montana scouts came on the body of a comrade horribly mutilated by the Indians.   They caught the culprits a few days afterwards.   Though the government report has no account of what happpened, traders say the bodies of the guilty Indians were found skinned and scalped by the white troops.

people to witness that hideous sight, which seriously may be called the image of Hell in this world."

The prisoners moved mournfully on. The Hurons chanted their death dirge. The Mohawk women uttered screams of mockery. Suddenly there broke from the throng of onlookers the Iroquois family that had adopted Radisson. Pushing through the crew of torturers, the mother caught Radisson by the hair, calling him by the name of her dead son, " Orimha ! Orimha ! " She cut the thongs that bound him to the poles, and wresting him free shoved him to her husband, who led Radisson to their own lodge.

" Thou fool," cried the old chief, " thou wast my son ! Thou makest thyself an enemy ! Thou lovest us not, though we saved thy life ! Wouldst kill me, too ? " Then, with a rough push to a mat on the ground, " Chagon — now, be merry ! It's a merry business you've got into ! Give him something to eat ! "

Trembling with fear, young Radisson put as bold a face on as he could and made a show of eating what the squaw placed before him. He was still relating his adventures when there came a roar of anger from the Mohawks outside, who had discovered his absence from the line. A moment later the rabble broke into the lodge. Jostling the friendly chief aside, the Mohawk warriors carried Radisson back to the orgies of the torture. The prisoners had been taken out of the stocks and placed on several scaffoldings. One poor Frenchman fell to the ground bruised and unable to rise. The Iroquois tore the scalp from his head and threw him into the fire. That was Radisson's first glimpse of what was in store for him. Then he, too, stood on the scaffolding among the other prisoners, who never ceased singing their death song. In the midst of these horrors — *diableries*, the Jesuits called them — as if the very elements had been moved with pity, there burst over the darkened forest a terrific hurricane of hail and rain. This put out the fires and drove all the tormentors away but a few impish children, who stayed to pluck nails from the hands and feet of the captives and shoot arrows with barbed points at the naked bodies. Every iniquity that cruelty could invent, these children practised on the captives. Red-hot spears were brought from the lodge fires and thrust into the prisoners. The mutilated finger ends were ground between stones. Thongs were twisted round wrists and ankles, by sticks put through a loop, till flesh was cut to the bone. As the rain ceased falling, a woman, who was probably the wife of one of the murdered Mohawks, brought her little boy to cut one of Radisson's fingers with a flint stone. The child was too young and ran away from the gruesome task.

Gathering darkness fell over the horrible spectacle. The exhausted captives, some in a delirium from pain, others unconscious, were led to separate lodges, or dragged over the ground, and left tied for the night. The next morning all were returned to the scaffolds, but the first day had glutted the Iroquois appetite for tortures. The friendly family was permitted to approach Radisson. The mother brought him food and told him that the Council Lodge had decided not to kill him for that day — they wanted the young white warrior for their own ranks; but even as the cheering hope was uttered, came a brave with a pipe of live coals, in which he thrust and held Radisson's thumb. No sooner had the tormentor left than the woman bound up the burn and oiled Radisson's wounds. He suffered no abuse that day till night, when the soles of both feet were burned. The majority of the captives were flung into a great bonfire. On the third day of torture he almost lost his life. First came a child to gnaw at his fingers. Then a man appeared armed for the ghastly work of mutilation. Both these the Iroquois father of Radisson sent away. Once, when none of the friendly family happened to be near, Radisson was seized and bound for burning, but by chance the lighted faggot scorched his executioner. A friendly hand slashed the thongs that bound him, and he was drawn back to the scaffold.

Past caring whether he lived or died, and in too great agony from the burns of his feet to realize where he was going, Radisson was conducted to the Great Council. Sixty old men sat on a circle of mats, smoking, round the central fire. Before them stood seven other captives. Radisson only was still bound. A gust of wind from the opening lodge door cleared the smoke for an instant and there entered Radisson's Indian father, clad in the regalia of a mighty chief. Tomahawk and calumet and medicine-bag were in his hands. He took his place in the circle of councillors. Judgment was to be given on the remaining prisoners.

After passing the Council Pipe from hand to hand in solemn silence, the sachems prepared to give their views. One arose, and offering the smoke of incense to the four winds of heaven to invoke witness to the justice of the trial, gave his opinion on the matter of life or death. Each of the chiefs in succession spoke. Without any warning whatever, one chief rose and summarily tomahawked three of the captives. That had been the sentence. The rest were driven, like sheep for the shambles, to life-long slavery.

Radisson was left last. His case was important. He had sanctioned the murder of three Mohawks. Not for a moment since he was recaptured had they dared to untie the hands of so dangerous a prisoner. Amid deathly silence, the Iroquois father stood up.

Flinging down medicine-bag, fur robe, wampum belts, and tomahawk, he pointed to the nineteen scars upon his side, each of which signified an enemy slain by his own hand. Then the old Mohawk broke into one of those impassioned rhapsodies of eloquence which delighted the savage nature, calling back to each of the warriors recollection of victories for the Iroquois. His eyes took fire from memory of heroic battle. The councillors shook off their imperturbable gravity and shouted "Ho, ho!" Each man of them had a memory of his part in those past glories. And as they applauded, there glided into the wigwam the mother, singing some battle-song of valor, dancing and gesticulating round and round the lodge in dizzy, serpentine circlings, that illustrated in pantomime those battles of long ago. Gliding ghostily from the camp-fire to the outer dark, she suddenly stopped, stood erect, advanced a step, and with all her might threw one belt of priceless wampum at the councillors' feet, one necklace over the prisoner's head.

Before the applause could cease or the councillors' ardor cool, the adopted brother sprang up, hatchet in hand, and sang of other victories. Then, with a delicacy of etiquette which white pleaders do not always observe, father and son withdrew from the Council Lodge to let the jury deliberate. The old sachems were disturbed. They had been moved more than their w.ont. Twenty withdrew to confer. Dusk gathered deeper and deeper over the forests of the Mohawk Valley. Tawny faces came peering at the doors, waiting for the decision. Outsiders tore the skins from the walls of the lodge that they, too, might witness the memorable trial of the boy prisoner. Sachem after sachem rose and spoke. Tobacco was sacrificed to the fire-god. Would the relatives of the dead Mohawks consider the wampum belts full compensation? Could the Iroquois suffer a youth to live who had joined the murderers of the Mohawks? Could the Mohawks afford to offend the great Iroquois chief who was the French youth's friend? As they deliberated, the other councillors returned, accompanied by all the members of Radisson's friendly family. Again the father sang and spoke. This time when he finished, instead of sitting down, he caught the necklace of wampum from Radisson's neck, threw it at the feet of the oldest sachem, cut the captive's bonds, and, amid shouts of applause, set the white youth free.

One of the incomprehensible things to civilization is how a white man *can* degenerate to savagery. Young Radisson's life is an illustration. In the first transports of his freedom, with the Mohawk women dancing and singing around him, the men shouting, he

leaped up, oblivious of pain; but when the flush of
ecstasy had passed, he sank to the mat of the Iroquois
lodge, and he was unable to use his burned feet for more
than a month.   During this time the Iroquois dressed
his wounds, brought him the choice portions of the
hunt, gave him clean clothing purchased at Orange
(Albany), and attended to his wants as if he had been

Albany, from an Old Print.

a prince.   No doubt the bright eyes of the swarthy
young French boy moved to pity the hearts of the
Mohawk mothers, and his courage had won him favor
among the warriors.   He was treated like a king.
The women waited upon him like slaves, and the men
gave him presents of firearms and ammunition — the
Indian's most precious possessions.   Between flattered

vanity and indolence, other white men, similarly treated, have lost their self-respect. Beckworth, of the Missouri, became to all intents and purposes a savage; and Bird, of the Blackfeet, degenerated lower than the Indians. Other Frenchmen captured from the St. Lawrence, and white women taken from the New England colonies, became so enamored of savage life that they refused to leave the Indian lodges when peace had liberated them. Not so Radisson. Though only seventeen, flattered vanity never caused him to forget the gratitude he owed the Mohawk family. Though he relates his life with a frankness that leaves nothing untold, he never at any time returned treachery for kindness. The very chivalry of the French nature endangered him all the more. Would he forget his manhood, his birthright of a superior race, his inheritance of nobility from a family that stood foremost among the *noblesse* of New France?

The spring of 1653 came with unloosening of the rivers and stirring of the forest sap and fret of the warrior blood. Radisson's Iroquois father held great feasts in which he heaved up the hatchet to break the kettle of sagamite against all enemies. Would Radisson go on the war-path with the braves, or stay at home with the women and so lose the respect of the tribe? In the hope of coming again within reach of

Three Rivers, he offered to join the Iroquois in their
wars.   The Mohawks were delighted with his spirit,
but they feared to lose their young warrior.   Accepting his offer, they refused to let him accompany them
to Quebec, but assigned him to a band of young
braves, who were to raid the border-lands between the
Huron country of the Upper Lakes and the St. Lawrence.   This was not what Radisson wanted, but he
could not draw back.   There followed months of
wild wanderings round the regions of Niagara.   The
band of young braves passed dangerous places with
great precipices and a waterfall, where the river was a
mile wide and unfrozen.   Radisson was constrained
to witness many acts against the Eries, which must
have one of two effects on white blood, — either turn
the white man into a complete savage, or disgust him
utterly with savage life.   Leaving the Mohawk village
amid a blare of guns and shouts, the young braves on
their maiden venture passed successively through the
lodges of Oneidas, Onondagas, Senecas, and Cayugas,
where they were feasted almost to death by the Iroquois Confederacy.[1]   Then they marched to the vast
wilderness of snow-padded forests and heaped windfall
between Lake Ontario and Lake Erie.

Snow still lay in great drifts under the shadow of

[1] Radisson puts the Senecas before the Cayugas, which is different from the order
given by the Jesuits.

hemlock and spruce; and the braves skimmed forward winged with the noiseless speed of snow-shoes.
When the snow became too soft from thaw for snow-
shoes, they paused to build themselves a skiff.   It
was too early to peel the bark off the birch, so they
made themselves a dugout of the walnut tree.   The
wind changed from north to south, clearing the lakes
of ice and filling the air with the earthy smells of up-
bursting growth.   "There was such a thawing,"
writes Radisson, "ye little brookes flowed like rivers,
which made us embark to wander over that sweet sea."
Lounging in their skiff all day, carried from shore to
shore with the waves, and sleeping round camp-fires
on the sand each night, the young braves luxuriated
in all the delights of sunny idleness and spring life.
But this was not war.   It was play, and play of the
sort that weans the white man from civilization to
savagery.

One day a scout, who had climbed to the top of
a tree, espied two strange squaws.   They were of a
hostile tribe.   The Mohawk bloodthirst was up as a
wolf's at the sight of lambs.   In vain Radisson tried
to save the women by warning the Iroquois that if there
were women, there must be men, too, who would exact
vengeance for the squaws' death.   The young braves
only laid their plans the more carefully for his warning
and massacred the entire encampment.   Prisoners were

taken, but when food became scarce they were brutally knocked on the head. These tribes had never heard guns before, and at the sound of shots fled as from diabolical enemies. It was an easy matter for the young braves in the course of a few weeks to take a score of scalps and a dozen prisoners. At one place more than two hundred beaver were trapped. At the end of the raid, the booty was equally divided. Radisson asked that the woman prisoner be given to him; and he saved her from torture and death on the return to the Mohawks by presenting her as a slave to his Indian mother. All his other share of booty he gave to the friendly family. The raid was over. He had failed of his main object in joining it. He had not escaped. But he had made one important gain. His valor had reëstablished the confidence of the Indians so that when they went on a free-booting expedition against the whites of the Dutch settlements at Orange (Albany), Radisson was taken with them. Orange, or Albany, consisted at that time of some fifty thatched log-houses surrounded by a settlement of perhaps a hundred and fifty farmers. This raid was bloodless. The warriors looted the farmers' cabins, emptied their cupboards, and drank their beer cellars dry to the last drop. Once more Radisson kept his head. While the braves entered Fort Orange roaring drunk, Radisson was alert and sober. A drunk Indian falls an easy

prey in the bartering of pelts.   The Iroquois wanted
guns.   The Dutch wanted pelts.   The whites treated
the savages like kings; and the Mohawks marched
from house to house feasting of the best.   Radisson
was dressed in garnished buckskin and had been
painted like a Mohawk.   Suspecting some design to

The Battery, New York, in Radisson's Time.

escape, his Iroquois friends never left him.   The
young Frenchman now saw white men for the first
time in almost two years; but the speech that he
heard was in a strange tongue.   As Radisson went
into the fort, he noticed a soldier among the Dutch.
At the same instant the soldier recognized him as a
Frenchman, and oblivious of the Mohawks' presence

blurted out his discovery in Iroquois dialect, vowing that for all the paint and grease, this youth was a white man below.   The fellow's blundering might have cost Radisson's life; but the youth had not been a captive among crafty Mohawks for nothing.   Radisson feigned surprise at the accusation.   That quieted the Mohawk suspicions and they were presently deep in the beer pots of the Dutch.   Again the soldier spoke, this time in French.   It was the first time that Radisson had heard his native tongue for months.   He answered in French.   At that the soldier emitted shouts of ac'ight, for he, too, was French, and these strangers in an alien land threw their arms about each other like a pair of long-lost brothers with exclamations of joy too great for words.

From that moment Radisson became the lion of Fort Orange.   The women dragged him to their houses and forced more dainties on him than he could eat.   He was conducted from house to house in triumph, to the amazed delight of the Indians.   The Dutch offered to ransom him at any price; but that would have exposed the Dutch settlement to the resentment of the Mohawks and placed Radisson under heavy obligation to people who were the enemies of New France.   Besides, his honor was pledged to return to his Indian parents; and it was a long way home to have to sail to Europe and back again to

Quebec.   Perhaps, too, there was deep in his heart
what he did not realize — a rooted love for the wilds
that was to follow him all through life.   By the
devious course of captivity, he had tasted of a new
freedom and could not give it up.   He declined the
offer of the Dutch.   In two days he was back among
the Mohawks ten times more a hero than he had
ever been.   Mother and sisters were his slaves.

But between love of the wilds and love of bar-
barism is a wide difference.   He had not been back
for two weeks when that glimpse of crude civilization
at Orange recalled torturing memories of the French
home in Three Rivers.   The filthy food, the smoky
lodges, the cruelties of the Mohawks, filled him with
loathing.   The nature of the white man, which had
been hidden under the grease and paint of the savage
— and in danger of total eclipse — now came upper-
most.   With Radisson, to think was to act.   He
determined to escape if it cost him his life.

Taking only a hatchet as if he were going to cut
wood, Radisson left the Indian lodge early one morning in the fall of 1653.   Once out of sight from
the village, he broke into a run, following the trail
through the dense forests of the Mohawk Valley
toward Fort Orange.   On and on he ran, all that day,
without pause to rest or eat, without backward glance,
with eye ever piercing through the long leafy vistas

of the forest on the watch for the fresh-chipped bark
of the trees that guided his course, or the narrow
indurated path over the spongy mould worn by running warriors. And when night filled the forest with
the hoot of owl, and the far, weird cries of wild creatures
on the rove, there sped through the aisled columns
of star light and shadow, the ghostly figure of the
French boy slim, and lithe as a willow, with muscles tense
as ironwood, and step silent as the mountain-cat.   All
that night he ran without a single stop. Chill daybreak found him still staggering on, over rocks slippery
with the night frost, over windfall tree on tree in a
barricade, through brawling mountain brooks where
his moccasins broke the skim of ice at the edge, past
rivers where he half waded, half swam.   He was now
faint from want of food; but fear spurred him on.
The morning air was so cold that he found it better
to run than rest.   By four of the afternoon he came
to a clearing in the forest, where was the cabin of
a settler.   A man was chopping wood.   Radisson
ascertained that there were no Iroquois in the cabin,
and, hiding in it, persuaded the settler to carry a
message to Fort Orange, two miles farther on. While
he waited Indians passed the cabin, singing and shouting.   The settler's wife concealed him behind sacks
of wheat and put out all lights.   Within an hour
came a rescue party from Orange, who conducted

him safely to the fort.   For three days Radisson hid
in Orange, while the Mohawks wandered through
the fort, calling him by name.

Gifts of money from the Jesuit, Poncet, and from a
Dutch merchant, enabled Radisson to take ship from
Orange to New York, and from New York to Europe.

This view of Fort Amsterdam on the Manhattan is copied from an ancient
engraving executed in Holland.   The fort was erected in 1623 but
finished upon the above model by Governor Van Twiller in 1635.

Père Poncet had been captured by the Mohawks the
preceding summer, but had escaped to Orange.[1]   Embarking on a small sloop, Radisson sailed down the
Hudson to New York, which then consisted of some
five hundred houses, with stores, barracks, a stone church,

[1] The fact that Radisson confessed his sins to this priest seems pretty well to prove
that Pierre was a Catholic and not a Protestant, as has been so often stated.

and a dilapidated fort. 'Central Park was a forest; goats and cows pastured on what is now Wall Street; and to east and west was a howling wilderness of marsh and woods. After a stay of three weeks, Radisson embarked for Amsterdam, which he reached in January, 1654.

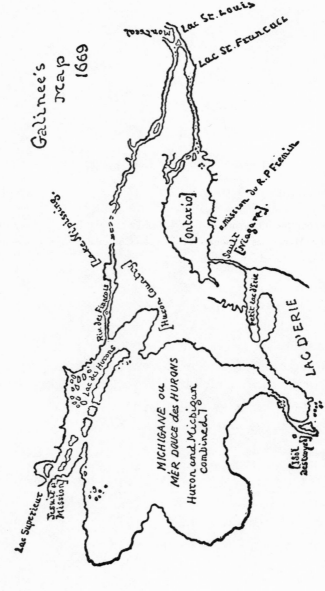

Galinee's map 1669

Lac St. Louis

Montreal

Lac St. Francace

Lac St Pierre?

[Ontario]

Mission du R.P Fremin

Sault [Niagara].

Petit sac d'Erie

LAC D'ERIE

Lac des Nipissing

Riv. de Francois

[Georgian] [Huron]

Lac des Hurons

MICHIGANE ou MER DOUCE des HURONS

Huron and Michigan combined?

[Sat destroyed]

Jesuites Mission

Lac Superieur

One of the Earliest Maps of the Great Lakes.

CHAPTER II

RADISSON'S SECOND VOYAGE

Radisson returns to Quebec, where he joins the Jesuits to go to the Iroquois Mission — He witnesses the Massacre of the Hurons among the Thousand Islands — Besieged by the Iroquois, they pass the Winter as Prisoners of War — Conspiracy to massacre the French foiled by Radisson.

FROM Amsterdam Radisson took ship to Rochelle. Here he found himself a stranger in his native land. All his kin of whom there is any record — Pierre Radisson, his father, Madeline Hénault, his mother, Marguerite and Françoise, his elder and younger sisters, his uncle and aunt, with their daughter, Elizabeth — were now living at Three Rivers in New France.[1]

---

[1] The uncle, Pierre Esprit Radisson, is the one with whom careless writers have confused the young hero, owing to identity of name.   Madeline Hénault has been described as the explorer's first wife, notwithstanding genealogical impossibilities which make the explorer's daughter thirty-six years old before he was seventeen.   Even the infallible Tanguay trips on Radisson's genealogy.   I have before me the complete record of the family taken from the parish registers of Three Rivers and Quebec, by the inde-fatigable Mr. Sulte, whose explanation of the case is this : that Radisson's mother, Madeline Hénault, first married Sebastien Hayet, of St. Malo, to whom was born Marguerite about 1630 ; that her second husband was Pierre Esprit Radisson of Paris, to whom were born our hero and the sisters Françoise and Elizabeth.

Embarking with the fishing fleet that yearly left
France for the Grand Banks, Radisson came early
in the spring of 1654 to Isle Percée at the mouth of
the St. Lawrence.   He was still a week's journey from
Three Rivers, but chance befriended him.   Algonquin canoes were on the way up the river to war on
the Iroquois.   Joining the Indian canoes, he slipped
past the hilly shores of the St. Lawrence and in five
days was between the main bank on the north side
and the muddy shallows of the Isle of Orleans.
Sheering out where the Montmorency roars over a
precipice in a shining cataract, the canoes glided across
St. Charles River among the forests of masts heaving
to the tide below the beetling heights of Cape Diamond, Quebec.

It was May, 1651, when he had first seen the turrets
and spires of Quebec glittering on the hillside in the
sun; it was May, 1652, that the Iroquois had carried
him off from Three Rivers; and it was May, 1654,
when he came again to his own.   He was welcomed
back as from the dead.   Changes had taken place
in the interval of his captivity.   A truce had been
arranged between the Iroquois and the French.
Now that the Huron missions had been wiped out by
Iroquois wars, the Jesuits regarded the truce as a
Divine provision for a mission among the Iroquois.
The year that Radisson escaped from the Mohawks,

Jesuit priests had gone among them.   A still greater
change that was to affect his life more vitally had
taken place in the Radisson family.   The year that
Radisson had been captured, the outraged people of
Three Rivers had seized a Mohawk chief and burned
him to death.   In revenge, the Mohawks murdered
the governor of Three Rivers and a company of
Frenchmen.   Among the slain was the husband of
Radisson's sister, Marguerite.   When Radisson returned, he found that his widowed sister had married
Médard Chouart Groseillers, a famous fur trader of
New France, who had passed his youth as a lay helper
to the Jesuit missions of Lake Huron.[1]   Radisson was
now doubly bound to the Jesuits by gratitude and
family ties.   Never did pagan heart hear an evangel
more gladly than the Mohawks heard the Jesuits.
The priests were welcomed with acclaim, led to the
Council Lodge, and presented with belts of wampum.
Not a suspicion of foul play seems to have entered the
Jesuits' mind.   When the Iroquois proposed to in-
corporate into the Confederacy the remnants of the
Hurons, the Jesuits discerned nothing in the plan
but the most excellent means to convert pagan Iro-

---

[1] I have throughout referred to Médard Chouart, Sieur des Groseillers, as simply
" Groseillers," because that is the name referring to him most commonly used in the
State Papers and old histories.   He was from Charly-Saint-Cyr, near Meaux, and is
supposed to have been born about 1621.   His first wife was Helen Martin, daughter
of Abraham Martin, who gave his name to the Plains of Abraham.

quois by Christian Hurons. Having gained an inch, the Iroquois demanded the proverbial ell. They asked that a French settlement be made in the Iroquois country. The Indians wanted a supply of firearms to war against all enemies; and with a French settlement miles away from help, the Iroquois could wage what war they pleased against the Algonquins without fear of reprisals from Quebec — the settlement of white men among hostiles would be hostage of generous treatment from New France. Of these designs, neither priests nor governor had the slightest suspicion. The Jesuits were thinking only of the Iroquois' soul; the French, of peace with the Iroquois at any cost.

In 1656 Major Dupuis and fifty Frenchmen had established a French colony among the Iroquois.[1] The hardships of these pioneers form no part of Radisson's life, and are, therefore, not set down here. Peace not bought by a victory is an unstable foundation for Indian treaty. The Mohawks were jealous that their confederates, the Onondagas, had obtained

[1] This is the story of Onondaga which Parkman has told. Unfortunately, when Parkman's account was written, *Radisson's Journals* were unknown and Mr. Parkman had to rely entirely on the *Letters of Marie de l' Incarnation* and the *Jesuit Relations*. After the discovery of *Radisson's Journals*, Parkman added a footnote to his account of Onondaga, *quoting* Radisson in confirmation. If Radisson may be quoted to corroborate Parkman, Radisson may surely be accepted as authentic. At the same time, I have compared this journal with Father Ragueneau's of the same party; and the two tally in every detail.

the French settlement. In 1657, eighty Iroquois came to Quebec to escort one hundred Huron refugees back to Onondaga for adoption into the Confederacy. These Hurons were Christians, and the two Jesuits, Paul Ragueneau and François du Péron, were appointed to accompany them to their new abode. Twenty young Frenchmen joined the party to seek their fortunes at the new settlement; but a man was needed who could speak Iroquois. Glad to repay his debt to the Jesuits, young Radisson volunteered to go as a *donné*, that is, a lay helper vowed to gratuitous services.

It was midsummer before all preparations had been made. On July 26, the party of two hundred, made up of twenty Frenchmen, eighty Iroquois, and a hundred Hurons, filed out of the gates of Montreal, and winding round the foot of the mountain followed a trail through the forest that took them past the Lachine Rapids. The Onondaga *voyageurs* carried the long birch canoes inverted on their shoulders, two Indians at each end; and the other Iroquois trotted over the rocks with the Frenchmen's baggage on their backs. The day was hot, the *portage* long and slippery with dank moisture. The Huron children fagged and fell behind. At nightfall, thirty of the haughty Iroquois lost patience, and throwing down their bundles made off for Quebec with the avowed purpose of raiding the Algonquins. On the way, they paused to scalp three Frenchmen at Montreal, cynically explaining that if the French persisted in taking Algonquins into their arms, the white men need not be surprised if the blow aimed at an Algonquin sometimes struck a Frenchman. That act opened the eyes of the French to the real meaning of the peace made with the Iroquois; but the little colony was beyond recall. To insure the safety of the French among the Onondagas, the French governor at Quebec seized a dozen Iroquois and kept them as hostages of good conduct.

Meanwhile, all was confusion on Lake St. Louis, where the last band of colonists had encamped. The Iroquois had cast the Frenchmen's baggage on the rocks and refused to carry it farther. Leaving the whites all embarrassed, the Onondagas hurriedly embarked the Hurons and paddled quickly out of sight. The act was too suddenly unanimous not to have been premeditated. Why had the Iroquois carried the Hurons away from the Frenchmen? Father Ragueneau at once suspected some sinister purpose. Taking only a single sack of flour for food, he called for volunteers among the twenty Frenchmen to embark in a leaky, old canoe and follow the treacherous Onondagas. Young Radisson was one of the first to offer himself. Six others followed his example; and the seven Frenchmen led by the priest struck across the lake, leaving the others to gather up the scattered baggage.

The Onondagas were too deep to reveal their plots with seven armed Frenchmen in pursuit.   The Indians permitted the French boats to come up with the main band.   All camped together in the most friendly fashion that night; but the next morning one Iroquois offered passage in his canoe to one Frenchman, another Iroquois to another of the whites, and by the third day, when they came to Lake St. Francis, the old canoe had been abandoned.   The French were scattered promiscuously among the Iroquois, with no two whites in one boat.   The Hurons were quicker to read the signs of treachery than the French. There were rumors of one hundred Mohawks lying in ambush at the Thousand Islands to massacre the coming Hurons.   On the morning of August 3 four Huron warriors and two women seized a canoe, and to the great astonishment of the encampment launched out before they could be stopped.   Heading the canoe back for Montreal, they broke out in a war chant of defiance to the Iroquois.

The Onondagas made no sign, but they evidently took council to delay no longer.   Again, when they embarked, they allowed no two whites in one canoe. The boats spread out.   Nothing was said to indicate anything unusual.   The lake lay like a silver

E

mirror in the August sun.   The water was so clear
that the Indians frequently paused to spear fish
lying below on the stones.   At places the canoes
skirted close to the wood-fringed shore, and braves
landed to shoot wild-fowl.   Radisson and Ragueneau
seemed simultaneously to have noticed the same
thing.   Without any signal, at about four in the afternoon, the Onondagas steered their canoes for a wooded

Paddling past Hostiles.

island in the middle of the St. Lawrence.   With
Radisson were three Iroquois and a Huron.   As the
canoe grated shore, the bowman loaded his musket
and sprang into the thicket.   Naturally, the Huron
turned to gaze after the disappearing hunter.   Instantly, the Onondaga standing directly behind buried
his hatchet in the Huron's head.   The victim fell
quivering across Radisson's feet and was hacked to
pieces by the other Iroquois.   Not far along the shore

from Radisson, the priest was landing. He noticed
an Iroquois chief approach a Christian Huron girl.
If the Huron had not been a convert, she might have
saved her life by becoming one of the chief's many
slaves; but she had repulsed the Onondaga pagan.
As Ragueneau looked, the girl fell dead with her skull
split by the chief's war-axe. The Hurons on the lake
now knew what awaited them; and a cry of terror
arose from the children. Then a silence of numb
horror settled over the incoming canoes. The
women were driven ashore like lambs before wolves;
but the valiant Hurons would not die without striking
one blow at their inveterate and treacherous enemies.
They threw themselves together back to back, prepared to fight. For a moment this show of resistance
drove off the Iroquois. Then the Onondaga chieftain
rushed forward, protesting that the two murders had
been a personal quarrel. Striking back his own warriors with a great show of sincerity, he bade the
Hurons run for refuge to the top of the hill. No
sooner had the Hurons broken rank, than there
rushed from the woods scores of Iroquois, daubed in
war-paint and shouting their war-cry. This was the
hunt to which the young braves had dashed from
the canoes to be in readiness behind the thicket.
Before the scattered Hurons could get together for
defence, the Onondagas had closed around the hilltop

in a cordon.   The priest ran here, there, everywhere,
— comforting the dying, stopping mutilation, defend-
ing the women.   All the Hurons were massacred
but one man, and the bodies were thrown into the
river.   With blankets drawn over their heads that
they might not see, the women huddled together,
dumb with terror.   When the Onondagas turned
toward the-women, the Frenchmen stood with muskets levelled.   The Onondagas halted, conferred, and
drew off.

The fight lasted for four hours.   Darkness and the
valor of the little French band saved the women for
the time.   The Iroquois kindled a fire and gathered
to celebrate their victory.   Then the old priest
took his life in his hands.   Borrowing three belts of
wampum, he left the huddling group of Huron
women and Frenchmen and marched boldly into the
circle of hostiles.   The lives of all the French and
Hurons hung by a thread.   Ragueneau had been the
spiritual guide of the murdered tribe for twenty years ;
and he was now sobbing like a child.   The Iroquois
regarded his grief with sardonic scorn ; but they
misjudged the manhood below the old priest's tears.
Ragueneau asked leave to speak.   They grunted
permission.   Springing up, he broke into impassioned,
fearless reproaches of the Iroquois for their treachery.
Casting one belt of wampum at the Onondaga chief's

feet, the priest demanded pledges that the massacre cease. A second belt was given to register the Onondaga's vow to conduct the women and children safely to the Iroquois country. The third belt was for the safety of the French at Onondaga.

The Iroquois were astonished. They had looked for womanish pleadings. They had heard stern demands coupled with fearless threats of punishment. When Ragueneau sat down, the Onondaga chief bestirred himself to counteract the priest's powerful impression. Lounging to his feet, the Onondaga impudently declared that the governor of Quebec had instigated the massacre. Ragueneau leaped up with a denial that took the lie from the scoundrel's teeth. The chief sat down abashed. The Council grunted " Ho, ho ! " accepting the wampum and promising all that the Jesuit had asked.

Among the Thousand Islands, the French who had remained behind to gather up the baggage again joined the Onondagas. They brought with them from the Isle of Massacres a poor Huron woman, whom they had found lying insensible on a rock. During the massacre she had hidden in a hollow tree, where she remained for three days. In this region, Radisson almost lost his life by hoisting a blanket sail to his canoe. The wind drifted the boat so far out that Radisson had to throw all ballast overboard to keep from being swamped. As they turned from the St. Lawrence and Lake Ontario up the Oswego River for Onondaga, they met other warriors of the Iroquois nation. In spite of pledges to the priest, the meeting was celebrated by torturing the Huron women to entertain the newcomers. Not the sufferings of the early Christians in Rome exceeded the martyrdom of the Christian Hurons among the Onondagas. As her mother mounted the scaffold of tortures, a little girl who had been educated by the Ursulines of Quebec broke out with loud weeping. The Huron mother turned calmly to the child : —

"Weep not my death, my little daughter! We shall this day be in heaven," said she ; "God will pity us to all eternity. The Iroquois cannot rob us of that."

As the flames crept about her, her voice was heard chanting in the crooning monotone of Indian death dirge : " Jesu — have pity on us ! Jesu — have pity on us ! " The next moment the child was thrown into the flames, repeating the same words.

The Iroquois recognized Radisson. He sent presents to his Mohawk parents, who afterwards played an important part in saving the French of Onondaga. Having passed the falls, they came to the French fort situated on the crest of a hill above a lake. Two

high towers loopholed for musketry occupied the
centre of the courtyard.   Double walls, trenched
between, ran round a space large enough to enable the
French to keep their cattle inside the fort. The *voyageurs* were welcomed to Onondaga by Major Dupuis,
fifty Frenchmen, and several Jesuits.

The pilgrims had scarcely settled at Onondaga before signs of the dangers that were gathering became
too plain for the blind zeal of the Jesuits to ignore.
Cayugas, Onondagas, and Senecas, togged out in war-
gear, swarmed outside the palisades.   There was no
more dissembling of hunger for the Jesuits' evangel.
The warriors spoke no more soft words, but spent
their time feasting, chanting war-songs, heaving up the
war-hatchet against the kettle of sagamite — which
meant the rupture of peace.   Then came four hundred
Mohawks, who not only shouted their war-songs, but
built their wigwams before the fort gates and established themselves for the winter like a besieging army.
That the intent of the entire Confederacy was hostile
to Onondaga could not be mistaken ; but what was
holding the Indians back?   Why did they delay the
massacre ?   Then Huron slaves brought word to the
besieged fort of the twelve Iroquois hostages held at
Quebec.   The fort understood what stayed the
Iroquois blow.   The Confederacy dared not attack

the isolated fort lest Quebec should take terrible vengeance on the hostages.

The French decided to send messengers to Quebec for instructions before closing navigation cut them off

Jogues, the Jesuit missionary, who was tortured by the Mohawks. From a painting in Château de Ramezay, Montreal.

for the winter. Thirteen men and one Jesuit left the fort the first week of September. Mohawk spies knew of the departure and lay in ambush at each side of the narrow river to intercept the party ; but the messengers eluded the trap by striking through the forests back from the river directly to the St. Lawrence. Then the little fort closed its gates and awaited an answer from Quebec. Winter settled over the land, blocking the rivers with ice and the forest trails with drifts of snow ; but no messengers came back from Quebec. The Mohawks had missed the outgoing scouts :

but they caught the return *coureurs* and destroyed the letters.   Not a soul could leave the fort but spies dogged his steps.   The Jesuits continued going from lodge to lodge, and in this way Onondaga gained vague knowledge of the plots outside the fort.   The French could venture out only at the risk of their lives, and spent the winter as closely confined as prisoners of war.   Of the ten drilled soldiers, nine threatened to desert.   One night an unseen hand plunged through the dark, seized the sentry, and dragged him from the gate.   The sentry drew his sword and shouted, " To arms ! "   A band of Frenchmen sallied from the gates with swords and muskets. In the tussle the sentry was rescued, and gifts were sent out in the morning to pacify the wounded Mohawks.   Fortunately the besieged had plenty of food inside the stockades ; but the Iroquois knew there could be no escape till the ice broke up in spring, and were quite willing to exchange ample supplies of corn for tobacco and firearms.   The Huron slaves who carried the corn to the fort acted as spies among the Mohawks for the French.

In the month of February the vague rumors of conspiracy crystallized into terrible reality.   A dying Mohawk confessed to a Jesuit that the Iroquois[1] Council had determined to massacre half the company

1 See *Jesuit Relations*, 1657–1658.

of French and to hold the other half till their own
Mohawk hostages were released from Quebec. Among
the hostiles encamped before the gates was Radisson's
Indian father. This Mohawk was still an influential
member of the Great Council. He, too, reported that
the warriors were bent on destroying Onondaga.[1]
What was to be done? No answer had come from
Quebec, and no aid could come till the spring. The
rivers were still blocked with ice; and there were not
sufficient boats in the fort to carry fifty men down to
Quebec. "What could we do?" writes Radisson.
"We were in their hands. It was as hard to get
away from them as for a ship in full sea without a
pilot."

They at once began constructing two large flat-
bottomed boats of light enough draft to run the rapids
in the flood-tide of spring. Carpenters worked hidden in an attic; but when the timbers were mortised
together, the boats had to be brought downstairs,
where one of the Huron slaves caught a glimpse of
them. Boats of such a size he had never before seen.
Each was capable of carrying fifteen passengers with
full complement of baggage. Spring rains were falling in floods. The convert Huron had heard the
Jesuits tell of Noah's ark in the deluge. Returning
to the Mohawks, he spread a terrifying report of an

[1] *Letters of Marie de l'Incarnation.*

impending flood and of strange arks of refuge built by
the white men.   Emissaries were appointed to visit the
French fort; but the garrison had been forewarned.
Radisson knew of the coming spies from his Indian
father; and the Jesuits had learned of the Council
from their converts.   Before the spies arrived, the
French had built a floor over their flatboats, and to
cover the fresh floor had heaped up a dozen canoes.
The spies left the fort satisfied that neither a deluge
nor an escape was impending.   Birch canoes would
be crushed like egg-shells if they were run through
the ice jams of spring floods.   Certain that their
victims were trapped, the Iroquois were in no haste
to assault a double-walled fort, where musketry could
mow them down as they rushed the hilltop.   The
Indian is bravest under cover; so the Mohawks
spread themselves in ambush on each side of the
narrow river and placed guards at the falls where any
boats must be *portaged*.

Of what good were the boats?   To allay suspicion
of escape, the Jesuits continued to visit the wigwams.[1]
The French were in despair.   They consulted Radisson, who could go among the Mohawks as with a
charmed life, and who knew the customs of the Confederacy so well.   Radisson proposed a way to out-
wit the savages.   With this plan the priests had

---

[1] See Ragueneau's account.

nothing to do.   To the harum-scarum Radisson belong the sole credit and discredit of the escapade. On his device hung the lives of fifty innocent men. These men must either escape or be massacred.   Of bloodshed, Radisson had already seen too much ; and the youth of twenty-one now no more proposed to stickle over the means of victory than generals who wear the Victoria cross stop to stickle over means to-day.

Radisson knew that the Indians had implicit faith in dreams ; so Radisson had a dream.[1]   He realized as critics of Indian customs fail to understand that the fearful privations of savage life teach the crime of waste.   The Indian will eat the last morsel of food set before him if he dies for it.   He believes that the gods punish waste of food by famine.   The belief is a religious principle and the feasts — *festins à tout manger* — are a religious act ; so Radisson dreamed — whether sleeping or waking — that the white men were to give a great festival to the Iroquois.   This dream he related to his Indian father.   The Indian like his white brother can clothe a vice under religious mantle. The Iroquois were gluttonous on a religious principle. Radisson's dream was greeted with joy.   *Coureurs* ran through the forest, bidding the Mohawks to the feast.   Leaving ambush of forest and waterfall, the

[1] See *Marie de l'Incarnation* and Dr. Dionne's modern monograph.

warriors hastened to the walls of Onondaga. To
whet their appetite, they were kept waiting outside for
two whole days. The French took turns in enter-
taining the waiting guests. Boisterous games, songs,
dances, and music kept the Iroquois awake and hilari-

Château de Ramezay, Montreal, for years the residence of the governor,
and later the storehouse of the fur companies.

ous to the evening of the second day. Inside the fort
bedlam reigned. Boats were dragged from floors to a
sally-port at the rear of the courtyard. Here firearms, ammunition, food, and baggage were placed in
readiness. Guns which could not be taken were

burned or broken.   Ammunition was scattered in the
snow.   All the stock but one solitary pig, a few
chickens, and the dogs was sacrificed for the feast,
and in the barracks a score of men were laboring over
enormous kettles of meat.   Had an Indian spy
climbed to the top of a tree and looked over the
palisades, all would have been discovered; but the
French entertainers outside kept their guests busy.

On the evening of the second day a great fire was
kindled in the outer enclosure, between the two walls.
The trumpets blew a deafening blast.   The Mohawks
answered with a shout.   The French clapped their
hands.   The outer gates were thrown wide open, and
in trooped several hundred Mohawk warriors, seating
themselves in a circle round the fire.   Another blare
of trumpets, and twelve enormous kettles of mince-
meat were carried round the circle of guests.   A
Mohawk chief rose solemnly and gave his deities of
earth, air, and fire profuse thanks for having brought
such generous people as the French among the Iroquois.   Other chiefs arose and declaimed to their
hearers that earth did not contain such hosts as the
French.   Before they had finished speaking there
came a second and a third and a fourth relay of kettles
round the circle of feasters.   Not one Iroquois dared
to refuse the food heaped before him.   By the time
the kettles of salted fowl and venison and bear had

passed round the circle, each Indian was glancing furtively sideways to see if his neighbor could still eat.   He who was compelled to forsake the feast first was to become the butt of the company.   All the while the French kept up a din of drums and trumpets and flageolets, dancing and singing and shouting to drive off sleep.   The eyes of the gorging Indians began to roll.   Never had they attempted to demolish such a banquet.   Some shook their heads and drew back.   Others fell over in the dead sleep that results from long fasting and overfeeding and fresh air.   Radisson was everywhere, urging the Iroquois to "Cheer up! cheer up! If sleep overcomes you, you must awake!   Beat the drum!   Blow the trumpet!   Cheer up!   Cheer up!"

But the end of the repulsive scene was at hand. By midnight the Indians had — in the language of the white man — "gone under the mahogany." They lay sprawled on the ground in sodden sleep. Perhaps, too, something had been dropped in the flesh-pots to make their sleep the sounder.   Radisson does not say no, neither does the priest, and they two were the only whites present who have written of the episode.[1]

---

[1] This account is drawn mainly from *Radisson's Journal*, partly from *Father Ragueneau*, and in one detail from a letter of *Marie de l'Incarnation*.   Garneau says the feasters were drugged; but I cannot find his authority for this, though from my knowledge of fur traders' escapes, I fancy it would hardly have been human nature not to add a sleeping potion to the kettles.

But the French would hardly have been human if they had not assured their own safety by drugging the feasters.   It was a common thing for the fur traders of a later period to prevent massacre and quell riot by administering a quietus to Indians with a few drops of laudanum.

The French now retired to the inner court.   The main gate was bolted and chained.   Through the loop-hole of this gate ran a rope attached to a bell that was used to summon the sentry.   To this rope the mischievous Radisson tied the only remaining pig, so that when the Indians would pull the rope for admission, the noise of the disturbed pig would give the impression of a sentry's tramp-tramp on parade.   Stuffed effigies of soldiers were then stuck about the barracks. If a spy climbed up to look over the palisades, he would see Frenchmen still in the fort.   While Radisson was busy with these precautions to delay pursuit, the soldiers and priests, led by Major Dupuis, had broken open the sally-port, forced the boats through sideways, and launched out on the river.   Speaking in whispers, they stowed the baggage in the flat-boats, then brought out skiffs — dugouts to withstand the ice jam — for the rest of the company.   The night was raw and cold.   A skim of ice had formed on the margins of the river.   Through the pitchy darkness fell a sleet of rain and snow that washed out the foot-

steps of the fugitives. The current of mid-river ran
a noisy mill-race of ice and log drift; and the *voyageurs* could not see one boat length ahead.

To men living in savagery come temptations that
can neither be measured nor judged by civilization.
To the French at Onondaga came such a temptation
now. Their priests were busy launching the boats.
The departing soldiers seemed simultaneously to have
become conscious of a very black suggestion. Cooped
up against the outer wall in the dead sleep of torpid
gluttony lay the leading warriors of the Iroquois
nation. Were these not the assassins of countless
Frenchmen, the murderers of women, the torturers of
children? Had Providence not placed the treacherous Iroquois in the hands of fifty Frenchmen? If
these warriors were slain, it would be an easy matter
to march to the villages of the Confederacy, kill the
old men, and take prisoners the women. New France
would be forever free of her most deadly enemy.
Like the Indians, the white men were trying to justify
a wrong under pretence of good. By chance, word
of the conspiracy was carried to the Jesuits. With
all the authority of the church, the priests forbade
the crime. "Their answer was," relates Radisson,
"that they were sent to instruct in the faith of
Jesus Christ and not to destroy, and that the cross
must be their sword."

F

Locking the sally-port, the company — as the Jesuit father records — "shook the dust of Onondaga from their feet," launched out on the swift-flowing, dark river and escaped "as the children of Israel escaped by night from the land of Egypt." They had not gone far through the darkness before the roar of waters told them of a cataract ahead. They were four hours carrying baggage and boats over this *portage.* Sleet beat upon their backs. The rocks were slippery with glazed ice; and through the rotten, half-thawed snow, the men sank to mid-waist. Navigation became worse on Lake Ontario; for the wind tossed the lake like a sea, and ice had whirled against the St. Lawrence in a jam. On the St. Lawrence, they had to wait for the current to carry the ice out. At places they cut a passage through the honeycombed ice with their hatchets, and again they were compelled to *portage* over the ice. The water was so high that the rapids were safely ridden by all the boats but one, which was shipwrecked, and three of the men were drowned.

They had left Onondaga on the 20th of March, 1658. On the evening of April 3d they came to Montreal, where they learned that New France had all winter suffered intolerable insolence from the Iroquois, lest punishment of the hostiles should endanger the French at Onondaga. The fleeing colonists waited twelve days at Montreal for the ice to clear, and were again held back by a jam at Three Rivers; but on April 23 they moored safely under the heights of Quebec.

Coureurs from Onondaga brought word that the Mohawks had been deceived by the pig and the ringing bell and the effigies for more than a week. Crowing came from the chicken yard, dogs bayed in their kennels, and when a Mohawk pulled the bell at the gate, he could hear the sentry's measured march.   At the end of seven days not a white man had come from the fort.   At first the Mohawks had thought the " black robes " were at prayers; but now suspicions of trickery flashed on the Iroquois.   Warriors climbed the palisades and found the fort empty. Two hundred Mohawks set out in pursuit; but the bad weather held them back.   And that was the way Radisson saved Onondaga.[1]

---

[1] The *festins à tout manger* must not be too sweepingly condemned by the self-righteous white man as long as drinking bouts are a part of civilized customs; and at least one civilized nation has the gross proverb, '' Better burst than waste.''

CHAPTER III

1658–1660

RADISSON'S THIRD VOYAGE

The Discovery of the Great Northwest — Radisson and his Brother-in-law, Groseillers, visit what are now Wisconsin, Minnesota, Dakota, and the Canadian Northwest — Radisson's Prophecy on first beholding the West — Twelve Years before Marquette and Jollïet, Radisson sees the Mississippi — The Terrible Remains of Dollard's Fight seen on the Way down the Ottawa — Why Radisson's Explorations have been ignored

WHILE Radisson was among the Iroquois, the little world of New France had not been asleep. Before Radisson was born, Jean Nicolet of Three Rivers had passed westward through the straits of Mackinaw and coasted down Lake Michigan as far as Green Bay.[1] Some years later the great Jesuit martyr, Jogues, had preached to the Indians of Sault Ste. Marie; but beyond the Sault was an unknown world that beckoned the young adventurers of New France as with the hands of a siren. Of the great beyond — known to-day as the Great Northwest — nothing had been learned but this: from it came the priceless stores of

[1] Mr. Benjamin Sulte establishes this date as 1634.

beaver pelts yearly brought down the Ottawa to Three
Rivers by the Algonquins, and in it dwelt strange, wild
races whose territory extended northwest and north to
unknown nameless seas.

The Great Beyond held the two things most
coveted by ambitious young men of New France, —
quick wealth by means of the fur trade and the
immortal fame of being a first explorer. Nicolet had
gone only as far as Green Bay and Fox River; Jogues
not far beyond the Sault. What secrets lay in the
Great Unknown? Year after year young Frenchmen,
fired with the zeal of the explorer, joined wandering
tribes of Algonquins going up the Ottawa, in the hope
of being taken beyond the Sault. In August, 1656,
there came from Green Bay two young Frenchmen
with fifty canoes of Algonquins, who told of far-distant
waters called Lake "Ouinipeg," and tribes of wandering hunters called "Christinos" (Crees), who spent
their winters in a land bare of trees (the prairie),
and their summers on the North Sea (Hudson's Bay). They also told of other tribes, who
were great warriors, living to the south, — these were
the Sioux. But the two Frenchmen had not gone
beyond the Great Lakes.[1] These Algonquins were

[1] See *Jesuit Relations*, 1656–57–58. I have purposely refrained from entering
into the heated controversy as to the identity of these two men. It is apart from the
subject, as there is no proof these men went beyond the Green Bay region.

received at Château St. Louis, Quebec, with pompous firing of cannon and other demonstrations of

A Cree brave, with the wampum string.

welcome. So eager were the French to take possession of the new land that thirty young men equipped themselves to go back with the Indians; and the Jesuits sent out two priests, Leonard Gareau and Gabriel Dreuillettes, with a lay helper, Louis Boësme. The sixty canoes left Quebec with more firing of guns for a God-speed; but at Lake St. Peter the Mohawks ambushed the flotilla. The enterprise of exploring the Great Beyond was abandoned by all the French but two. Gareau, who was mortally wounded on the Ottawa, probably by a Frenchman or renegade hunter, died at Montreal; and Dreuillettes did not go farther than Lake Nipissing. Here, Dreuillettes learned much of the Unknown from an old Nipissing chief. He heard of six overland routes to the bay of the North, whence came such store of peltry.[1] He, too, like the two Frenchmen from Green Bay, heard of wandering tribes who had no settled lodge like the Hurons and Iroquois, but lived by the chase, — Crees and Sioux and Assiniboines of the prairie, at constant war round a lake called " Ouinipegouek."

By one of those curious coincidences of destiny which mark the lives of nations and men, the young Frenchman who had gone with the Jesuit, Dreuillettes, to Lake Nipissing when the other Frenchmen turned back, was Médard Chouart Groseillers, the fur trader married to Radisson's widowed sister, Marguerite.[2]

When Radisson came back from Onondaga, he found his brother-in-law, Groseillers, at Three Rivers, with ambitious designs of exploration in the unknown land of which he had heard at Green Bay and on Lake Nipissing. Jacques Cartier had discovered only one great river, had laid the foundations of only one small province; Champlain had only made the circuit of the St. Lawrence, the Ottawa, and the Great

---

[1] These routes were : (1) By the Saguenay, (2) by Three Rivers and the St. Maurice, (3) by Lake Nipissing, (4) by Lake Huron, through the land of the Sautaux, (5) by Lake Superior overland, (6) by the Ottawa. See *Jesuit Relations* for detailed accounts of these routes. Dreuillettes went farther west to the Crees a few years later, but that does not concern this narrative.

[2] The dispute as to whether eastern Minnesota was discovered on the 1654–55–56 trip, and whether Groseillers discovered it, is a point for savants, but will, I think, remain an unsettled dispute.

Lakes; but here was a country — if the Indians spoke the truth — greater than all the empires of Europe together, a country bounded only by three great seas, the Sea of the North, the Sea of the South, and the Sea of Japan, a country so vast as to stagger the utmost conception of little New France.

It was unnecessary for Groseillers to say more. The ambition of young Radisson took fire. Long ago, when a captive among the Mohawks, he had cherished boyish dreams that it was to be his " destiny to discover many wild nations "; and here was that destiny opening the door for him, pointing the way, beckoning to the toils and dangers and glories of the discoverer's life. Radisson had been tortured among the Mohawks and besieged among the Onondagas. Groseillers had been among the Huron missions that were destroyed and among the Algonquin canoes that were attacked. Both explorers knew what perils awaited them; but what youthful blood ever chilled at prospect of danger when a single *coup* might win both wealth and fame? Radisson had not been home one month; but he had no sooner heard the plan than he " longed to see himself in a boat."

A hundred and fifty Algonquins had come down the Ottawa from the Great Beyond shortly after Radisson returned from Onondaga. Six of these Algonquins had brought their furs to Three Rivers.

Some emissaries had gone to Quebec to meet the governor; but the majority of the Indians remained at Montreal to avoid the ambuscade of the Mohawks on Lake St. Peter. Radisson and Groseillers were not the only Frenchmen conspiring to wrest fame and fortune from the Upper Country. When the Indians came back from Quebec, they were accompanied by thirty young French adventurers, gay as boys out of school or gold hunters before the first check to their plans. There were also two Jesuits sent out to win the new domain for the cross.[1] As ignorant as children of the hardships ahead, the other treasure-seekers kept up nonchalant boasting that roused the irony of such seasoned men as Radisson and Groseillers. "What fairer bastion than a good tongue," Radisson demands cynically, "especially when one sees his own chimney smoke? . . . It is different when food is wanting, work necessary day and night, sleep taken on the bare ground or to mid-waist in water, with an empty stomach, weariness in the bones, and bad weather overhead."

Giving the slip to their noisy companions, Radisson and Groseillers stole out from Three Rivers late one night in June, accompanied by Algonquin guides.

---

[1] The *Relations* do not give the names of these two Jesuits, probably owing to the fact that the enterprise failed. They simply state that two priests set out, but were compelled to remain behind owing to the caprice of the savages.

Travelling only at night to avoid Iroquois spies, they
came to Montreal in three days.   Here were gathered
one hundred and forty Indians from the Upper
Country, the thirty French, and the two priests.   No
gun was fired at Montreal, lest the Mohawks should
get wind of the departure; and the flotilla of sixty
canoes spread over Lake St. Louis for the far venture
of the *Pays d'en Haut*.   Three days of work had
silenced the boasting of the gay adventurers; and the
voyageurs, white and red, were now paddling in swift
silence.   Safety engendered carelessness.   As the fleet
seemed to be safe from Iroquois ambush, the canoes
began to scatter.   Some loitered behind.   Hunters
went ashore to shoot.   The hills began to ring with
shot and call.   At the first *portage* many of the
canoes were nine and ten miles apart.   Enemies could
have set on the Algonquins in some narrow defile and
slaughtered the entire company like sheep in a pen.
Radisson and Groseillers warned the Indians of the
risk they were running.   Many of these Algonquins
had never before possessed firearms.   With the
muskets obtained in trade at Three Rivers, they
thought themselves invincible and laughed all warning
to scorn.   Radisson and Groseillers were told that
they were a pair of timid squaws; and the canoes
spread apart till not twenty were within call.   As they
skirted the wooded shores, a man suddenly dashed

from the forest with an upraised war-hatchet in one hand and a blanket streaming from his shoulders. He shouted for them to come to him. The Algonquins were panic-stricken. Was the man pursued by Mohawks, or laying a trap to lure them within shooting range? Seeing them hesitate, the Indian threw down blanket and hatchet to signify that he was defenceless, and rushed into the water to his armpits.

" I would save you," he shouted in Iroquois.

The Algonquins did not understand. They only knew that he spoke the tongue of the hated enemy and was unarmed. In a trice, the Algonquins in the nearest canoe had thrown out a well-aimed lasso, roped the man round the waist, and drawn him a captive into the canoe.

" Brothers," protested the captive, who seems to have been either a Huron slave or an Iroquois magician, " your enemies are spread up and down! Sleep not! They have heard your noise! They wait for you! They are sure of their prey! Believe me — keep together! Spend not your powder in vain to frighten your enemies by noise! See that the stones of your arrows be not bent! Bend your bows! Keep your hatchets sharp! Build a fort! Make haste!"

But the Algonquins, intoxicated with the new power of firearms, would hear no warning. They did not understand his words and refused to heed Radisson's interpretation. Beating paddles on their canoes

and firing off guns, they shouted derisively that the
man was " a dog and a hen." All the same, they did
not land to encamp that night, but slept in midstream,
with their boats tied to the rushes or on the lee side of
floating trees. The French lost heart. If this were
the beginning, what of the end ? Daylight had scarcely
broken when the paddles of the eager *voyageurs* were
cutting the thick gray mist that rose from the river to
get away from observation while the fog still hid the
fleet. From afar came the dull, heavy rumble of a
waterfall.[1]

There was a rush of the twelve foremost canoes to
reach the landing and cross the *portage* before the
thinning mist lifted entirely. Twelve boats had got
ashore when the fog was cleft by a tremendous crashing of guns, and Iroquois ambushed in the bordering
forest let go a salute of musketry. Everything was
instantly in confusion. Abandoning their baggage
to the enemy, the Algonquins and French rushed

[1] Whether they were now on the Ottawa or the St. Lawrence, it is impossible
to tell. Dr. Dionne thinks that the band went overland from Lake Ontario to Lake
Huron. I know both waters — Lake Ontario and the Ottawa — from many trips,
and I think Radisson's description here tallies with his other descriptions of the Ottawa.
It is certain that they must have been on the Ottawa before they came to the Lake of
the Castors or Nipissing. The noise of the waterfall seems to point to the Chaudière
Falls of the Ottawa. If so, the landing place would be the tongue of land running out
from Hull, opposite the city of Ottawa, and the *portage* would be the Aylmer Road
beyond the rapids above the fall: Mr. Benjamin Sulte, the scholarly historian, thinks
they went by way of the Ottawa, not Lake Ontario, as the St. Lawrence route was not
used till 1702.

for the woods to erect a barricade. This would protect the landing of the other canoes. The Iroquois immediately threw up a defence of fallen logs likewise, and each canoe that came ashore was greeted with a cross fire between the two barricades. Four canoes were destroyed and thirteen of the Indians from the Upper Country killed. As day wore on, the Iroquois' shots ceased, and the Algonquins celebrated the truce by killing and devouring all the prisoners they had taken, among whom was the magician who had given them warning. Radisson and Groseillers wondered if the Iroquois were reserving their powder for a night raid. The Algonquins did not wait to know. As soon as darkness fell, there was a wild scramble for the shore. A long, low trumpet call, such as hunters use, signalled the Algonquins to rally and rush for the boats. The French embarked as best they could. The Indians swam and paddled for the opposite shore of the river. Here, in the dark, hurried council was taken. The most of the baggage had been lost. The Indians refused to help either the Jesuits or the French, and it was impossible for the white *voyageurs* to keep up the pace in the dash across an unknown *portage* through the dark. The French adventurers turned back for Montreal. Of the white men, Radisson and Groseillers alone went on.

Frightened into their senses by the encounter, the Algonquins now travelled only at night till they were far beyond range of the Iroquois. All day the fugitive band lay hidden in the woods. They could not hunt, lest Mohawk spies might hear the gunshots. Provisions dwindled. In a short time the food consisted of *tripe de roche* — a greenish moss boiled into a soup — and the few fish that might be caught during hurried nightly launch or morning landing. Sometimes they hid in a berry patch, when the fruit was gathered and boiled, but camp-fires were stamped out and covered. Turning westward, they crossed the barren region of iron-capped rocks and dwarf growth between the Upper Ottawa and the Great Lakes. Now they were farther from the Iroquois, and staved off famine by shooting an occasional bear in the berry patches. For a thousand miles they had travelled against stream, carrying their boats across sixty *portages*. Now they glided with the current westward to Lake Nipissing. On the lake, the Upper Indians always *cached* provisions. Fish, otter, and beaver were plentiful; but again they refrained from using firearms, for Iroquois footprints had been found on the sand.

From Lake Nipissing they passed to Lake Huron, where the fleet divided. Radisson and Groseillers went with the Indians, who crossed Lake Huron for Green Bay on Lake Michigan. The birch canoes could not venture across the lake in storms; so the boats rounded southward, keeping along the shore of Georgian Bay. Cedar forests clustered down the sandy reaches of the lake. Rivers dark as cathedral aisles rolled their brown tides through the woods to the blue waters of Lake Huron. At one point Groseillers recognized the site of the ruined Jesuit missions. The Indians waited the chance of a fair day, and paddled over to the straits at the entrance to Lake Michigan. At Manitoulin Island were Huron refugees, among whom were, doubtless, the waiting families of the Indians with Radisson. All struck south for Green Bay. So far Radisson and Groseillers had travelled over beaten ground. Now they were at the gateway of the Great Beyond, where no white man had yet gone.

The first thing done on taking up winter quarters on Green Bay was to appease the friends of those warriors slain by the Mohawks. A distribution of gifts had barely dried up the tears of mourning when news came of Iroquois on the war-path. Radisson did not wait for fear to unman the Algonquin warriors. Before making winter camp, he offered to lead a band of volunteers against the marauders. For two days he followed vague tracks through the autumn-tinted forests. Here were markings of the dead leaves turned freshly up; there a moccasin print on the sand: and now the ashes of a hidden camp-fire lying in almost imperceptible powder on fallen logs told where the Mohawks had bivouacked. On the third day Radisson caught the ambushed band unprepared, and fell upon the Iroquois so furiously that not one escaped.

After that the Indians of the Upper Country could not do too much for the white men. Radisson and Groseillers were conducted from camp to camp in triumph. Feasts were held. Ambassadors went ahead with gifts from the Frenchmen; and companies of women marched to meet the explorers, chanting songs of welcome. " But our mind was not to stay here," relates Radisson, " but to know the remotest people; and, because we had been willing to die in their defence, these Indians consented to conduct us."

Before the opening of spring, 1659, Radisson and Groseillers had been guided across what is now Wisconsin to "a mighty river, great, rushing, profound, and comparable to the St. Lawrence." [1] On the shores of the river they found a vast nation — " the people of the fire," prairie tribes, a branch of the Sioux, who received them well.[2] This river was undoubtedly the Upper Mississippi, now for the first time seen by white men. Radisson and Groseillers had discovered

[1] *Jesuit Relations*, 1660.
[2] *Jesuit Relations*, 1660, and *Radisson's Journal*. These "people of the fire," or Mascoutins, were in three regions, (1) Wisconsin, (2) Nebraska, (3) on the Missouri. See Appendix E.

An Old-time Buffalo Hunt on the Plains among the Sioux.

the Great Northwest.[1] They were standing on the threshold of the Great Beyond. They saw before them not the Sea of China, as speculators had dreamed, not kingdoms for conquest, which the princes of Europe coveted ; not a short road to Asia, of which savants had spun a cobweb of theories. They saw what every Westerner sees to-day, — illimitable reaches of prairie and ravine, forested hills sloping to mighty rivers, and open meadow-lands watered by streams looped like a ribbon. They saw a land waiting for its people, wealth waiting for possessors, an empire waiting for the nation builders.

What were Radisson's thoughts? Did he realize the importance of his discovery? Could he have the vaguest premonition that he had opened a door of escape from stifled older lands to a higher type of manhood and freedom than the most sanguine dreamer had ever hoped?[2] After an act has come to fruition, it is easy to read into the actor's mind fuller purpose than he could have intended. Columbus could not have realized to what the discovery of America would

[1] Benjamin Sulte unequivocally states that the river was the Mississippi. Of writers contemporaneous with Radisson, the Jesuits, Marie de l'Incarnation, and Charlevoix corroborate Radisson's account. In the face of this, what are we to think of modern writers with a reputation to lose, who brush Radisson's exploits aside as a possible fabrication ? The only conclusion is that they have not read his *Journal*.

[2] I refer to Radisson alone, because for half the time in 1659 Groseillers was ill at the lake, and we cannot be sure that he accompanied Radisson in all the journeys south and west, though Radisson generously always includes him as " we." Besides, Groseillers seems to have attended to the trading, Radisson to the exploring.

G

lead.   Did Radisson realize what the discovery of the Great Northwest meant?

Here is what he says, in that curious medley of idioms which so often results when a speaker knows many languages but is master of none : —

"The country was so pleasant, so beautiful, and so fruitful, that it grieved me to see that the world could not discover such inticing countries to live in. This, I say, because the Europeans fight for a rock in the sea against one another, or for a steril land . . . where the people by changement of air engender sickness and die. . . .   Contrariwise, these kingdoms are so delicious and under so temperate a climate, plentiful of all things, and the earth brings forth its fruit twice a year, that the people live long and lusty and wise in their way.   What a conquest would this be, at little or no cost?   What pleasure should people have . . . instead of misery and poverty !   Why should not men reap of the love of God here?   Surely, more is to be gained converting souls here than in differences of creed, when wrongs are committed under pretence of religion ! . . .   It is true, I confess, . . . that access here is difficult . . . but nothing is to be gained without labor and pains." [1]

---

[1] If any one cares to render Radisson's peculiar jumble of French, English, Italian, and Indian idioms into more intelligent form, they may try their hand at it.   His meaning is quite clear ; but the words are a medley.   The passage is to be found on pp. 150–151, of the *Prince Society Reprint.*   See also *Jesuit Relations,* 1660.

Here Radisson foreshadows all the best gains that
the West has accomplished for the human race.
What are they?   Mainly room, — room to live and
room for opportunity; equal chances for all classes,

Father Marquette, from an old painting discovered in Montreal by
Mr. McNab.   The date on the picture is 1669.

high and low; plenty for all classes, high and low; the
conquests not of war but of peace. The question arises,
— when Radisson discovered the Great Northwest ten

years before Marquette and Jolliet, twenty years before La Salle, a hundred years before De la Vérendrye, why has his name been slurred over and left in
oblivion?[1] The reasons are plain. Radisson was a
Christian, but he was not a slave to any creed. Such
liberality did not commend itself to the annalists of an
age that was still rioting in a very carnival of religious
persecution. Radisson always invoked the blessing of
Heaven on his enterprises and rendered thanks for his
victories; but he was indifferent as to whether he was
acting as lay helper with the Jesuits, or allied to the
Huguenots of London and Boston. His discoveries
were too important to be ignored by the missionaries.
They related his discoveries, but refrained from men-
tioning his name, though twice referring to Groseillers.
What hurt Radisson's fame even more than his indifference to creeds was his indifference to nationality.
Like Columbus, he had little care what flag floated
at the prow, provided only that the prow pushed on
and on and on, — into the Unknown. He sold his

---

[1] It will be noted that what I claim for Radisson is the honor of discovering the
Great Northwest, and refrain from trying to identify his movements with the modern
place names of certain states.   I have done this intentionally — though it would have
been easy to advance opinions about Green Bay, Fox River, and the Wisconsin, and
so become involved in the childish quarrel that has split the western historical societies
and obscured the main issue of Radisson's feat.   Needless to say, the world does not
care whether Radisson went by way of the Menominee, or snow-shoed across country.
The question is : Did he reach the Mississippi Valley before Marquette and Jolliet and
La Salle ?   That question this chapter answers.

services alternately to France and England till he had
offended both governments; and, in addition to with-
standing a conspiracy of silence on the part of the
Church, his fame encountered the ill-will of state
historians. He is mentioned as "the adventurer,"
"the hang-dog," "the renegade." Only in 1885,
when the manuscript of his travels was rescued from
oblivion, did it become evident that history must be
rewritten. Here was a man whose discoveries were
second only to those of Columbus, and whose explorations were more far-ranging and important than those
of Champlain and La Salle and De la Vérendrye put
together.

The spring of 1659 found the explorers still among
the prairie tribes of the Mississippi. From these people Radisson learned of four other races occupying
vast, undiscovered countries. He heard of the Sioux,
a warlike nation to the west, who had no fixed abode
but lived by the chase and were at constant war with
another nomadic tribe to the north — the Crees. The
Crees spent the summer time round the shores of salt
water, and in winter came inland to hunt. Between
these two was a third, — the Assiniboines, — who used
earthen pots for cooking, heated their food by throwing
hot stones in water, and dressed themselves in buckskin.
These three tribes were wandering hunters; but the

people of the fire told Radisson of yet another nation,
who lived in villages like the Iroquois, on "a great
river that divided itself in two," and was called "the
Forked River," because "it had two branches, the
one toward the west, the other toward the south,
. . . toward Mexico." These people were the Mandans or Omahas, or Iowas, or other people of the
Missouri.[1]

A whole world of discoveries lay before them. In
what direction should they go? "We desired not to
go to the north till we had made a discovery in the
south," explains Radisson. The people of the fire
refused to accompany the explorers farther; so the
two "put themselves in hazard," as Radisson relates,
and set out alone. They must have struck across
the height of land between the Mississippi and the
Missouri; for Radisson records that they met several
nations having villages, "all amazed to see us and very

[1] I have refrained from quoting Radisson's names for the different Indian tribes because it would only be "caviare to the general." If Radisson's manuscript be consulted
it will be seen that the crucial point is the whereabouts of the Mascoutins — or people of
the fire.   Reference to the last part of Appendix E will show that these people extended
far beyond the Wisconsin to the Missouri.   It is ignorance of this fact that has created
such bitter and childish controversy about the exact direction taken by Radisson west-
north-west of the Mascoutins.   The exact words of the document in the Marine
Department are : "In the lower Missipy there are several other nations very numerous
with whom we have no commerce who are trading yet with nobody.   Above Missoury
river which is in the Mississippi below the river Illinois, to the south, there are the
Mascoutins, Nadoessioux (Sioux) with whom we trade and who are numerous."   Benjamin Sulte was one of the first to discover that the Mascoutins had been in Nebraska,
though he does not attempt to trace this part of Radisson's journey definitely.

civil. The farther we sojourned, the delightfuller the land became. I can say that in all my lifetime I have never seen a finer country, for all that I have been in Italy. The people have very long hair. They reap twice a year. They war against the Sioux and the Cree. . . . It was very hot there. . . . Being among the people they told us . . . of men that built great cabins and have beards and have knives like the French." The Indians showed Radisson a string of beads only used by Europeans. These people must have been the Spaniards of the south. The tribes on the Missouri were large men of well-formed figures. There were no deformities among the people. Radisson saw corn and pumpkins in their gardens. "Their arrows were not of stone, but of fish bones. . . . Their dishes were made of wood. . . . They had great calumets of red and green stone . . . and great store of tobacco. . . . They had a kind of drink that made them mad for a whole day." [1] "We had not yet seen the Sioux,"

[1] The entire account of the people on "the Forked River" is so exact an account of the Mandans that it might be a page from Catlin's descriptions two centuries later. The long hair, the two crops a year, the tobacco, the soap-stone calumets, the stationary villages, the knowledge of the Spaniards, the warm climate — all point to a region far south of the Northern States, to which so many historians have stupidly and with almost wilful ignorance insisted on limiting Radisson's travels. Parkman has been thoroughly honest in the matter. His *La Salle* had been written before the discovery of the *Radisson Journals*; but in subsequent editions he acknowledges in a footnote that Radisson had been to "the Forked River." Other writers (with the exception of five) have been content to quote from Radisson's enemies instead of going directly to his journals. Even Garneau slurs over Radisson's explorations; but Garneau, too, wrote before the

relates Radisson. " We went toward the south and
came back by the north."   The *Jesuit Relations* are
more explicit.   Written the year that Radisson returned to Quebec, they state : " Continuing their wanderings, our two young Frenchmen visited the Sioux,
where they found five thousand warriors.   They then
left this nation for another warlike people, who with
bows and arrows had rendered themselves redoubtable."
These were the Crees, with whom, say the Jesuits, wood
is so rare and small that nature has taught them to
make fire of a kind of coal and to cover their cabins
with skins of the chase.   The explorers seem to have
spent the summer hunting antelope, buffalo, moose,
and wild turkey.   The Sioux received them cordially,
supplied them with food, and gave them an escort to
the next encampments.   They had set out southwest
to the Mascoutins, Mandans, and perhaps, also, the
Omahas.   They were now circling back northeastward
toward the Sault between Lake Michigan and Lake
Superior.   How far westward had they gone ?   Only
two facts gave any clew.   Radisson reports that moun-

discovery of the Radisson papers.   Abbé Tanguay, who is almost infallible on French-
Canadian matters, slips up on Radisson, because his writings preceded the publication
of the *Radisson Relations*.   The five writers who have attempted to redeem Radisson's
memory from ignominy are : Dr. N. E. Dionne, of the Parliamentary Library, Quebec ;
Mr. Justice Prudhomme, of St. Boniface, Manitoba ; Dr. George Bryce, of Winnepeg ;
Mr. Benjamin Sulte, of Ottawa ; and Judge J. V. Brower, of St. Paul.   If ever a monument be erected to Radisson — as one certainly ought in every province and state west
of the Great Lakes — the names of these four champions should be engraved upon it.

tains lay far inland; and the Jesuits record that the explorers were among tribes that used coal. This must have been a country far west of the Mandans and Mascoutins and within sight of at least the Bad Lands, or that stretch of rough country between the prairie and outlying foothills of the Rockies.[1] The course of the first exploration seems to have circled over the territory now known as Wisconsin, perhaps eastern Iowa and Nebraska, South Dakota, Montana, and back over North Dakota and Minnesota to the north shore of Lake Superior. "The lake toward the north is full of rocks, yet great ships can ride in it without danger," writes Radisson. At the Sault they found the Crees and Sautaux in bitter war. They also heard of a French establishment, and going to visit it found that the Jesuits had established a mission.

Radisson had explored the Southwest. He now decided to essay the Northwest. When the Sautaux

[1] This claim will, I know, stagger preconceived ideas. In the light of only Radisson's narrative, the third voyage has usually been identified with Wisconsin and Minnesota; but in the light of the *Jesuit Relations*, written the year that Radisson returned, to what tribes could the descriptions apply? Even Parkman's footnote acknowledged that Radisson was among the people of the Missouri. Grant that, and the question arises, What people on the Missouri answer the description? The Indians of the far west use not only coal for fire, but raw galena to make bullets for their guns. In fact, it was that practice of the tribes of Idaho that led prospectors to find the Blue Bell Mine of Kootenay. Granting that the Jesuit account — which was of course, from hearsay — mistook the use of turf, dry grass, or buffalo refuse for a kind of coal, the fact remains that only the very far western tribes had this custom.

were at war with the Crees, he met the Crees and heard of the great salt sea in the north. Surely this was the Sea of the North — Hudson Bay — of which the Nipissing chief had told Groseillers long ago. Then the Crees had great store of beaver pelts; and trade must not be forgotten. No sooner had peace been arranged between Sautaux and Crees, than Cree hunters flocked out of the northern forests to winter on Lake Superior. A rumor of Iroquois on the warpath compelled Radisson and Groseillers to move their camp back from Lake Superior higher up the chain of lakes and rivers between what is now Minnesota and Canada, toward the country of the Sioux. In the fall of 1659 Groseillers' health began to fail from the hardships; so he remained in camp for the winter, attending to the trade, while Radisson carried on the explorations alone.

This was one of the coldest winters known in Canada.[1] The snow fell so heavily in the thick pine woods of Minnesota that Radisson says the forest became as sombre as a cellar. The colder the weather the better the fur, and, presenting gifts to insure safe conduct, Radisson set out with a band of one hundred and fifty Cree hunters for the Northwest. They travelled on snow-shoes, hunting moose on the way and sleeping at night round a camp-fire under the stars. League

---

[1] *Letters of Marie de l' Incarnation.*

after league, with no sound through the deathly white forest but the soft crunch-crunch of the snow-shoes, they travelled two hundred miles toward what is now Manitoba. When they had set out, the snow was like a cushion. Now it began to melt in the spring sun, and clogged the snow-shoes till it was almost impossible to travel. In the morning the surface was glazed ice, and they could march without snow-shoes. Spring thaw called a halt to their exploration. The Crees encamped for three weeks to build boats. As soon as the ice cleared, the band launched back down-stream for the appointed rendez-vous on Green Bay. All that Radisson learned on this trip was that the Bay of the North lay much farther from Lake Superior than the old Nipissing chief had told Dreuillettes and Groseillers.[1]

Groseillers had all in readiness to depart for Quebec; and five hundred Indians from the Upper Country had come together to go down the Ottawa and St. Lawrence with the explorers. As they were about to embark, *coureurs* came in from the woods with news that more than a thousand Iroquois were on the war-path, boasting that they would exterminate the French.[2] Somewhere along the Ottawa a small band of Hurons had been massacred. The Indians with

[1] *Jesuit Relations,* 1658.
[2] See Marie de l' Incarnation, Dollier de Casson, and Abbé Belmont.

Groseillers and Radisson were terrified. A council of the elders was called.

" Brothers, why are ye so foolish as to put yourselves in the hands of those that wait for you?" demanded an old chief, addressing the two white men. " The Iroquois will destroy you and carry you away captive. Will you have your brethren, that love you, slain? Who will baptize our children?" (Radisson and Groseillers had baptized more than two hundred children.[1]) " Stay till next year! Then you may freely go! Our mothers will send their children to be taught in the way of the Lord!"

Fear is like fire. It must be taken in the beginning, or it spreads. The explorers retired, decided on a course of action, and requested the Indians to meet them in council a second time. Eight hundred warriors assembled, seating themselves in a circle. Radisson and Groseillers took their station in the centre.[2]

[1] *Jesuit Relations*, 1660.

[2] It may be well to state as nearly as possible exactly *what* tribes Radisson had met in this trip. Those rejoined on the way up at Manitoulin Island were refugee Hurons and Ottawas. From the Hurons, Ottawas, and Algonquins of Green Bay, Radisson went west with Pottowatomies; from them to the Escotecke or Sioux of the Fire, namely a branch of the Mascoutins. From these Wisconsin Mascoutins, he learns of the Nadoneceroron, or Sioux proper, and of the Christinos or Crees. Going west with the Mascoutins, he comes to "sedentary" tribes. Are these the Mandans? He compares this country to Italy. From them he hears of white men, that he thinks may be Spaniards. This tribe is at bitter war with Sioux and Crees. At Green Bay he hears of the Sautaux in war with Crees. His description of buffalo hunts among the Sioux tallies exactly with the Pembina hunts of a later day. Oldmixon says that it was from Crees and Assiniboines visiting at Green Bay that Radisson learned of a way overland to the great game country of Hudson Bay.

"Who am I ? " demanded Groseillers, hotly. "Am
I a foe or a friend ?   If a foe, why did you suffer me
to live ?   If a friend, listen what I say ! You know
that we risked our lives for you ! If we have no courage, why did you not tell us ?   If you have more wit
than we, why did you not use it to defend yourselves
against the Iroquois ?   How can you defend your
wives and children unless you get arms from the
French ! "

"Fools," cried Radisson, striking a beaver skin
across an Indian's shoulder, "will you fight the Iroquois with beaver pelts ? Do you not know the
French way ? We fight with guns, not robes. The
Iroquois will coop you up here till you have used all
your powder, and then despatch you with ease ! Shall
your children be slaves because you are cowards ?   Do
what you will ! For my part I choose to die like a
man rather than live like a beggar. Take back your
beaver robes. We can live without you — " and the
white men strode out from the council.

Consternation reigned among the Indians. There
was an uproar of argument. For six days the fate of the
white men hung fire. Finally the chiefs sent word that
the five hundred young warriors would go to Quebec
with the white men. Radisson did not give their ardor
time to cool. They embarked at once. The fleet of
canoes crossed the head of the lakes and came to the

Upper Ottawa without adventure. Scouts went ahead
to all the *portages*, and great care was taken to avoid
an ambush when passing overland. Below the Chaudière Falls the scouts reported that four Iroquois
boats had crossed the river. Again Radisson did not
give time for fear. He sent the lightest boats in pursuit ; and while keeping the enemy thus engaged with
half his own company on guard at the ends of the long
portage, he hurriedly got cargoes and canoes across the
landing. The Iroquois had fled. By that Radisson
knew they were weak. Somewhere along the Long
Sault Rapids, the scouts saw sixteen Iroquois canoes.
The Indians would have thrown down their goods
and fled, but Radisson instantly got his forces in hand
and held them with a grip of steel. Distributing
loaded muskets to the bravest warriors, he pursued the
Iroquois with a picked company of Hurons, Algonquins, Sautaux, and Sioux. Beating their paddles,
Radisson's company shouted the war-cry till the hills
rang ; but all the warriors were careful not to waste an
ounce of powder till within hitting range. The Iroquois were not used to this sort of defence. They
fled. The Long Sault was always the most dangerous
part of the Ottawa. Radisson kept scouts to rear and
fore, but the Iroquois had deserted their boats and
were hanging on the flanks of the company to attempt
an ambush. It was apparent that a fort had been

erected at the foot of the rapids. Leaving half the
band in their boats, Radisson marched overland with
two hundred warriors. Iroquois shots spattered from
each side ; but the Huron muskets kept the assailants
at a distance, and those of Radisson's warriors who
had not guns were armed with bows and arrows, and
wore a shield of buffalo skin dried hard as metal.
The Iroquois rushed for the barricade at the foot of

Voyageurs running the Rapids of the Ottawa River.

the Sault. Five of them were picked off as they ran.
For a moment the Iroquois were out of cover, and
their weakness was betrayed. They had only one
hundred and fifty men, while Radisson had five hundred ; but the odds would not long be in his favor.
Ammunition was running out, and the enemy must be
dislodged without wasting a shot. Radisson called back
encouragement to his followers. They answered with a
shout. Tying the beaver pelts in great bundles, the

Indians rolled the fur in front nearer and nearer the Iroquois boats, keeping under shelter from the shots of the fort. The Iroquois must either lose their boats and be cut off from escape, or retire from the fort. It was not necessary for Radisson's warriors to fire a shot. Abandoning even their baggage and glad to get off with their lives, the Iroquois dashed to save their boats.

A terrible spectacle awaited Radisson inside the enclosure of the palisades.[1] The scalps of dead Indians flaunted from the pickets. Not a tree but was spattered with bullet marks as with bird shot. Here and there burnt holes gaped in the stockades like wounds. Outside along the river bank lay the charred bones of captives who had been burned. The scarred fort told its own tale. Here refugees had been penned up by the Iroquois till thirst and starvation did their work. In the clay a hole had been dug for water by the parched victims, and the ooze through the mud eagerly scooped up. Only when he reached Montreal did Radisson learn the story of the dismantled fort. The rumor carried to the explorers on Lake Michigan of a thousand Iro-

---

[1] There is a mistake in Radisson's account here, which is easily checked by contemporaneous accounts of Marie de l'Incarnation and Dollier de Casson. Radisson describes Dollard's fight during his fourth trip in 1664, when it is quite plain that he means 1660. The fight has been so thoroughly described by Mr. Parkman, who drew his material from the two authorities mentioned, and the *Jesuit Relations*, that I do not give it in detail. I give a brief account of Radisson's description of the tragedy.

quois going on the war-path to exterminate the French had been only too true. Half the warriors were to assault Quebec, half to come down on Montreal from the Ottawa. One thing only could save the French — to keep the bands apart. Those on the Ottawa had been hunting all winter and must necessarily be short of powder. To intercept them, a gallant band of seventeen French, four Algonquins, and sixty Hurons led by Dollard took their stand at the Long Sault. The French and their Indian allies were boiling their kettles when two hundred Iroquois broke from the woods. There was no time to build a fort. Leaving their food, Dollard and his men threw themselves into the rude palisades which Indians had erected the previous year. The Iroquois kept up a constant fire and sent for reënforcements of six hundred warriors, who were on the Richelieu. In defiance the Indians fighting for the French sallied out, scalped the fallen Iroquois, and hoisted the sanguinary trophies on long poles above the pickets. The enraged Iroquois redoubled their fury. The fort was too small to admit all the Hurons; and when the Iroquois came up from the Richelieu with Huron renegades among their warriors, the Hurons deserted their French allies and went over in a body to the enemy. For two days the French had fought against two hundred Iroquois. For five more days they fought against

H

eight hundred. "The worst of it was," relates Radisson, "the French had no water, as we plainly saw;
for they had made a hole in the ground out of which
they could get but little because the fort was on a
hill. It was pitiable. There was not a tree but what
was shot with bullets. The Iroquois had rushed to
make a breach (in the wall). . . . The French set fire
to a barrel of powder to drive the Iroquois back . . .
but it fell inside the fort. . . . Upon this, the Iroquois entered . . . so that not one of the French
escaped. . . . It was terrible . . . for we came there
eight days after the defeat." [1]

Without a doubt it was Dollard's splendid fight that
put fear in the hearts of the Iroquois who fled before
Radisson. The passage to Montreal was clear. The
boats ran the rapids without unloading; but Groseillers almost lost his life. His canoe caught on a rock
in midstream, but righting herself shot down safely to
the landing with no greater loss than a damaged keel.
The next day, after two years' absence, Radisson and
Groseillers arrived at Montreal. A brief stop was
made at Three Rivers for rest till twenty citizens had

---

[1] It will be noticed that Radisson's account of the battle at the Long Sault — which
I have given in his own words as far as possible — differs in details from the only other
accounts written by contemporaries; namely, Marie de l'Incarnation, Dollier de Casson,
the Abbé Belmont, and the Jesuits. All these must have written from hearsay, for
they were at Quebec and Montreal. Radisson was on the spot a week after the
tragedy; so that his account may be supposed to be as accurate as any.

fitted out two shallops with cannon to escort the discoverers in fitting pomp to Quebec.   As the fleet of
canoes glided round Cape Diamond, battery and bastion thundered a welcome.   Welcome they were, and
thrice welcome ; for so ceaseless had been the Iroquois
wars that the three French ships lying at anchor would
have returned to France without a single beaver skin
if the explorers had not come.   Citizens shouted from
the terraced heights of Château St. Louis, and bells
rang out the joy of all New France over the discoverers' return.   For a week Radisson and Groseillers
were fêted.   Viscomte d'Argenson, the new governor,
presented them with gifts and sent two brigantines to
carry them home to Three Rivers.   There they rested
for the remainder of the year, Groseillers at his seigniory with his wife, Marguerite; Radisson, under the
parental roof.[1]

[1] Mr. Benjamin Sulte states that the explorers wintered on Green Bay, 1658–1659,
then visited the tribes between Milwaukee and the river Wisconsin in the spring of
1659. Here they learn of the Sioux and the Crees. They push southwest first, where
they see the Mississippi between April and July, 1659.   Thence they come back
to the Sault.   Then they winter, 1659–1660, among the Sioux.   I have not
attempted to give the dates of the itinerary ; because it would be a matter of speculation
open to contradiction ; but if we accept Radisson's account at all — and that account
is corroborated by writers contemporaneous with him — we must then accept *his*
account of *where* he went, and not the casual guesses of modern writers who have
given his journal one hurried reading, and then sat down, without consulting documents contemporaneous with Radisson, to inform the world of *where* he went.
Because this is such a very sore point with two or three western historical societies, I
beg to state the reasons why I have set down Radisson's itinerary as much farther west
than has been generally believed, though how far west he went does not efface the main

and essential fact *that Radisson was the true discoverer of the Great Northwest.* For that, let us give him a belated credit and not obscure the feat by disputes. (1) The term "Forked River" referred to the Missouri and Mississippi, not the Wisconsin and Mississippi. (2) No other rivers in that region are to be compared to the Ottawa and St. Lawrence but the Missouri and Mississippi. (3) The Mascoutins, or People of the Fire, among whom Radisson found himself when he descended the Wisconsin from Green Bay, conducted him westward only as far as the tribes allied to them, the Mascoutins of the Missouri or Nebraska. Hence, Radisson going west-north-west to the Sioux — as he says he did — must have skirted much farther west than Wisconsin and Minnesota. (4) His descriptions of the Indians who knew tribes in trade with the Spaniards must refer to the Indians south of the Big Bend of the Missouri. (5) His description of the climate refers to the same region. (6) The *Jesuit Relations* confirm beyond all doubt that he was among the main body of the great Sioux Confederacy. (7) Both his and the Jesuit reference is to the treeless prairie, which does not apply to the wooded lake regions of eastern Minnesota or northern Wisconsin.

To me, it is simply astounding — and that is putting it mildly — that any one pretending to have read *Radisson's Journal* can accuse him of "claiming" to have "descended to the salt sea" (Gulf of Mexico). Radisson makes no such claim ; and to accuse him of such is like building a straw enemy for the sake of knocking him down, or stirring up muddy waters to make them look deep. The exact words of Radisson's narrative are : "We went into ye great river that divides itself in 2, where the hurrons with some Ottauake . . . had retired. . . . This nation have warrs against those of the Forked River . . . so called because it has 2 branches the one towards the west, the other towards the South, wch. we believe runns towards Mexico, by the tokens they gave us . . . they told us the prisoners they take tells them that they have warrs against a nation . . . that have great beards and such knives as we have " . . . etc., etc., etc. . . . . "which made us believe they were Europeans." This statement is *no* claim that Radisson went to Mexico, but only that he met tribes who knew tribes trading with Spaniards of Mexico. And yet, on the careless reading of this statement, one historian brands Radisson as a liar for "having claimed he went to Mexico." The thing would be comical in its impudence if it were not that many such misrepresentations of what Radisson wrote have dimmed the glory of his real achievements.

Montreal in 1760: 1, the St. Lawrence; 20, the Dock; 18–19, Arsenal; 16, the Church; 13–15, the Convent and Hospital; 8–12, Sally-ports, River Side; 17, Cannon and Wall; 3–4–5, Houses on Island.

CHAPTER IV

1661–1664

RADISSON'S FOURTH VOYAGE

The Success of the Explorers arouses Envy — It becomes known
that they have heard of the Famous Sea of the North — When
they ask Permission to resume their Explorations, the French Governor refuses except on Condition of receiving Half the Profits — In
Defiance, the Explorers steal off at Midnight — They return with
a Fortune and are driven from New France

RADISSON was not yet twenty-six years of age, and
his explorations of the Great Northwest had won
him both fame and fortune. As Spain sought gold
in the New Word, so France sought precious furs.
Furs were the only possible means of wealth to the
French colony, and for ten years the fur trade had
languished owing to the Iroquois wars. For a year
after the migration of the Hurons to Onondaga, not a
single beaver skin was brought to Montreal. Then
began the annual visits of the Indians from the Upper
Country to the forts of the St. Lawrence. Sweeping
down the northern rivers like wild-fowl, in far-spread,
desultory flocks, came the Indians of the *Pays d'en*

Haut. Down the Ottawa to Montreal, down the St. Maurice to Three Rivers, down the Saguenay and round to Quebec, came the treasure-craft, — light fleets of birch canoes laden to the water-line with beaver skins. Whence came the wealth that revived the languishing trade of New France? From a vague, far Eldorado somewhere round a sea in the North. Hudson had discovered this sea half a century before Radisson's day; Jean Bourdon, a Frenchman, had coasted up Labrador in 1657 seeking the Bay of the North; and on their last trip the explorers had learned from the Crees who came through the dense forests of the hinterland that there lay round this Bay of the North a vast country with untold wealth of furs. The discovery of a route overland to the north sea was to become the lodestar of Radisson's life.[1]

"We considered whether to reveal what we had learned," explains Radisson, "for we had *not* been in the Bay of the North, knowing only what the Crees told us. We wished to discover it ourselves and have assurance before revealing anything." But the secret leaked out. Either Groseillers told his wife, or the

---

[1] The childish dispute whether Bourdon sailed into the bay and up to its head, or only to 50° N. latitude, does not concern Radisson's life, and, therefore, is ignored. One thing I can state with absolute certainty from having been up the coast of Labrador in a most inclement season, that Bourdon could not possibly have gone to and back from the inner waters of Hudson Bay between May 2 and August 11. J. Edmond Roy and Mr. Sulte both pronounce Bourdon a myth, and his trip a fabrication.

Jesuits got wind of the news from the Indians ; for it was announced from Quebec that two priests, young La Vallière, the son of the governor at Three Rivers, six other Frenchmen, and some Indians would set out for the Bay of the North up the Saguenay.   Radisson was invited to join the company as a guide.   Needless to say that a man who had already discovered the Great Northwest and knew the secret of the road to the North, refused to play a second part among amateur explorers.   Radisson promptly declined.   Nevertheless, in May, 1661, the Jesuits, Gabriel Dreuillettes and Claude Dablon, accompanied by Couture, La Vallière, and three others, set out with Indian guides for the discovery of Hudson's Bay by land.   On June 1 they began to ascend the Saguenay, pressing through vast solitudes below the sombre precipices of the river. The rapids were frequent, the heat was terrific, and the *portages* arduous.   Owing to the obstinacy of the guides, the French were stopped north of Lake St. John.   Here the priests established a mission, and messengers were sent to Quebec for instructions.

Meanwhile, Radisson and Groseillers saw that no time must be lost.   If they would be first in the North, as they had been first in the West, they must set out at once.   Two Indian guides from the Upper Country chanced to be in Montreal. Groseillers secured them by bringing both to Three

Rivers. Then the explorers formally applied to the French governor, D'Avaugour, for permission to go on the voyage of discovery. New France regulated the fur trade by license. Imprisonment, the galleys for life, even death on a second offence, were the punishments of those who traded without a license. The governor's answer revealed the real animus behind his enthusiasm for discovery. He would give the explorers a license if they would share half the profits of the trip with him and take along two of his servants as auditors of the returns. One can imagine the indignation of the dauntless explorers at this answer. Their cargo of furs the preceding year had saved New France from bankruptcy. Offering to venture their lives a second time for the extension of the French domain, they were told they might do so if they would share half the profits with an avaricious governor. Their answer was characteristic. Discoverers were greater than governors ; still, if the Indians of the Upper Country invited his Excellency, Radisson and Groseillers would be glad to have the honor of his company ; as for his servants — men who went on voyages of discovery had to act as both masters and servants.

D'Avaugour was furious. He issued orders forbidding the explorers to leave Three Rivers without his express permission. Radisson and Groseillers knew the penalties of ignoring this order. They

asked the Jesuits to intercede for them. Though
Gareau had been slain trying to ascend the Ottawa and
Father Ménard had by this time preached in the
forests of Lake Michigan, the Jesuits had made no
great discoveries in the Northwest.   All they got for
their intercessions was a snub.[1]

While messages were still passing between the governor and the explorers, there swept down the St.
Lawrence to Three Rivers seven canoes of Indians
from the Upper Country, asking for Radisson and
Groseillers.   The explorers were honorable to a
degree.   They notified the governor of Quebec that
they intended to embark with the Indians.   D'Avaugour stubbornly ordered the Indians to await the return
of his party from the Saguenay.   The Indians made
off to hide in the rushes of Lake St. Peter.   The
sympathy of Three Rivers was with the explorers.
Late one night in August Radisson and Groseillers —
who was captain of the soldiers and carried the keys
of the fort — slipped out from the gates, with a third
Frenchman called Larivière.   As they stepped into
their canoe, the sentry demanded, " Who goes ? "

" Groseillers," came the answer through the dark.

" God give you a good voyage, sir," called the
sentry, faithful to his captain rather than the governor.

---

[1] " Shame put upon them," says Radisson.   Ménard did *not* go out with Radisson
and Groseillers, as is erroneously recorded.

The skiff pushed out on the lapping tide. A bend in the river — and the lights of the fort glimmering in long lines across the water had vanished behind. The prow of Radisson's boat was once more heading up-stream for the Unknown. Paddling with all swiftness through the dark, the three Frenchmen had come to the rushes of Lake St. Peter before daybreak. No Indians could be found. Men of softer mettle might have turned back. Not so Radisson. " We were well-armed and had a good boat," he relates, " so we resolved to paddle day and night to overtake the Indians." At the west end of the lake they came up with the north-bound canoes. For three days and nights they pushed on without rest. Naturally, Radisson did not pause to report progress at Montreal. Game was so plentiful in the surrounding forests that Iroquois hunters were always abroad in the regions of the St. Lawrence and Ottawa.[1] Once they heard guns. Turning a bend in the river, they discovered five Iroquois boats, just in time to avoid them. That night the Frenchman, Larivière, dreamed that he had been captured by the Mohawks, and he shouted out in

---

[1] I have purposely avoided stating whether Radisson went by way of Lake Ontario or the Ottawa. Dr. Dionne thinks that he went by Ontario and Niagara because Radisson refers to vast waterfalls under which a man could walk. Radisson gives the height of these falls as forty feet. Niagara are nearer three hundred; and the Chaudière of the Ottawa would answer Radisson's description better, were it not that he says a man could go under the falls for a quarter of a mile. " The Lake of the Castors " plainly points to Lake Nipissing.

such terror that the alarmed Indians rushed to embark. The next day they again came on the trail of Iroquois. The frightened Indians from the Upper Country shouldered their canoes and dashed through the woods. Larivière could not keep up and was afraid to go back from the river lest he should lose his bearings. Fighting his way over windfall and rock, he sank exhausted and fell asleep. Far ahead of the Iroquois boats the Upper Country Indians came together again. The Frenchman was nowhere to be found. It was dark. The Indians would not wait to search. Radisson and Groseillers dared not turn back to face the irate governor. Larivière was abandoned. Two weeks afterwards some French hunters found him lying on the rocks almost dead from starvation. He was sent back to Three Rivers, where D'Avaugour had him imprisoned. This outrage the inhabitants of Three Rivers resented. They forced the jail and rescued Larivière.

Three days after the loss of Larivière Radisson and Groseillers caught up with seven more canoes of Indians from the Upper Country. The union of the two bands was just in time, for the next day they were set upon at a *portage* by the Iroquois. Ordering the Indians to encase themselves in bucklers of matting and buffalo hide, Radisson led the assault on the Iroquois barricade. Trees were cut down, and

the Upper Indians rushed the rude fort with timbers
extemporized into battering-rams.   In close range of
the enemy, Radisson made a curious discovery.
Frenchmen were directing the Iroquois warriors.
Who had sent these French to intercept the explorers?   If Radisson suspected treachery on the part

Château St. Louis, Quebec, 1669, from one of the oldest prints in
existence.

of jealous rivals from Quebec, it must have redoubled
his fury; for the Indians from the Upper Country threw
themselves in the breached barricade with such force
that the Iroquois lost heart and tossed belts of wampum
over the stockades to supplicate peace.   It was almost
night.   Radisson's Indians drew off to consider the
terms of peace.   When morning came, behold an

empty fort! The French renegades had fled with their Indian allies.

Glad to be rid of the first hindrance, the explorers once more sped north. In the afternoon, Radisson's scouts ran full tilt into a band of Iroquois laden with beaver pelts. The Iroquois were smarting from their defeat of the previous night; and what was Radisson's amusement to see his own scouts and the Iroquois running from each other in equal fright, while the ground between lay strewn with booty! Radisson rushed his Indians for the waterside to intercept the Iroquois' flight. The Iroquois left their boats and swam for the opposite shore, where they threw up the usual barricade and entrenched themselves to shoot on Radisson's passing canoes. Using the captured beaver pelts as shields, the Upper Indians ran the gantlet of the Iroquois fire with the loss of only one man.

The slightest defeat may turn well-ordered retreat into panic. If the explorers went on, the Iroquois would hang to the rear of the travelling Indians and pick off warriors till the Upper Country people became so weakened they would fall an easy prey. Not flight, but fight, was Radisson's motto. He ordered his men ashore to break up the barricade. Darkness fell over the forest. The Iroquois could not see to fire. " They spared not their powder," relates Radisson, " but they made more noise than hurt." Attaching a fuse to a barrel of powder, Radisson threw this over into the Iroquois fort. The crash of the explosion was followed by a blaze of the Iroquois musketry that killed three of Radisson's men. Radisson then tore the bark off a birch tree, filled the bole with powder, and in the darkness crept close to the Iroquois barricade and set fire to the logs. Red tongues of fire leaped up, there was a roar as of wind, and the Iroquois fort was on fire. Radisson's men dashed through the fire, hatchet in hand. The Iroquois answered with their death chant. Friend and foe merged in the smoke and darkness. "We could not know one another in that skirmish of blows," says Radisson. "There was noise to terrify the stoutest man." In the midst of the mêlée a frightful storm of thunder and sheeted rain rolled over the forest. "To my mind," writes the disgusted Radisson, "that was something extraordinary. I think the Devil himself sent that storm to let those wretches escape, so that they might destroy more innocents." The rain put out the fire. As soon as the storm had passed, Radisson kindled torches to search for the missing. Three of his men were slain, seven wounded. Of the enemy, eleven lay dead, five were prisoners. The rest of the Iroquois had fled to the forest. The Upper Indians burned their prisoners according to their custom, and the night was passed in mad orgies to celebrate the victory. " The sleep we took did not make our heads giddy," writes Radisson.

The next day they encountered more Iroquois. Both sides at once began building forts ; but when he could, Radisson always avoided war. Having gained victory enough to hold the Iroquois in check, he wanted no massacre. That night he embarked his men noiselessly ; and never once stopping to kindle camp-fire, they paddled from Friday night to Tuesday morning. The *portages* over rocks in the dark cut the *voyageurs'* moccasins to shreds. Every landing was marked with the blood of bruised feet. Sometimes they avoided leaving any trace of themselves by walking in the stream, dragging their boats along the edge of the rapids. By Tuesday the Indians were so fagged that they could go no farther without rest. Canoes were moored in the hiding of the rushes till the *voyageurs* slept. They had been twenty-two days going from Three Rivers to Lake Nipissing, and had not slept one hour on land.

It was October when they came to Lake Superior. The forests were painted in all the glory of autumn, and game abounded. White fish appeared under the clear, still waters of the lake like shoals of floating metal ; bears were seen hulking away from the watering places of sandy shores ; and wild geese whistled overhead. After the terrible dangers of the voyage, with scant sleep and scanter fare, the country seemed, as Radisson says, a terrestrial paradise. The Indians gave solemn thanks to their gods of earth and forest, "and we," writes Radisson, "to the God of gods." Indian summer lay on the land. November found the explorers coasting the south shore of Lake Superior. They passed the Island of Michilimackinac with its stone arches. Radisson heard from the Indians of the copper mines. He saw the pictured rocks that were to become famous for beauty. " I gave it the name of St. Peter because that was my name and I was the first Christian to see it," he writes of the stone arch. " There were in these places very deep caves, caused by the violence of the waves." Jesuits had been on the part of Lake Superior near the Sault, and poor Ménard perished in the forests of Lake Michigan; but Radisson and Groseillers were the first white men to cruise from south to west and west to north, where a chain of lakes and waterways leads from the Minnesota lake country to the prairies now known as Manitoba. Before the end of November the explorers rounded the western end of Lake Superior and proceeded northwest. Radisson records that they came to great winter encampments of the Crees; and the Crees did not venture east for fear of Sautaux and Iroquois. He mentions a river of Sturgeons, where was a great store of fish.

The Crees wished to conduct the two white men to the wooded lake region, northwest towards the land of the Assiniboines, where Indian families took refuge on islands from those tigers of the plains — the Sioux — who were invincible on horseback but less skilful in canoes.   The rivers were beginning to freeze. Boats were abandoned ; but there was no snow for snow-shoe travelling, and the explorers were unable to transport the goods brought for trade.   Bidding the Crees go to their families and bring back slaves to carry the baggage, Radisson and Groseillers built themselves the first fort and the first fur post between the Missouri and the North Pole.   It was evidently somewhere west of Duluth in either what is now Minnesota or northwestern Ontario.

This fur post was the first habitation of civilization in all the Great Northwest. Not the railway, not the cattle trail, not the path of forward-marching empire purposely hewing a way through the wilderness, opened the West.   It was the fur trade that found the West.   It was the fur trade that explored the West.   It was the fur trade that wrested the West from savagery.   The beginning was in the little fort built by Radisson and Groseillers.   No great factor in human progress ever had a more insignificant beginning.

The fort was rushed up by two men almost starving for food. It was on the side of a river, built in the shape of a triangle, with the base at the water side. The walls were of unbarked logs, the roof of thatched branches interlaced, with the door at the river side. In the middle of the earth floor, so that the smoke would curl up where the branches formed a funnel or chimney, was the fire. On the right of the fire, two hewn logs overlaid with pine boughs made a bed. On the left, another hewn log acted as a table. Jumbled everywhere, hanging from branches and knobs of branches, were the firearms, clothing, and merchandise of the two fur traders. Naturally, a fort two thousand miles from help needed sentries. Radisson had not forgotten his boyhood days of Onondaga. He strung carefully concealed cords through the grass and branches around the fort. To these bells were fastened, and the bells were the sentries. The two white men could now sleep soundly without fear of approach. This fort, from which sprang the buoyant, aggressive, prosperous, free life of the Great Northwest, was founded and built and completed in two days. The West had begun.[1]

[1] The two main reasons why I think that Radisson and Groseillers were now moving up that chain of lakes and rivers between Minnesota and Canada, connecting Lake of the Woods with Lake Winnipeg, are : (1) Oldmixon says it was the report of the Assiniboine Indians from Lake Assiniboine (Lake Winnipeg) that led Radisson to seek for the Bay of the North overland. These Assiniboines did not go to the bay by way

It was a beginning which every Western pioneer was to repeat for the next two hundred years : first, the log cabins ; then, the fight with the wilderness for food.

Radisson, being the younger, went into the woods to hunt, while Groseillers kept house. Wild geese and ducks were whistling south, but "the whistling that I made," writes Radisson, "was another music than theirs ; for I killed three and scared the rest." Strange Indians came through the forest, but were not admitted to the tiny fort, lest knowledge of the traders' weakness should tempt theft. Many a night the explorers were roused by a sudden ringing of the bells or crashing through the underbrush, to find that wild animals had been attracted by the smell of meat, and wolverine or wildcat was attempting to tear through the matted branches of the thatched roof. The desire for firearms has tempted Indians to murder many a trader ; so Radisson and Groseillers *cached* all the supplies that they did not need in a hole across the river. News of the two white men alone in the northern forest spread like wild-fire to the different Sautaux and Ojibway encampments ; and Radisson

of Lake Superior, but by way of Lake Winnipeg.   (2) A *mémoire* written by De la Chesnaye in 1696 — see *Documents Nouvelle France,* 1492-1712 — distinctly refers to a *coureur's* trail from Lake Superior to Lake Assiniboine or Lake Winnipeg.   There is no record of any Frenchmen but Radisson and Groseillers having followed such a trail to the land of the Assiniboines — the Manitoba of to-day — before 1676.

invented another protection in addition to the bells. He rolled gunpowder in twisted tubes of birch bark, and ran a circle of this round the fort. Putting a torch to the birch, he surprised the Indians by displaying to them a circle of fire running along the ground in a series of jumps. To the Indians it was magic. The two white men were engirt with a mystery that defended them from all harm. Thus white men passed their first winter in the Great Northwest.

Toward winter four hundred Crees came to escort the explorers to the wooded lake region yet farther west towards the land of the Assiniboines, the modern Manitoba. "We were Cæsars," writes Radisson. "There was no one to contradict us. We went away free from any burden, while those poor miserables thought themselves happy to carry our equipage in the hope of getting a brass ring, or an awl, or a needle. . . . They admired our actions more than the fools of Paris their king. . . .[1] They made a great noise, calling us gods and devils. We marched four days through the woods. The country was beautiful with clear parks. At last we came within a league of the Cree cabins, where we spent the night that we might enter the encampment with pomp the next day. The

[1] One can guess that a man who wrote in that spirit two centuries before the French Revolution would not be a sycophant in courts, — which, perhaps, helps to explain the conspiracy of silence that obscured Radisson's fame.

swiftest Indians ran ahead to warn the people of our coming." Embarking in boats, where the water was open, the two explorers came to the Cree lodges. They were welcomed with shouts. Messengers marched in front, scattering presents from the white men, — kettles to call all to a feast of friendship ; knives to encourage the warriors to be brave ; swords to signify that the white men would fight all enemies of the Cree ; and abundance of trinkets — needles and awls and combs and tin mirrors — for the women. The Indians prostrated themselves as slaves; and the explorers were conducted to a grand council of welcome. A feast was held, followed by a symbolic dance in celebration of the white men's presence.

Their entry to the Great Northwest had been a triumph : but they could not escape the privations of the explorer's life. Winter set in with a severity to make up for the long, late autumn. Snow fell continuously till day and night were as one, the sombre forests muffled to silence with the wild creatures driven for shelter to secret haunts. Four hundred men had brought the explorers north. Allowing an average of four to each family, there must have been sixteen hundred people in the encampment of Crees. To prevent famine, the Crees scattered to the winter hunting-grounds, arranging to come together again in two months at a northern rendezvous. When Radisson and Groseillers came to the rendezvous, they learned that the gathering hunters had had poor luck. Food was short. To make matters worse, heavy rains were followed by sharp frost. The snow became iced over, destroying rabbit and grouse, which feed the large game. Radisson noticed that the Indians often snatched food from the hands of hungry children. More starving Crees continued to come into camp. Soon the husbands were taking the wives' share of food, and the women were subsisting on dried pelts. The Crees became too weak to carry their snow-shoes, or to gather wood for fire. The cries of the dying broke the deathly stillness of the winter forest; and the strong began to dog the footsteps of the weak. "Good God, have mercy on these innocent people," writes Radisson; "have mercy on us who acknowledge Thee!" Digging through the snow with their rackets, some of the Crees got roots to eat. Others tore the bark from trees and made a kind of soup that kept them alive. Two weeks after the famine set in, the Indians were boiling the pulverized bones of the waste heap. After that the only food was the buckskin that had been tanned for clothing. "We ate it so eagerly," writes Radisson, "that our gums did bleed. . . . We became the image of death." Before the spring five hundred Crees had died of famine. Radisson and Groseillers scarcely

had strength to drag the dead from the tepees.   The
Indians thought that Groseillers had been fed by
some fiend, for his heavy, black beard covered his
thin face.   Radisson they loved, because his beardless
face looked as gaunt as theirs.[1]

Relief came with the breaking of the weather.   The
rain washed the iced snows away; deer began to
roam; and with the opening of the rivers came two
messengers from the Sioux to invite Radisson and
Groseillers to visit their nation.   The two Sioux
had a dog, which they refused to sell for all Radisson's gifts.   The Crees dared not offend the Sioux
ambassadors by stealing the worthless cur on which
such hungry eyes were cast, but at night Radisson
slipped up to the Sioux tepee.   The dog came prowling out.   Radisson stabbed it so suddenly that it
dropped without a sound.   Hurrying back, he boiled
and fed the meat to the famishing Crees.   When the
Sioux returned to their own country, they sent a score
of slaves with food for the starving encampment.   No
doubt Radisson had plied the first messengers with

[1] My reason for thinking that this region was farther north than Minnesota is the
size of the Cree winter camp; but I have refrained from trying to localize this part of
the trip, except to say it was west and north of Duluth.   Some writers recognize in the
description parts of Minnesota, others the hinterland between Lake Superior and
James Bay.   In the light of the *mémoire* of 1696 sent to the French government, I
am unable to regard this itinerary as any other than the famous fur traders' trail between
Lake Superior and Lake Winnipeg by way of Sturgeon River and the Lake of the
Woods.

gifts; for the slaves brought word that thirty picked
runners from the Sioux were coming to escort the
white men to the prairie. To receive their bene-
factors, and also, perhaps, to show that they were
not defenceless, the Crees at once constructed a fort;
for Cree and Sioux had been enemies from time immemorial. In two days came the runners, clad only
in short garments, and carrying bow and quiver.
The Crees led the young braves to the fort. Kettles
were set out. Fagged from the long run, the Sioux
ate without a word. At the end of the meal one
rose. Shooting an arrow into the air as a sign that
he called Deity to witness the truth of his words, he
proclaimed in a loud voice that the elders of the
Sioux nation would arrive next day at the fort to
make a treaty with the French.

The news was no proof of generosity. The Sioux
were the great warriors of the West. They knew
very well that whoever formed an alliance with the
French would obtain firearms; and firearms meant
victory against all other tribes. The news set the
Crees by the ears. Warriors hastened from the forests
to defend the fort. The next day came the elders
of the Sioux in pomp. They were preceded by the
young braves bearing bows and arrows and buffalo-
skin shields on which were drawn figures portraying
victories. Their hair was turned up in a stiff crest

A Parley on the Plains.

surmounted by eagle feathers, and their bodies were painted bright vermilion.   Behind came the elders, with medicine-bags of rattlesnake skin streaming from their shoulders and long strings of bears' claws hanging from neck and wrist.   They were dressed in buckskin, garnished with porcupine quills, and wore moccasins of buffalo hide, with the hair dangling from the heel.   In the belt of each was a skull-cracker — a sort of sling stone with a long handle — and a war-hatchet.   Each elder carried a peace pipe set with precious stones, and stuck in the stem were the quills of the war eagle to represent enemies slain.   Women slaves followed, loaded with skins for the elders' tents.

A great fire had been kindled inside the court of the Cree stockades.   Round the pavilion the Sioux elders seated themselves.   First, they solemnly smoked the calumet of peace.   Then the chief of the Sioux rose and chanted a song, giving thanks for their safe journey.   Setting aside gifts of rare beaver pelts, he declared that the Sioux had come to make friends with the French, who were masters of peace and war; that the elders would conduct the white men back to the Sioux country; that the mountains were levelled and the valleys cast up, and the way made smooth, and branches strewn on the ground for the white men's feet, and streams bridged, and the doors of the tepees

open.   Let the French come to the Sioux!   The Indians would die for the French.   A gift was presented
to invoke the friendship of the Crees.   Another rich
gift of furs let out the secret of the Sioux' anxiety:
it was that the French might give the Sioux "thunder
weapons," meaning guns.

The speech being finished, the Crees set a feast
before their guests.   To this feast Radisson and
Groseillers came in a style that eclipsed the Sioux.
Cree warriors marched in front, carrying guns.   Radisson and Groseillers were dressed in armor.[1]   At their
belts they wore pistol, sword, and dagger.   On their
heads were crowns of colored porcupine quills.   Two
pages carried the dishes and spoons to be used at the
feast; and four Cree magicians followed with smoking
calumets in their hands.   Four Indian maids carried
bearskins to place on the ground when the two explorers deigned to sit down.   Inside the fort more
than six hundred councillors had assembled.   Outside were gathered a thousand spectators.   As Radisson and Groseillers entered, an old Cree flung a peace
pipe at the explorers' feet and sang a song of thanks-
giving to the sun that he had lived to see "those
terrible men whose words (guns) made the earth
quake."   Stripping himself of his costly furs, he
placed them on the white men's shoulders, shouting:

[1] *Radisson Relations*, p. 207.

"Ye are masters over us: dead or alive, dispose of us as you will."

Then Radisson rose and chanted a song, in which he declared that the French took the Crees for brethren and would defend them. To prove his words, he threw powder in the fire and had twelve guns shot off, which frightened the Sioux almost out of their senses. A slave girl placed a coal in the calumet. Radisson then presented gifts: the first to testify that the French adopted the Sioux for friends; the second as a token that the French also took the Crees for friends; the third as a sign that the French "would reduce to powder with heavenly fire" any one who disturbed the peace between these tribes. The fourth gift was in grateful recognition of the Sioux' courtesy in granting free passage through their country. The gifts consisted of kettles and hatchets and awls and needles and looking-glasses and bells and combs and paint, but *not* guns. Radisson's speech was received with "Ho, ho's" of applause. Sports began. Radisson offered prizes for racing, jumping, shooting with the bow, and climbing a greased post. All the while, musicians were singing and beating the tom-tom, a drum made of buffalo hide stretched on hoops and filled with water.

Fourteen days later Radisson and Groseillers set out for the Sioux country, or what are now known as the

Northwestern states.[1]   On the third voyage Radisson came to the Sioux from the south.   On this voyage, he came to them from the northeast.   He found that the tribe numbered seven thousand men of fighting age. He remarked that the Sioux used a kind of coke or peat for fire instead of wood.   While he heard of the tribes that used coal for fire, he does not relate that he went to them on this trip.   Again he heard of the mountains far inland, where the Indians found copper and lead and a kind of stone that was transparent.[2] He remained six weeks with the Sioux, hunting buffalo and deer.   Between the Missouri and the Saskatchewan ran a well-beaten trail northeastward, which was used by the Crees and the Sioux in their wars. It is probable that the Sioux escorted Radisson back to the Crees by this trail, till he was across what is now the boundary between Minnesota and Canada, and could strike directly eastward for the Lake of the Woods region, or the hinterland between James Bay and Lake Superior.

In spring the Crees went to the Bay of the North, which Radisson was seeking; and after leaving the

[1] We are now on safe ground.   There was a well-known trail from what is now known as the Rat Portage region to the great Sioux camps west of the Mississippi and Red River valleys.   But again I refuse to lay myself open to controversy by trying definitely to give either the dates or exact places of this trip.

[2] If any proof is wanted that Radisson's journeyings took him far west of the Mississippi, these details afford it.

Sioux, the two explorers struck for the little fort north of Lake Superior, where they had *cached* their goods. Spring in the North was later than spring in the South; but the shore ice of the Northern lakes had already become soft. To save time they cut across the lakes of Minnesota, dragging their sleighs on the ice. Groseillers' sleigh was loaded with pelts obtained from the Sioux, and the elder man began to fag. Radisson took the heavy sleigh, giving Groseillers the lighter one. About twelve miles out from the shore, on one of these lakes, the ice suddenly gave, and Radisson plunged through to his waist. It was as dangerous to turn back as to go on. If they deserted their merchandise, they would have nothing to trade with the Indians; but when Radisson succeeded in extricating himself, he was so badly strained that he could not go forward another step. There was no sense in risking both their lives on the rotten ice. He urged Groseillers to go on. Groseillers dared not hesitate. Laying two sleds as a wind-break on each side of Radisson, he covered the injured man with robes, consigned him to the keeping of God, and hurried over the ice to obtain help from the Crees.

The Crees got Radisson ashore, and there he lay in agony for eight days. The Indians were preparing to set out for the North. They invited Radisson to go with them. His sprain had not healed; but he could not miss the opportunity of approaching the Bay of the North. For two days he marched with the hunters, enduring torture at every step. The third day he could go no farther and they deserted him. Groseillers had gone hunting with another band of Crees. Radisson had neither gun nor hatchet, and the Indians left him only ten pounds of pemmican. After a short rest he journeyed painfully on, following the trail of the marching Crees. On the fifth day he found the frame of a deserted wigwam. Covering it with branches of trees and kindling a fire to drive off beasts of prey, he crept in and lay down to sleep. He was awakened by a crackling of flame. The fire had caught the pine boughs and the tepee was in a blaze. Radisson flung his snow-shoes and clothing as far as he could, and broke from the fire-trap. Half-dressed and lame, shuddering with cold and hunger, he felt through the dark over the snow for his clothing. A far cry rang through the forest like the bay of the wolf pack. Radisson kept solitary watch till morning, when he found that the cry came from Indians sent out to find him by Groseillers. He was taken to an encampment, where the Crees were building canoes to go to the Bay of the North.

The entire band, with the two explorers, then launched on the rivers flowing north. "We were in danger to perish a thousand times from the ice jam," writes

Radisson. ". . . At last we came full sail from a deep bay . . . we came to the seaside, where we found an old house all demolished and battered with bullets. . . . They (the Crees) told us about Europeans. . . . We went from isle to isle all that summer. . . . This region had a great store of cows (caribou). . . . We went farther to see the place that the Indians were to pass the summer. . . . The river (where they went) came from the lake that empties itself in . . . the Saguenay . . . a hundred leagues from the great river of Canada (the St. Lawrence) . . . to where we were in the Bay of the North. . . . We passed the summer quietly coasting the seaside. . . . The people here burn not their prisoners, but knock them on the head. . . . They have a store of turquoise. . . . They find green stones, very fine, at the same Bay of the Sea (labradorite). . . . We went up another river to the Upper Lake (Winnipeg)."[1]

For years the dispute has been waged with zeal worthy of a better cause whether Radisson referred to Hudson Bay in this passage. The French claim that he did; the English that he did not. "The house demolished with bullets" was probably an old trading post, contend the English; but there was no trading post except Radisson's west of Lake Superior at that time, retort the French. By "cows" Radisson

---

[1] *Radisson's Journal*, pp. 224, 225, 226.

meant buffalo, and no buffalo were found as far east as Hudson Bay, say the English; by "cows" Radisson meant caribou and deer, and herds of these frequented the shores of Hudson Bay, answer the French. No river comes from the Saguenay to Hudson Bay, declare the English; yes, but a river comes from the direction of the Saguenay, and was followed by subsequent explorers, assert the French.[1] The stones of turquoise and green were agates from Lake Superior, explain the English; the stones were labradorites from the east coast of the Bay, maintain the French. So the childish quarrel has gone on for two centuries. England and France alike conspired to crush the man while he lived; and when he died they quarrelled over the glory of his discoveries. The point is not whether Radisson actually wet his oars in the different indentations of Hudson and James bays. The point is that he found where it lay from the Great Lakes, and discovered the watershed sloping north from the Great Lakes to Hudson Bay. This was new ground, and entitled Radisson to the fame of a discoverer.

[1] Mr. A. P. Low, who has made the most thorough exploration of Labrador and Hudson Bay of any man living, says, "Rupert River forms the discharge of the Mistassini lakes . . . and empties into Rupert Bay close to the mouth of the Nottoway River, and rises in a number of lakes close to the height of land dividing it from the St. Maurice River, which joins the St. Lawrence at Three Rivers."

From the Indians of the bay, Radisson heard of another lake leagues to the north, whose upper end was always frozen. This was probably some vague story of the lakes in the region that was to become known two centuries later as Mackenzie River. The spring of 1663 found the explorers back in the Lake of the Woods region accompanied by seven hundred Indians of the Upper Country. The company filled three hundred and sixty canoes. Indian girls dived into the lake to push the canoes off, and stood chanting a song of good-speed till the boats had glided out of sight through the long, narrow, rocky gaps of the Lake of the Woods. At Lake Superior the company paused to lay up a supply of smoked sturgeon. At the Sault four hundred Crees turned back. The rest of the Indians hoisted blankets on fishing-poles, and, with a west wind, scudded across Lake Huron to Lake Nipissing. From Lake Nipissing they rode safely down the Ottawa to Montreal. Cannon were fired to welcome the discoverers, for New France was again on the verge of bankruptcy from a beaver famine.

A different welcome awaited them at Quebec. D'Argenson, the governor, was about to leave for France, and nothing had come of the Jesuit expedition up the Saguenay. He had already sent Couture, for a second time, overland to find a way to

K

Hudson Bay; but no word had come from Couture, and the governor's time was up. The explorers had disobeyed him in leaving without his permission. Their return with a fortune of pelts was the salvation of the impecunious governor. From 1627 to 1663 five distinct fur companies, organized under the patronage of royalty, had gone bankrupt in New France.[1] Therefore, it became a loyal governor to protect his Majesty's interests. Besides, the revenue collectors could claim one-fourth of all returns in beaver except from posts farmed expressly for the king. No sooner had Radisson and Groseillers come home than D'Argenson ordered Groseillers imprisoned. He then fined the explorers $20,000, to build a fort at Three Rivers, giving them leave to put their coats-of-arms on the gate; a $30,000 fine was to go to the public treasury of New France; $70,000 worth of beaver was seized as the tax due the revenue. Of a cargo worth $300,000 in modern money, Radisson and Groseillers had less than $20,000 left.[2]

[1] *Les Compagnies de Colonisation sous l'ancien régime*, by Chailly-Bert.

[2] Oldmixon says : "Radisson and Groseillers met with some savages on the Lake of Assiniboin, and from them they learned that they might go by land to the bottom of Hudson's Bay, where the English had not been yet, at James Bay; upon which they desired them to conduct them thither, and the savages accordingly did it. They returned to the Upper Lake the same way they came, and thence to Quebec, where they offered the principal merchants to carry ships to Hudson's Bay; but their project was rejected." Vol. I, p. 548. Radisson's figures are given as "pounds"; but by £ did he mean English "pound" or French livre, that is 17¢ ? A franc in 1660 equalled the modern dollar.

Had D'Argenson and his successors encouraged instead of persecuted the discoverers, France could have claimed all North America but the narrow strip of New England on the east and the Spanish settlements on the south. Having repudiated Radisson and Groseillers, France could not claim the fruits of deeds which she punished.[1]

[1] The exact tribes mentioned in the *Mémoire of 1696*, with whom the French were in trade in the West are: On the "Missoury" and south of it, the Mascoutins and Sioux; two hundred miles beyond the "Missisipy" the Issaguy, the Octbatons, the Omtouŝ, of whom were Sioux capable of mustering four thousand warriors; south of Lake Superior, the Sauteurs; on "Sipisagny, the river which is the discharge of Lake Asemipigon" (Winnipeg), the "Nation of the Grand Rat," Algonquins numbering two thousand, who traded with the English of Hudson Bay; De la Chesnaye adds in his *mémoire* details of the trip from Lake Superior to the lake of the Assiniboines. Knowing what close co-workers he and Radisson were, we can guess where he got his information.

CHAPTER V

1664–1676

RADISSON RENOUNCES ALLEGIANCE TO TWO CROWNS

Rival Traders thwart the Plans of the Discoverers — Entangled in Lawsuits, the two French Explorers go to England — The Organization of the Hudson's Bay Fur Company — Radisson the Storm-centre of International Intrigue — Boston Merchants in the Struggle to capture the Fur Trade

HENCEFORTH Radisson and Groseillers were men without a country. Twice their return from the North with cargoes of beaver had saved New France from ruin. They had discovered more of America than all the other explorers combined. Their reward was jealous rivalry that reduced them to beggary; injustice that compelled them to renounce allegiance to two crowns; obloquy during a lifetime; and oblivion for two centuries after their death. The very force of unchecked impulse that carries the hero over all obstacles may also carry him over the bounds of caution and compromise that regulate the conduct of other men. This was the case with Radisson and

Groseillers. They were powerless to resist the extortion of the French governor. The Company of One Hundred Associates had given place to the Company of the West Indies. This trading venture had been organized under the direct patronage of the king.[1] It had been proclaimed from the pulpits of France. Privileges were promised to all who subscribed for the stock. The Company was granted a blank list of titles to bestow on its patrons and servants. No one else in New France might engage in the beaver trade; no one else might buy skins from the Indians and sell the pelts in Europe; and one-fourth of the trade went for public revenue. In spite of all the privileges, fur company after fur company failed in New France; but to them Radisson had to sell his furs, and when the revenue officers went over the cargo, the minions of the governor also seized a share under pretence of a fine for trading without a license.

Groseillers was furious, and sailed for France to demand restitution; but the intriguing courtiers proved too strong for him. Though he spent £10,000, nothing was done. D'Avaugour had come back to France, and stockholders of the jealous fur company were all-powerful at court. Groseillers then relinquished all idea of restitution, and tried to interest merchants in another expedition to Hudson Bay by

[1] Chailly-Bert.

way of the sea.[1]   He might have spared himself the
trouble.   His enthusiasm only aroused the quiet smile
of supercilious indifference.   His plans were regarded
as chimerical.   Finally a merchant of Rochelle half
promised to send a boat to Isle Percée at the mouth

Martello Tower of Refuge in Time of Indian Wars — Three Rivers.

of the St. Lawrence in 1664.   Groseillers had already
wasted six months.   Eager for action, he hurried back
to Three Rivers, where Radisson awaited him.   The

---

[1] The Jesuit expeditions of Dablon and Dreuillettes in 1661 had failed to reach the
bay overland.   Cabot had coasted Labrador in 1497 ;   Captain Davis had gone north of
Hudson Bay in 1585–1587;   Hudson had lost his life there in 1610.   Sir Thomas
Button had explored Baffin's Land, Nelson River, and the Button Islands in 1612 ;
Munck, the Dane, had found the mouth of the Churchill River in 1619; James and
Fox had explored the inland sea in 1631 ; Shapley had brought a ship up from Boston
in 1640 ; and Bourdon, the Frenchman, had gone up to the straits in 1656–1657.

two secretly took passage in a fishing schooner to
Anticosti, and from Anticosti went south to Isle
Percée. Here a Jesuit just out from France bore the
message to them that no ship would come. The
promise had been a put-off to rid France of the
enthusiast. New France had treated them with
injustice, Old France with mockery. Which way
should they turn? They could not go back to Three
Rivers. This attempt to go to Hudson Bay without
a license laid them open to a second fine. Baffled,
but not beaten, the explorers did what ninety-nine
men out of a hundred would have done in similar
circumstances — they left the country. Some rumor
of their intention to abandon New France must have
gone abroad; for when they reached Cape Breton,
their servants grumbled so loudly that a mob of
Frenchmen threatened to burn the explorers. Dismissing their servants, Radisson and Groseillers
escaped to Port Royal, Nova Scotia.

In Port Royal they met a sea-captain from Boston,
Zechariah Gillam, who offered his ship for a voyage
to Hudson Bay, but the season was far spent when
they set out. Captain Gillam was afraid to enter the
ice-locked bay so late in summer. The boat turned
back, and the trip was a loss. This run of ill-luck
had now lasted for a year. They still had some
money from the Northern trips, and they signed a

contract with ship-owners of Boston to take two
vessels to Hudson Bay the following spring. Provisions must be laid up for the long voyage. One of
the ships was sent to the Grand Banks for fish.
Rounding eastward past the crescent reefs of Sable
Island, the ship was caught by the beach-combers and
totally wrecked on the drifts of sand. Instead of
sailing for Hudson Bay in the spring of 1665, Radisson and Groseillers were summoned to Boston to
defend themselves in a lawsuit for the value of the
lost vessel. They were acquitted; but lawsuits on
the heels of misfortune exhausted the resources of the
adventurers. The exploits of the two Frenchmen had
become the sensation of Boston. Sir Robert Carr,
one of the British commissioners then in the New
England colonies, urged Radisson and Groseillers to
renounce allegiance to a country that had shown only
ingratitude, and to come to England.[1] When Sir
George Cartwright sailed from Nantucket on August 1, 1665, he was accompanied by Radisson and
Groseillers.[2] Misfortune continued to dog them.
Within a few days' sail of England, their ship en-

---

[1] George Carr, writing to Lord Arlington on December 14, 1665, says : " Hearing
some Frenchmen discourse in New England . . . of a great trade of beaver, and afterward making proof of what they had said, he thought them the best present he could
possibly make his Majesty and persuaded them to come to England."

[2] Colonel Richard Nicolls, writing on July 31, 1665, says he " supposes Col. Geo.
Cartwright is now at sea."

countered the Dutch cruiser *Caper*. For two
hours the ships poured broadsides of shot into each
other's hulls. The masts were torn from the English
vessel. She was boarded and stripped, and the
Frenchmen were thoroughly questioned. Then the
captives were all landed in Spain. Accompanied by
the two Frenchmen, Sir George Cartwright hastened
to England early in 1666. The plague had driven
the court from London to Oxford. Cartwright laid
the plans of the explorers before Charles II. The
king ordered 40*s.* a week paid to Radisson and
Groseillers, for the winter. They took chambers
in London. Later they followed the court to Windsor, where they were received by King Charles.

The English court favored the project of trade in
Hudson Bay, but during the Dutch war nothing
could be done. The captain of the Dutch ship
Caper had sent word of the French explorers to
De Witt, the great statesman. De Witt despatched a
spy from Picardy, France, one Eli Godefroy Touret,
who chanced to know Groseillers, to meet the explorers in London. Masking as Groseillers' nephew,
Touret tried to bribe both men to join the Dutch.
Failing this, he attempted to undermine their credit
with the English by accusing Radisson and Groseillers
of counterfeiting money; but the English court
refused to be deceived, and Touret was imprisoned.

Owing to the plague and the war, two years passed without the vague promises of the English court taking shape.   Montague, the English ambassador to France, heard of the explorers' feats, and wrote to Prince Rupert.   Prince Rupert was a soldier of fortune, who could enter into the spirit of the explorers.   He had fought on the losing side against Cromwell, and then taken to the high seas to replenish broken fortunes by piracy.   The wealth of the beaver trade appealed to him.   He gave all the influence of his *prestige* to the explorers' plans.   By the spring of 1668 money enough had been advanced to fit out two boats for Hudson Bay.   In the *Eagle*, with Captain Stannard, went Radisson ; in the *Nonsuch*, with Captain Zechariah Gillam of Boston, went Groseillers. North of Ireland furious gales drove the ships apart. Radisson's vessel was damaged and driven back to London ; but his year was not wasted.   It is likely that the account of his first voyages was written while Groseillers was away.[1]   Sometime during his stay in London he married Mary Kirke, a daughter of the Huguenot John Kirke, whose family had long ago gone from Boston and captured Quebec.

Gillam's journal records that the *Nonsuch* left Gravesend the 3d of June, 1668, reached Resolution

[1] It plainly could not have been written while *en route* across the Atlantic with Sir George Cartwright, for it records events after that time.

Island on August 4, and came to anchor at the south of James Bay on September 29.[1] It was here that Radisson had come overland five years before, when he thought that he discovered a river flowing from the direction of the St. Lawrence. The river was Nemisco. Groseillers called it Rupert in honor of his patron. A palisaded fort was at once built, and named King Charles after the English monarch. By December, the bay was locked in the deathly silence of northern frost. Snow fell till the air became darkened day after day, a ceaseless fall of muffling snow; the earth — as Gillam's journal says — "seemed frozen to death." Gillam attended to the fort, Groseillers to the trade. Dual command was bound to cause a clash. By April, 1669, the terrible cold had relaxed. The ice swept out of the river with a roar. Wild fowl came winging north in myriad flocks. By June the fort was sweltering in almost tropical heat. The *Nonsuch* hoisted anchor and sailed for England, loaded to the water-line with a cargo of furs. Honors awaited Groseillers in London. King Charles created him a *Knight de la Jarretière*, an order for princes of the royal blood.[2] In addition, he was granted a sum of money. Prince Rupert and Radisson had, meanwhile, been busy organizing a fur com-

---

[1] Robson's *Hudson Bay.*

[2] See Dr. N. E. Dionne; also Marie de l'Incarnation; but Sulte discredits this granting of a title.

pany.   The success of Groseillers' voyage now assured
this company a royal charter, which was granted in
May, 1670.   Such was the origin of the Hudson's
Bay Company.   Prince Rupert was its first governor;
Charles Bayly was appointed resident governor on the
bay.   Among the first shareholders were Prince Rupert, the Duke of York, Sir George Cartwright, the
Duke of Albermarle, Shaftesbury, Sir Peter Colleton,
who had advanced Radisson a loan during the long
period of waiting, and Sir John Kirke, whose daughter had married Radisson.

That spring, Radisson and Groseillers again sailed
for the bay.   In 1671, three ships were sent out from
England, and Radisson established a second post
westward at Moose.   With Governor Bayly, he sailed
up and met the Indians at what was to become the
great fur capital of the north, Port Nelson, or York.
The third year of the company's existence, Radisson
and Groseillers perceived a change.   Not so many
Indians came down to the English forts to trade.
Those who came brought fewer pelts and demanded
higher prices.   Rivals had been at work.   The English learned that the French had come overland and
were paying high prices to draw the Indians from the
bay.   In the spring a council was held.[1]   Should they

[1] See Robson's *Hudson Bay*, containing reference to the journal kept by Gorst,
Bayly's secretary, at Rupert Fort.

continue on the east side of the bay, or move west, where there would be no rivalry ? Groseillers boldly counselled moving inland and driving off French competition. Bayly was for moving west. He even hinted that Groseillers' advice sprang from disloyalty to the English. The clash that was inevitable from divided command was this time avoided by compromise. They would all sail west, and all come back to Rupert's River. When they returned, they found that the English ensign had been torn down and the French flag raised.[1] A veteran Jesuit missionary of the Saguenay, Charles Albanel, two French companions, and some Indian guides had ensconced themselves in the empty houses.[2] The priest now presented Governor Bayly with letters from Count Frontenac

[1] See State Papers, Canadian Archives, 1676, January 26, Whitehall: Memorial of the Hudson Bay Company complaining of Albanel, a Jesuit, attempting to seduce Radisson and Groseillers from the company's services; in absence of ships pulling down the British ensign and tampering with the Indians.

[2] I am inclined to think that Albanel may not have been aware of the documents which he carried from Quebec to the traders being practically an offer to bribe Radisson and Groseillers to desert England. Some accounts say that Albanel was accompanied by Groseillers' son, but I find no authority for this. On the other hand, Albanel does not mention the Englishmen being present. Just as Radisson and Groseillers, ten years before, had taken possession of the old house battered with bullets, so Albanel took possession of the deserted huts. Here is what his account says (Cramoisy edition of the *Relations*): " Le 28 June à peine avions nous avancé un quart de lieue, que nous rencontrasmes à main gauche dans un petit ruisseau un heu avec ses agrez de dix ou dou tonneaux, qui portoit le Pavillon Anglois et la voile latine ; delà à la portée du fusil, nous entrasmes dans deux maisons desertes . . . nous rencontrasmes deux ou trois cabanes et un chien abandonné. . . ." His tampering with the Indians was simply the presentation of gifts to attract them to Quebec.

commending the French to the good offices of Governor Bayly.[1]

France had not been idle.

When it was too late, the country awakened to the injustice done Radisson and Groseillers. While Radisson was still in Boston, all restrictions were taken from the beaver trade, except the tax of one-fourth to the revenue. The Jesuit Dablon, who was near the western end of Lake Superior, gathered all the information he could from the Indians of the way to the Sea of the North. Father Marquette learned of the Mississippi from the Indians. The Western tribes had been summoned to the Sault, where Sieur de Saint-Lusson met them in treaty for the French; and the French flag was raised in the presence of Père Claude Allouez, who blessed the ceremony. M. Colbert sent instructions to M. Talon, the intendant of New France, to grant titles of nobility to Groseillers' nephew in order to keep him in the country.[2] On the Saguenay was a Jesuit, Charles Albanel, loyal to the French and of English birth, whose devotion to the Indians during the small-pox scourge of 1670 had given him unbounded influence. Talon, the intendant of New France, was keen to retrieve in the North what D'Ar-

---

[1] See State Papers, Canadian Archives : M. Frontenac, the commander of French (?) king's troops at Hudson Bay, introduces and recommends Father Albanel.

[2] State Papers, Canadian Archives.

genson's injustice had lost. Who could be better qualified to go overland to Hudson Bay than the old missionary, loyal to France, of English birth, and beloved by the Indians? Albanel was summoned to Quebec and gladly accepted the commission. He chose for companions Saint-Simon and young Couture, the son of the famous guide to the Jesuits. The company left Quebec on August 6, 1671, and secured a guide at Tadoussac. Embarking in canoes, they ascended the shadowy cañon of the Saguenay to Lake St. John. On the 7th of September they left the forest of Lake St. John and mounted the current of a winding river, full of cataracts and rapids, toward Mistassini. On this stream they met Indians who told them that two European vessels were on Hudson Bay. The Indians showed Albanel tobacco which they had received from the English.

It seemed futile to go on a voyage of discovery where English were already in possession. The priest sent one of the Frenchmen and two Indians back to Quebec for passports and instructions. What the instructions were can only be guessed by subsequent developments. The messengers left the depth of the forest on the 19th of September, and had returned from Quebec by the 10th of October. Snow was falling. The streams had frozen, and the Indians had gone into camp for the winter. Going from wigwam to wigwam through the drifted forest, Father Albanel passed the winter preaching to the savages. Skins of the chase were laid on the wigwams. Against the pelts, snow was banked to close up every chink. Inside, the air was blue with smoke and the steam of the simmering kettle. Indian hunters lay on the moss floor round the central fires. Children and dogs crouched heterogeneously against the sloping tent walls. Squaws plodded through the forest, setting traps and baiting the fish-lines that hung through air-holes of the thick ice. In these lodges Albanel wintered. He was among strange Indians and suffered incredible hardships. Where there was room, he, too, sat crouched under the crowded tent walls, scoffed at by the braves, teased by the unrebuked children, eating when the squaws threw waste food to him, going hungry when his French companions failed to bring in game. Sometimes night overtook him on the trail. Shovelling a bed through the snow to the moss with his snow-shoes, piling shrubs as a wind-break, and kindling a roaring fire, the priest passed the night under the stars.

When spring came, the Indians opposed his passage down the river. A council was called. Albanel explained that his message was to bring the Indians down to Quebec and keep them from going to the English for trade. The Indians, who had acted as middlemen between Quebec traders and the Northern tribes, saw the advantage of undermining the English trade.   Gifts were presented by the Frenchmen, and the friendship of the Indians was secured.   On June 1, 1672, sixteen savages embarked with the three Frenchmen.   For the next ten days, the difficulties were almost insurmountable.   The river tore through a deep gorge of sheer precipices which the *voyageurs* could pass only by clinging to the rock walls with hands and feet.   One *portage* was twelve miles long over a muskeg of quaking moss that floated on water. At every step the travellers plunged through to their waists.   Over this the long canoes and baggage had to be carried.   On the 10th of June they reached the height of land that divides the waters of Hudson Bay from the St. Lawrence.   The watershed was a small plateau with two lakes, one of which emptied north, the other, south.   As they approached Lake Mistassini, the Lake Indians again opposed their free passage down the rivers.

" You must wait," they said, " till we notify the elders of your coming."   Shortly afterwards, the French met a score of canoes with the Indians all painted for war.   The idea of turning back never occurred to the priest.   By way of demonstrating his joy at meeting the warriors, he had ten volleys of musketry fired off, which converted the war into a

L

council of peace. At the assemblage, Albanel dis- tributed gifts to the savages.

"Stop trading with the English at the sea," he cried; "they do not pray to God; come to Lake St. John with your furs; there you will always find a *robe noire* to instruct you and baptize you."

The treaty was celebrated by a festival and a dance. In the morning, after solemn religious services, the French embarked. On the 18th of June they came to Lake Mistassini, an enormous body of water similar to the Great Lakes.[1] From Mistassini, the course was down-stream and easier. High water enabled them to run many of the rapids; and on the 28th of June, after a voyage of eight hundred leagues, four hundred rapids, and two hundred waterfalls, they came to the deserted houses of the English. The very next day they found the Indians and held religious services, making solemn treaty, presenting presents, and hoisting the French flag. For the first three weeks of July they coasted along the shores of James Bay, taking possession of the country in the name of the French king. Then they cruised back to King Charles Fort on Rupert's River.[2] They were just in time to meet the returned Englishmen.

---

[1] For some years there were sensational reports that Mistassini was larger than Lake Superior. Mr. Low, of the Canadian Geological Survey, in a very exhaustive report, shows this is not so. Still, the lake ranks with the large lakes of America. Mr. Low gives its dimensions as one hundred miles long and twelve miles wide.

[2] There is a discrepancy in dates here which I leave savants to worry out. *Albanel's*

Governor Bayly of the Hudson's Bay Company
was astounded to find the French at Rupert's River.
Now he knew what had allured the Indians from the
bay, but he hardly relished finding foreigners in possession of his own fort. The situation required deli-
cate tact. Governor Bayly was a bluff tradesman with
an insular dislike of Frenchmen and Catholics common
in England at a time when bigoted fanaticism ran
riot. King Charles was on friendly terms with France.
Therefore, the Jesuit's passport must be respected; so
Albanel was received with at least a show of courtesy.
But Bayly was the governor of a fur company; and
the rights of the company must be respected. To
make matters worse, the French *voyageurs* brought
letters to Groseillers and Radisson from their relatives
in Quebec. Bayly, no doubt, wished the Jesuit guest far
enough. Albanel left in a few weeks. Then Bayly's
suspicions blazed out in open accusations that the two
French explorers had been playing a double game and
acting against English interests. In September came

Relation (Cramoisy) is of 1672. Thomas Gorst, secretary to Governor Bayly, says
that the quarrel took place in 1674. Oldmixon, who wrote from hearsay, says in
1673. Robson, who had access to Hudson's Bay records, says 1676; and I am
inclined to think they all agree. In a word, Radisson and Groseillers were on bad
terms with the local Hudson's Bay Company governor from the first, and the open
quarrel took place only in 1675. Considering the bigotry of the times, the quarrel was
only natural. Bayly was governor, but he could not take precedence over Radisson
and Groseillers. He was Protestant and English. They were Catholics and French.
Besides, they were really at the English governor's mercy; for they could not go back
to Canada until publicly pardoned by the French king.

the company ship to the fort with Captain Gillam, who
had never agreed with Radisson from the time that
they had quarrelled about going from Port Royal to
the straits of Hudson Bay.   It has been said that, at
this stage, Radisson and Groseillers, feeling the preju-
dice too strong against them, deserted and passed
overland through the forests to Quebec.   The records
of the Hudson's Bay Company do not corroborate this
report.   Bayly in the heat of his wrath sent home
accusations with the returning ship.   The ship that
came out in 1674 requested Radisson to go to England and report.   This he did, and so completely
refuted the charges of disloyalty that in 1675 the company voted him £100 a year; but Radisson would
not sit quietly in England on a pension.   Owing to
hostility toward him among the English employees of
the company, he could not go back to the bay.
Meantime he had wife and family and servants to maintain on £100 a year.   If England had no more need
of him, France realized the fact that she had.   Debts
were accumulating.   Restless as a caged tiger, Radisson found himself baffled until a message came from
the great Colbert of France, offering to pay all his
debts and give him a position in the French navy.
His pardon was signed and proclaimed.   In 1676,
France granted him fishing privileges on the island of
Anticosti; but the lodestar of the fur trade still drew

him, for that year he was called to Quebec to meet a company of traders conferring on the price of beaver.[1] In that meeting assembled, among others, Jolliet, La Salle, Groseillers, and Radisson — men whose names were to become immortal.

It was plain that the two adventurers could not long rest.[2]

[1] State Papers, Canadian Archives, October 20, 1676, Quebec : Report of proceedings regarding the price of beaver . . . by an ordinance, October 19, 1676, M. Jacques Duchesneau, Intendant, had called a meeting of the leading fur traders to consult about fixing the price of beaver. There were present, among others, Robert, Cavelier de la Salle, . . . Charles le Moyne, . . . two Godefroys of Three Rivers, . . . Groseillers, . . . Jolliet, . . . Pierre Radisson.

[2] Mr. Low's geological report on Labrador contains interesting particulars of the route followed by Father Albanel. He speaks of the gorge and swamps and difficult *portages* in precisely the same way as the priest, though Albanel must have encountered the worst possible difficulties on the route, for he went down so early in the spring.

CHAPTER VI

1682–1684

RADISSON GIVES UP A CAREER IN THE NAVY FOR THE FUR TRADE

Though opposed by the Monopolists of Quebec, he secures Ships for a Voyage to Hudson Bay — Here he encounters a Pirate Ship from Boston and an English Ship of the Hudson's Bay Company — How he plays his Cards to win against Both Rivals

A CLEVER man may be a dangerous rival. Both France and England recognized this in Radisson. The Hudson's Bay Company distrusted him because he was a foreigner. The fur traders of Quebec were jealous. The Hudson's Bay Company had offered him a pension of £100 a year to do nothing. France had pardoned his secession to England, paid his debts, and given him a position in the navy, and when the fleet was wrecked returning from the campaign against Dutch possessions in the West Indies, the French king advanced money for Radisson to refit himself; but France distrusted the explorer because he had an English wife. All that France and England wanted Radisson to do was to keep quiet. What the haughty

spirit of Radisson would *not* do for all the fortunes
which two nations could offer to bribe him — was to
keep quiet. He cared more for the game than the
winnings ; and the game of sitting still and drawing a
pension for doing nothing was
altogether too tame for Radisson.
Groseillers gave up the struggle
and retired for the time to his
family at Three Rivers. At Quebec, in 1676, Radisson heard of
others everywhere reaping where he
had sown. Jolliet and La Salle
were preparing to push the fur
trade of New France westward

"Skin for Skin," Coat of
Arms and Motto, Hud-
son's Bay Company.

of the Great Lakes, where Radisson had penetrated
twenty years previously. Fur traders of Quebec, who
organized under the name of the Company of the
North, yearly sent their canoes up the Ottawa, St.
Maurice, and Saguenay to the forests south of Hudson
Bay, which Radisson had traversed. On the bay
itself the English company were entrenched. North,
northwest, and west, Radisson had been the explorer ;
but the reward of his labor had been snatched by
other hands.

Radisson must have served meritoriously on the
fleet, for after the wreck he was offered the command
of a man-of-war ; but he asked for a commission to

New France.   From this request there arose complications.   His wife's family, the Kirkes, had held
claims against New France from the days when the
Kirkes of Boston had captured Quebec.   These
claims now amounted to £40,000.   M. Colbert, the
great French statesman, hesitated to give a commission
to a man allied by marriage with the enemies of New
France.   Radisson at last learned why preferment had
been denied him.   It was on account of his wife.
Twice Radisson journeyed to London for Mary
Kirke.   Those were times of an easy change in faith.
Charles II was playing double with Catholics and
Protestants.   The Kirkes were closely attached to the
court ; and it was, perhaps, not difficult for the Huguenot wife to abjure Protestantism and declare herself a
convert to the religion of her husband.   But when
Radisson proposed taking her back to France, that
was another matter.   Sir John Kirke forbade his
daughter's departure till the claims of the Kirke
family against New France had been paid.   When
Radisson returned without his wife, he was reproached
by M. Colbert for disloyalty.   The government refused its patronage to his plans for the fur trade ; but
M. Colbert sent him to confer with La Chesnaye, a
prominent fur trader and member of the Council in
New France, who happened to be in Paris at that time.
La Chesnaye had been sent out to Canada to look

after the affairs of a Rouen fur-trading company. Soon he became a commissioner of the West Indies Company; and when the merchants of Quebec organized the Company of the North, La Chesnaye became a director. No one knew better than he how bitterly the monopolists of Quebec would oppose Radisson's plans for a trip to Hudson Bay; but the prospects were alluring. La Chesnaye was deeply involved in the fur trade and snatched at the chance of profits to stave off the bankruptcy that reduced him to beggary a few years later. In defiance of the rival companies and independent of those with which he was connected, he offered to furnish ships and share profits with Radisson and Groseillers for a voyage to Hudson Bay.

M. Colbert did not give his patronage to the scheme; but he wished Radisson a God-speed. The Jesuits advanced Radisson money to pay his passage; and in the fall of 1681, he arrived in Quebec. La Chesnaye met him, and Groseillers was summoned. The three then went to the Château Saint-Louis to lay their plans before the governor. Though the privileges of the West Indies Company had been curtailed, the fur trade was again regulated by license.[1]

---

[1] Within ten years so many different regulations were promulgated on the fur trade that it is almost impossible to keep track of them. In 1673 orders came from Paris forbidding French settlers of New France from wandering in the woods for longer than twenty-four hours. In 1672 M. Frontenac forbade the selling of merchandise to *coureurs du bois*, or the purchase of furs from them. In 1675 a decree of the Council

Frontenac had granted a license to the Company of the North for the fur trade of Hudson Bay. He could not openly favor Radisson; but he winked at the expedition by granting passports to the explorers, and the three men who were to accompany him, Jean Baptiste, son of Groseillers, Pierre Allemand, the pilot who was afterward given a commission to explore the Eskimo country, and Jean Godefroy, an interpreter.[1] Jean Baptiste, Radisson's nephew, invested £500 in goods for barter. Others of Three Rivers and Quebec advanced money to provision the ship.[2] Ten days after Radisson's arrival in Quebec, the explorers had left the high fortress of the St. Lawrence to winter in Acadia. When spring came, they went with the fishing fleets to Isle Percée, where La Chesnaye was to send the ships. Radisson's ship, the *St. Pierre*,

of State awarded to M. Jean Oudiette one-fourth of all beaver, with the exclusive right of buying and selling in Canada. In 1676 Frontenac withdrew from the *Cie Indes Occidentales* all the rights it had over Canada and other places. An ordinance of October 1, 1682, forbade all trade except under license. An ordinance in 1684 ordered all fur traders trading in Hudson Bay to pay one-fourth to Farmers of the Revenue.

[1] It is hard to tell who this Godefroy was. Of all the famous Godefroys of Three Rivers (according to Abbé Tanguay) there was only one, Jean Batiste, born 1658, who might have gone with Radisson; but I hardly think so. The Godefroys descended from the French nobility and themselves bore titles from the king, but in spite of this, were the best canoemen of New France, as ready — according to Mr. Sulte — to *faire la cuisine* as to command a fort. Radisson's Godefroy evidently went in the capacity of a servant, for his name is not mentioned in the official list of promoters. On the other hand, parish records do not give the date of Jean Batiste Godefroy's death; so that he may have gone as a servant and died in the North.

[2] State Papers, 1683, state that Dame Sorel, La Chesnaye, Chaujon, Gitton, Foret, and others advanced money for the goods.

— named after himself, — came first, a rickety sloop of fifty tons with a crew of twelve mutinous, ill-fed men, a cargo of goods for barter, and scant enough supply of provisions. Groseillers' ship, the *St. Anne*, was smaller and better built, with a crew of fifteen. The explorers set sail on the 11th of July. From the first there was trouble with the crews. Fresh-water *voyageurs* make bad ocean sailors. Food was short. The voyage was to be long. It was to unknown waters, famous for disaster. The sea was boisterous. In the months of June and July, the North Atlantic is beset with fog and iceberg. The ice sweeps south in mountainous bergs that have thawed and split before they reach the temperate zones.[1] On the 30th of July the two ships passed the Straits of Belle Isle. Fog-banks hung heavy on the blue of the far watery horizon. Out of the fog, like ghosts in gloom, drifted the shadowy ice-floes. The coast of Labrador consists of bare, domed, lonely hills alternated with rock walls rising sheer from the sea as some giant masonry. Here the rock is buttressed by a sharp angle knife-edged in a precipice. There, the beetling walls are guarded by long reefs like the teeth of a saw. Over these reefs, the drifting tide breaks with multitudinous

[1] In 1898, when up the coast of Labrador, I was told by the superintendent of a northern whaling station — a man who has received royal decorations for his scientific research of ocean phenomena — that he has frequently seen icebergs off Labrador that. were nine miles long.

voices. The French *voyageurs* had never known such seafaring. In the wail of the white-foamed reefs, their superstition heard the shriek of the demons. The explorers had anchored in one of the sheltered harbors, which the sailors call "holes-in-the-wall." The crews mutinied. They would go no farther through ice-drift and fog to an unknown sea. Radisson never waited for the contagion of fear to work. He ordered anchors up and headed for open sea. Then he tried to encourage the sailors with promises. They would not hear him; for the ship's galley was nearly empty of food. Then Radisson threatened the first mutineer to show rebellion with such severe punishment as the hard customs of the age permitted. The crew sulked, biding its time. At that moment the lookout shouted "Sail ho!'

All hands discerned a ship with a strange sail, such as Dutch and Spanish pirates carried, bearing down upon them shoreward. The lesser fear was forgotten in the greater. The *St. Pierre's* crew crowded sail. Heading about, the two explorers' ships threaded the rock reefs like pursued deer. The pirate came on full speed before the wind. Night fell while Radisson was still hiding among the rocks. Notwithstanding reefs and high seas, while the pirate ship hove to for the night, Radisson stole out in the dark and gave his pursuer the slip. The chase had saved him a mutiny.

As the vessels drove northward, the ice drifted past like a white world afloat. When Radisson approached the entrance to Hudson Bay, he met floes in impenetrable masses. So far the ships had avoided delay by tacking along the edges of the ice-fields, from lake to lake of ocean surrounded by ice. Now the ice began to crush together, driven by wind and tide with furious enough force to snap the two ships like egg-shells. Radisson watched for a free passage, and, with a wind to rear, scudded for shelter of a hole-in-the-wall. Here he met the Eskimo, and provisions were replenished; but the dangers of the ice-fields had frightened the crews again. In two days Radisson put to sea to avoid a second mutiny. The wind was landward, driving the ice back from the straits, and they passed safely into Hudson Bay. The ice again surrounded them; but it was useless for the men to mutiny. Ice blocked up all retreat. Jammed among the floes, Groseillers was afraid to carry sail, and fell behind. Radisson drove ahead, now skirting the ice-floes, now pounded by breaking icebergs, now crashing into surface brash or puddled ice to the fore. " We were like to have perished," he writes, " but God was pleased to preserve us."

On the 26th of August, six weeks after sailing from Isle Percée, Radisson rode triumphantly in on the tide to Hayes River, south of Nelson River, where he had been with the English ships ten years before. Two weeks later the *Ste. Anne,* with Groseillers, arrived. The two ships cautiously ascended the river, seeking a harbor. Fifteen miles from salt water, Radisson anchored. At last he was back in his native element, the wilderness, where man must set himself to conquer and take dominion over earth.

Groseillers was always the trader, Radisson the explorer. Leaving his brother-in-law to build the fort, Radisson launched a canoe on Hayes River to explore inland. Young Jean Groseillers accompanied him to look after the trade with the Indians.[1] For eight days they paddled up a river that was destined to be the path of countless traders and pioneers for two centuries, and that may yet be destined to become the path of a northern commerce. By September the floodtide of Hayes River had subsided. In a week the *voyageurs* had travelled probably three hundred miles, and were within the region of Lake Winnipeg, where the Cree hunters assemble in October for the winter. Radisson had come to this region by way of Lake Superior with the Cree hunters twenty years before, and his visit had become a tradition among the tribes. Beaver are busy in October gnawing down young saplings for winter food. Radisson observed chips floating past the canoe. Where there are beaver,

---

[1] Jean was born in 1654 and was, therefore, twenty-eight.

there should be Indians; so the *voyageurs* paddled on. One night, as they lay round the camp-fire, with canoes overturned, a deer, startled from its evening drinking-place, bounded from the thicket. A sharp whistle — and an Indian ran from the brush of an island opposite the camp, signalling the white men to head the deer back; but when Radisson called from the waterside, the savage took fright and dashed for the woods.

All that night the *voyageurs* kept sleepless guard. In the morning they moved to the island and kindled a signal-fire to call the Indians. In a little while canoes cautiously skirted the island, and the chief of the band stood up, bow and arrow in hand. Pointing his arrows to the deities of north, south, east, and west, he broke the shaft to splinters, as a signal of peace, and chanted his welcome : —

> " Ho, young men, be not afraid !
> The sun is favorable to us !
> Our enemies shall fear us !
> This is the man we have wished
> Since the days of our fathers ! "

With a leap, the chief sprang into the water and swam ashore, followed by all the canoes. Radisson called out to know who was commander. The chief, with a sign as old and universal as humanity, bowed his head in servility. Radisson took the Indian by the hand, and, seating him by the fire, chanted an answer in Cree : —

> " I know all the earth !
> Your friends shall be my friends !
> I come to bring you arms to destroy your enemies !
> Nor wife nor child shall die of hunger !
> For I have brought you merchandise !
> Be of good cheer !
> I will be thy son !
> I have brought thee a father !
> He is yonder below building a fort
> Where I have two great ships ! " [1]

The chief kept pace with the profuse compliments by vowing the life of his tribe in service of the white man. Radisson presented pipes and tobacco to the Indians. For the chief he reserved a fowling-piece with powder and shot. White man and Indian then exchanged blankets. Presents were sent for the absent wives. The savages were so grateful that they cast all their furs at Radisson's feet, and promised to bring their hunt to the fort in spring. In Paris and London Radisson had been harassed by jealousy. In

---

[1] I have written both addresses as the Indians would chant them. To be sure, they will not scan according to the elephantine grace of the pedant's iambics ; but then, neither will the Indian songs scan, though I know of nothing more subtly rhythmical. Rhythm is so much a part of the Indian that it is in his walk, in the intonation of his words, in the gesture of his hands. I think most Westerners will bear me out in saying that it is the exquisitely musical intonation of words that betrays Indian blood to the third and fourth generation.

the wilderness he was master of circumstance; but a surprise awaited him at Groseillers' fort.

The French habitation — called Fort Bourbon — had been built on the north shore of Hayes or Ste. Therese River. Directly north, overland, was another broad river with a gulflike entrance. This was the Nelson. Between the two rivers ran a narrow neck of swampy, bush-grown land. The day that Radisson returned to the newly erected fort, there rolled across the marshes the ominous echo of cannon-firing. Who could the newcomers be? A week's sail south at the head of the bay were the English establishments of the Hudson's Bay Company. The season was far advanced. Had English ships come to winter on Nelson River? Ordering Jean Groseillers to go back inland to the Indians, Radisson launched down Hayes River in search of the strange ship. He went to the salt water, but saw nothing. Upon returning, he found that Jean Groseillers had come back to the fort with news of more cannonading farther inland. Radisson rightly guessed that the ship had sailed up Nelson River, firing cannon as she went to notify Indians for trade. Picking out three intrepid men, Radisson crossed the marsh by a creek which the Indian canoes used, to go to Nelson River.[1] Through the brush the scout spied a white tent on an island.

[1] See Robson's map.

M

All night the Frenchmen lay in the woods, watching their rivals and hoping that some workman might pass close enough to be seized and questioned. At noon, next day, Radisson's patience was exhausted. He paddled round the island, and showed himself a cannon-shot distant from the fort. Holding up a pole, Radisson waved as if he were an Indian afraid to approach closer in order to trade. The others hallooed a welcome and gabbled out Indian words from a guide-book. Radisson paddled a length closer. The others ran eagerly down to the water side away from their cannon. In signal of friendship, they advanced unarmed. Radisson must have laughed to see how well his ruse worked.

"Who are you?" he demanded in plain English, "and what do you want?" The traders called back that they were Englishmen come for beaver. Again the crafty Frenchman must have laughed; for he knew very well that all English ships except those of the Hudson's Bay Company were prohibited by law from coming here to trade.[1] Though the strange ship displayed an English ensign, the flag did not show the magical letters "H. B. C."

"Whose commission have you?" pursued Radisson.

---

[1] State Papers: "The Governor of New England is ordered to seize all vessels trading in Hudson Bay contrary to charter —"

"No commission — New Englanders," answered the others.

"Contrabands," thought Radisson to himself. Then he announced that he had taken possession of all that country for France, had built a strong fort, and expected more ships. In a word, he advised the New Englanders to save themselves by instant flight; but his canoe had glided nearer. To Radisson's surprise, he discovered that the leader of the New Eng-

Hudson's Bay Company Coins, made of Lead melted from Tea Chests at York Factory, each Coin representing so many Beaver Skins.

land poachers was Ben Gillam of Boston, son of Captain Gillam, the trusted servant of the Hudson's Bay Company, who had opposed Radisson and Groseillers on Rupert's River. It looked as if the contraband might be a venture of the father as well as the son.[1] Radisson and young Gillam recognized each other with a show of friendliness, Gillam inviting Radisson to inspect the ship with much the same motive that the fabled spider invited the fly. Radis-

[1] *Radisson's Journal*, p. 277.

son took tactful precaution for his own liberty by graciously asking that two of the New England servants go down to the canoe with the three Frenchmen. No sooner had Radisson gone on the New England ship than young Gillam ordered cannon fired and English flags run up. Having made that brave show of strength, the young man proposed that the French and the New Englanders should divide the traffic between them for the winter. Radisson diplomatically suggested that such an important proposal be laid before his colleagues. In leaving, he advised Gillam to keep his men from wandering beyond the island, lest they suffer wrong at the hands of the French soldiers. Incidentally, that advice would also keep the New Englanders from learning how desperately weak the French really were. Neither leader was in the slightest deceived by the other; each played for time to take the other unawares, and each knew the game that was being played.

Instead of returning by the creek that cut athwart the neck of land between the two rivers, Radisson decided to go down Nelson River to the bay, round the point, and ascend Hayes River to the French quarters. Cogitating how to frighten young Gillam out of the country or else to seize him, Radisson glided down the swift current of Nelson River toward salt water. He had not gone nine miles from the New Englanders when he was astounded by the spectacle of a ship breasting with full-blown sails up the tide of the Nelson directly in front of the French canoe. The French dashed for the hiding of the brushwood on shore. From their concealment they saw that the ship was a Hudson's Bay Company vessel, armed with cannon and commission for lawful trade. If once the Hudson's Bay Company ship and the New Englanders united, the English would be strong enough to overpower the French.

The majority of leaders would have escaped the impending disaster by taking ingloriously to their heels. Radisson, with that adroit presence of mind which characterized his entire life, had provided for his followers' safety by landing them on the south shore, where the French could flee across the marsh to the ships if pursued. Then his only thought was how to keep the rivals apart. Instantly he had an enormous bonfire kindled. Then he posted his followers in ambush. The ship mistook the fire for an Indian signal, reefed its sails, and anchored. Usually natives paddled out to the traders' ships to barter. These Indians kept in hiding. The ship waited for them to come; and Radisson waited for the ship's hands to land. In the morning a gig boat was lowered to row ashore. In it were Captain Gillam,

Radisson's personal enemy, John Bridgar,[1] the new governor of the Hudson's Bay Company for Nelson River, and six sailors.   All were heavily armed, yet Radisson stood alone to receive them, with his three companions posted on the outskirts of the woods as if in command of ambushed forces.   Fortune is said to favor the dauntless, and just as the boat came within gunshot of the shore, it ran aground.   A sailor jumped out to drag the craft up the bank. They were all at Radisson's mercy — without cover. He at once levelled his gun with a shout of " Halt!" At the same moment his own men made as if to sally from the woods.   The English imagined themselves ambushed, and called out that they were the officers of the Hudson's Bay Company.   Radisson declared who he was and that he had taken possession of the country for France.   His musket was still levelled. His men were ready to dash forward.   The English put their heads together and decided that discretion was the better part of valor.   Governor Bridgar meekly requested permission to land and salute the commander of the French.   Then followed a pompous melodrama of bravado, each side affecting sham strength.   Radisson told the English all that he had told the New Englanders, going on board the Company's ship to dine, while English hostages remained

---

[1] Robson gives the commission to this governor.

with his French followers. For reasons which he did not reveal, he strongly advised Governor Bridgar not to go farther up Nelson River. Above all, he warned Captain Gillam not to permit the English sailors to wander inland. Having exchanged compliments, Radisson took gracious leave of his hosts, and with his three men slipped down the Nelson in their canoe. Past a bend in the river, he ordered the canoe ashore. The French then skirted back through the woods and lay watching the English till satisfied that the Hudson's Bay Company ship would go no nearer the island where Ben Gillam lay hidden.

Groseillers and his son looked after the trade that winter. Radisson had his hands full keeping the two English crews apart. Ten days after his return, he again left Hayes River to see what his rivals were doing. The Hudson's Bay Company ship had gone aground in the ooze a mile from the fort where Governor Bridgar had taken up quarters. That division of forces weakened the English fort. Introducing his man as captain of a French ship, Radisson entered the governor's house. The visitors drained a health to their host and fired off muskets to learn whether sentinels were on guard. No attention was paid to the unwonted noise. "I judged," writes Radisson, "that they were careless, and might easily be surprised." He then went across to the river flats, where the tide

had left the vessel, and, calmly mounting the ladder,
took a survey of Gillam's ship.   When the irate old
captain rushed up to know the meaning of the
intrusion Radisson suavely proffered provisions, of
which they were plainly in need.

The New Englanders had been more industrious.
A stoutly palisaded fort had been completed on young
Gillam's island, and cannon commanded all approach.
Radisson fired a musket to notify the sentry, and took
care to beach his canoe below the range of the guns.
Young Gillam showed a less civil front than before.
His lieutenant ironically congratulated Radisson on
his " safe " return, and invited him to visit the fort if
he would enter *alone*.   When Radisson would have
introduced his four followers, the lieutenant swore " if
the four French were forty devils, they could not take
the New Englanders' fort."   The safety of the French
habitation now hung by a hair.   Everything depended
on keeping the two English companies apart, and
they were distant only nine miles.   The scheme must
have flashed on Radisson in an intuition ; for he laid
his plans as he listened to the boastings of the
New Englanders.   If father and son could be brought
together through Radisson's favor, Captain Gillam
would keep the English from coming to the New
England fort lest his son should be seized for poach-
ing on the trade of the Company ; and Ben Gillam

would keep his men from going near the English fort
lest Governor Bridgar should learn of the contraband
ship from Boston. Incidentally, both sides would be
prevented from knowing the weakness of the French
at Fort Bourbon. At once Radisson told young
Gillam of his father's presence. Ben was eager to see
his father and, as he thought, secure himself from
detection in illegal trade. Radisson was to return
to the old captain with the promised provisions.
He offered to take young Gillam, disguised as a
bush-ranger. In return, he demanded (1) that the
New Englanders should not leave their fort ; (2) that
they should not betray themselves by discharging cannon ; (3) that they shoot any Hudson's Bay Company
people who tried to enter the New England fort. To
young Gillam these terms seemed designed for his
own protection. What they really accomplished was
the complete protection of the French from united
attack. Father and son would have put themselves
in Radisson's power. A word of betrayal to Bridgar,
the Hudson's Bay governor, and both the Gillams
would be arrested for illegal trade. Ben Gillam's
visit to his father was fraught with all the danger that
Radisson's daring could have desired. A seaman half
suspected the identity of the bush-ranger, and Governor Bridgar wanted to know how Radisson had returned so soon when the French fort was far away.

"I told him, smiling," writes Radisson, "that I could fly when there was need to serve my friends."

Young Gillam had begun to suspect the weakness of the French. When the two were safely out of the Hudson's Bay Company fort, he offered to go home part of the way with Radisson. This was to learn where the French fort lay. Radisson declined the kindly service and deliberately set out from the New Englanders' island in the wrong direction, coming down the Nelson past young Gillam's fort at night. The delay of the trick nearly cost Radisson his life. Fall rains had set in, and the river was running a mill-race. Great floes of ice from the North were tossing on the bay at the mouth of the Nelson River in a maelstrom of tide and wind. In the dark Radisson did not see how swiftly his canoe had been carried down-stream. Before he knew it his boat shot out of the river among the tossing ice-floes of the bay. Surrounded by ice in a wild sea, he could not get back to land. The spray drove over the canoe till the Frenchman's clothes were stiff with ice. For four hours they lay jammed in the ice-drift till a sudden upheaval crushed the canoe to kindling wood and left the men stranded on the ice. Running from floe to floe, they gained the shore and beat their way for three days through a raging hurricane of sleet and snow toward the French habitation. They were on the side of the Hayes opposite the French fort. Four *voyageurs* crossed for them, and the little company at last gained the shelter of a roof.

Radisson now knew that young Gillam intended to spy upon the French; so he sent scouts to watch the New Englanders' fort. The scouts reported that the young captain had sent messengers to obtain additional men from his father; but the New England soldiers, remembering Radisson's orders to shoot any one approaching, had levelled muskets to fire at the reën-forcements. The rebuffed men had gone back to Governor Bridgar with word of a fort and ship only nine miles up Nelson River. Bridgar thought this was the French establishment, and old Captain Gillam could not undeceive him. The Hudson's Bay Company governor had sent the two men back to spy on what he thought was a French fort. At once Radisson sent out men to capture Bridgar's scouts, who were found half dead with cold and hunger. The captives reported to Radisson that the English ship had been totally wrecked in the ice jam. Bridgar's people were starving. Many traders would have left their rivals to perish. Radisson supplied them with food for the winter. They were no longer to be feared; but there was still danger from young Gillam. He had wished to visit the French fort. Radisson decided to give him an opportunity. Ben Gillam was escorted down to Hayes River. A month passed quietly. The young captain had learned that the boasted forces of the French consisted of less than thirty men. His insolence knew no bounds. He struck a French servant, called Radisson a pirate, and gathering up his belongings prepared to go home. Radisson quietly barred the young man's way.

"You pitiful dog!" said the Frenchman, coolly. "You poor young fool! Why do you suppose you were brought to this fort? We brought you here because it suited us! We keep you here as long as it suits us! We take you back when it suits us!"

Ben Gillam was dumfounded to find that he had been trapped, when he had all the while thought that he was acting the part of a clever spy. He broke out in a storm of abuse. Radisson remanded the foolish young man to a French guard. At the mess-room table Radisson addressed his prisoner : —

"Gillam, to-day I set out to capture your fort."

At the table sat less than thirty men. Young Gillam gave one scornful glance at the French faces and laughed.

"If you had a hundred men instead of twenty," he jeered.

"How many have you, Ben?"

"Nine ; and they'll kill you before you reach the palisades."

Radisson was not talking of killing.

"Gillam," he returned imperturbably, "pick out nine of my men, and I have your fort within forty-eight hours."

Gillam chose the company, and Radisson took one of the Hudson Bay captives as a witness. The thing was done as easily as a piece of farcical comedy. French hostages had been left among the New Englanders as guarantee of Gillam's safety in Radisson's fort. These hostages had been instructed to drop, as if by chance, blocks of wood across the doors of the guard-room and powder house and barracks. Even these precautions proved unnecessary. Two of Radisson's advance guard, who were met by the lieutenant of the New England fort, reported that "Gillam had remained behind." The lieutenant led the two Frenchmen into the fort. These two kept the gates open for Radisson, who marched in with his band, unopposed. The keys were delivered and Radisson was in possession. At midnight the watch-dogs raised an alarm, and the French sallied out to find that a New Englander had run to the Hudson's Bay Company for aid, and Governor Bridgar's men were attacking the ships. All of the assailants fled but four, whom Radisson caught ransacking the ship's cabin. Radisson now had more captives than he could guard, so he loaded the Hudson's Bay Company men with provisions and sent them back to their own starving fort.

Radisson left the New England fort in charge of his Frenchmen and returned to the French quarters. Strange news was carried to him there. Bridgar had forgotten all benefits, waited until Radisson's back was turned, and, with one last desperate cast of the die to retrieve all by capturing the New England fort and ship for the fur company, had marched against young Gillam's island. The French threw open the gates for the Hudson's Bay governor to enter. Then they turned the key and told Governor Bridgar that he was a prisoner. Their *coup* was a complete triumph for Radisson. Both of his rivals were prisoners, and the French flag flew undisputed over Port Nelson.

Spring brought the Indians down to the bay with the winter's hunt. The sight of threescore Englishmen captured by twenty Frenchmen roused the war spirit of the young braves. They offered Radisson two hundred beaver skins to be allowed to massacre the English. Radisson thanked the savages for their good will, but declined their offer. Floods had damaged the water-rotted timbers of the two old hulls in which the explorers voyaged north. It was agreed to return to Quebec in Ben Gillam's boat. A vessel was constructed on one of the hulls to send the English prisoners to the Hudson's Bay Company forts at the south end of the bay.[1] Young Jean Groseillers was left, with seven men, to hold the French post till boats came in the following year. On the 27th of July the ships weighed anchor for the homeward voyage. Young Gillam was given a free passage by way of Quebec. Bridgar was to have gone with his men to the Hudson's Bay Company forts at the south of the bay, but at the last moment a friendly Englishman warned Radisson that the governor's design was to wait till the large ship had left, head the bark back for Hayes River, capture the fort, and put the Frenchmen to the sword. To prevent this Bridgar, too, was carried to Quebec. Twenty miles out the ship was caught in ice-floes that held her for a month, and Bridgar again conspired to cut the throats of the Frenchmen. Henceforth young Gillam and Bridgar were out on parole during the day and kept under lock at night.

The same jealousy as of old awaited Radisson at Quebec. The Company of the North was furious that La Chesnaye had sent ships to Hudson Bay, which the shareholders considered to be their territory by license.[2] Farmers of the Revenue beset the ship

[1] Later in Hudson Bay history, when another commander captured the forts, the prisoners were sold into slavery. Radisson's treatment of his rivals hardly substantiates all the accusations of rascality trumped up against him. Just how many prisoners he took in this *coup*, no two records agree.

[2] Archives, September 24, 1683 : Ordinance of M. de Meulles regarding the

to seize the cargo, because the explorers had gone
North without a permit.   La Chesnaye saved some of
the furs by transshipping them for France before the
vessel reached Quebec.   Then followed an intermi-
nable lawsuit, that exhausted the profits of the voyage.
La Barre had succeeded Frontenac as governor.   The
best friends of La Barre would scarcely deny that his
sole ambition as governor was to amass a fortune from
the fur trade of Canada.   Inspired by the jealous
Company of the North, he refused to grant Radisson
prize money for the capture of the contraband ship,
restored the vessel to Gillam, and gave him clearance
to sail for Boston.[1]   For this La Barre was sharply
reprimanded from France; but the reprimand did
not mend the broken fortunes of the two explorers,
who had given their lives for the extension of the
French domain.[2]   M. Colbert summoned Radisson

claims of persons interested in the expedition to Hudson Bay, organized by M. de la
Chesnaye, Gitton, Bruneau, Mme. Sorel. . . .   In order to avoid difficulties with the
Company of the North, they had placed a vessel at Isle Percée to receive the furs brought
back . . . and convey them to Holland and Spain. . . .   Joachims de Chalons, agent
of the Company of the North, sent a *bateau* to Percée to defeat the project.   De la
Chesnaye, summoned to appear before the intendant, maintained that the company had
no right to this trade, . . . that the enterprise involved so many risks that he could
not consent to divide the profits, if he had any.   The partners having been heard,
M. de Meulles orders that the boats from Hudson Bay be anchored at Quebec.

[1] Archives, October 25, 1683 :   M. de la Barre grants Benjamin Gillam of Boston
clearance for the ship *Le Garçon*, now in port at Quebec, although he had no license
from his Britannic Majesty permitting him to enter Hudson Bay.

[2] Such foundationless accusations have been written against Radisson by historians
who ought to have known better, about these furs, that I quote the final orders of the

and Groseillers to return to France and give an account of all they had done; but when they arrived in Paris, on January 15, 1684, they learned that the great statesman had died. Lord Preston, the English envoy, had lodged such complaints against them for the defeat of the Englishmen in Hudson Bay, that France hesitated to extend public recognition of their services.

government on the subject : November 5, 1683, M. de la Barre forbids Chalons, agent of La Ferme du Canada, confiscating the furs brought from Hudson Bay ; November 8 M. de la Chesnaye is to be paid for the furs seized.

CHAPTER VII

1684–1710

THE LAST VOYAGE OF RADISSON TO HUDSON BAY

France refuses to restore the Confiscated Furs and Radisson tries to redeem his Fortune — Reëngaged by England, he captures back Fort Nelson, but comes to Want in his Old Age — his Character

RADISSON was now near his fiftieth year. He had spent his entire life exploring the wilds. He had saved New France from bankruptcy with cargoes of furs that in four years amounted to half a million of modern money. In ten years he had brought half a million dollars worth of furs to the English company.[1] Yet he was a poor man, threatened with the sponging-house by clamorous creditors and in the power of avaricious statesmen, who used him as a tool for their own schemes. La Chesnaye had saved his furs ; but the half of the cargo that was the share of Radisson and Groseillers had been seized at Quebec.[2]

---

[1] Radisson's petition to the Hudson's Bay Company gives these amounts.

[2] See State Papers quoted in Chapter VI. I need scarcely add that Radisson did *not* steal a march on his patrons by secretly shipping furs to Europe. This is only another of the innumerable slanders against Radisson which State Papers disprove.

On arriving in France, Groseillers presented a memorial of their wrong to the court.[1]   Probably because England and France were allied by treaty at that time, the petition for redress was ignored.   Groseillers was now an old man.   He left the struggle to Radisson and retired to spend his days in quietness.[2] Radisson did not cease to press his claim for the return of confiscated furs.   He had a wife and four

---

[1] It seems impossible that historians with the slightest regard for truth should have branded this part of *Radisson's Relation* as a fabrication, too.   Yet such is the case, and of writers whose books are supposed to be reputable.   Since parts of Radisson's life appeared in the magazines, among many letters I received one from a well-known historian which to put it mildly was furious at the acceptance of *Radisson's Journal* as authentic.   In reply, I asked that historian how many documents contemporaneous with Radisson's life he had consulted before he branded so great an explorer as Radisson as a liar.   Needless to say, that question was not answered.   In corroboration of this part of Radisson's life, I have lying before me : (1) Chouart's letters — see Appendix. (2) A letter of Frontenac recording Radisson's first trip by boat for De la Chesnaye and the complications it would be likely to cause.   (3) A complete official account sent from Quebec to France of Radisson's doings in the bay, which tallies in every respect with *Radisson's Journal*.   (4) Report of M. de Meulles to the Minister on the whole affair with the English and New Englanders.   (5) An official report on the release of Gillam's boat at Quebec.   (6) The memorial presented by Groseillers to the French minister.   (7) An official statement of the first discovery of the bay overland. (8) A complete statement (official) of the complications created by Radisson's wife being English.   (9) A statement through a third party — presumably an official — by Radisson himself of these complications dated 1683.   (10) A letter from the king to the governor at Quebec retailing the English complaints of Radisson at Nelson River.

In the face of this, what is to be said of the historian who calls Radisson's adventures "a fabrication" ?   Such misrepresentation betrays about equal amounts of impudence and ignorance.

[2] From Charlevoix to modern writers mention is made of the death of these two explorers.   Different names are given as the places where they died.   This is all pure supposition.   Therefore I do not quote.   No records exist to prove where Radisson and Groseillers died.

children to support; but, in spite of all his services
to England and France, he did not own a shilling's
worth of property in the whole world.   From January to May he waited for the tardy justice of the
French court.   When his suit became too urgent, he
was told that he had offended the Most Christian
King by attacking the fur posts under the protection
of a friendly monarch, King Charles.   The hollow-
ness of that excuse became apparent when the French
government sanctioned the fitting out of two vessels
for Radisson to go to Hudson Bay in the spring.
Lord Preston, the English ambassador, was also playing a double game.   He never ceased to reproach
the French for the destruction of the fur posts on
Hudson Bay.   At the same time he besieged Radisson with offers to return to the service of the Hudson's
Bay Company.

Radisson was deadly tired of the farce.   From first
to last France had treated him with the blackest
injustice.   If he had wished to be rich, he could long
ago have accumulated wealth by casting in his lot with
the dishonest rulers of Quebec.   In England a strong
clique, headed by Bridgar, Gillam, and Dering opposed
him; but King Charles and the Duke of York,
Prince Rupert, when he was alive, Sir William
Young, Sir James Hayes, and Sir John Kirke were
in his favor.   His heart yearned for his wife and

children.   Just then letters came from England urging him to return to the Hudson's Bay Company. Lord Preston plied the explorer with fair promises. Under threat of punishment for molesting the English of Hudson Bay, the French government tried to force him into a contract to sail on a second voyage to the North on the same terms as in 1682–1683 — not to share the profits.   England and France were both playing double.   Radisson smiled a grim smile and took his resolution.   Daily he conferred with the French Marine on details of the voyage.   He permitted the date of sailing to be set for April 24. Sailors were enlisted, stores put on board, everything was in readiness.   At the last moment, Radisson asked leave of absence to say good-by to his family. The request was granted.   Without losing a moment, he sailed for England, where he arrived on the 10th of May and was at once taken in hand by Sir William Young and Sir James Hayes.   He was honored as his explorations entitled him to be.   King Charles and the Duke of York received him.   Both royal brothers gave him gifts in token of appreciation.   He took the oath of fealty and cast in his lot with the English for good.   It was characteristic of the enthusiast that he was, when Radisson did not sign a strictly business contract with the Hudson's Bay Company.   " I accepted their commission with the greatest pleasure in the world," he writes; ". . . without any precautions on my part for my own interests . . . since they had confidence in me, I wished to be generous towards them . . . in the hope they would render me all the justice due from gentlemen of honor and probity."

But to the troubles of the future Radisson always paid small heed. Glad to be off once more to the adventurous freedom of the wilds, he set sail from England on May 17, 1684, in the *Happy Return*, accompanied by two other vessels. No incident marked the voyage till the ships had passed through the straits and were driven apart by the ice-drift of the bay. About sixty miles out from Port Nelson, the *Happy Return* was held back by ice. Fearing trouble between young Jean Groseillers' men and the English of the other ships, Radisson embarked in a shallop with seven men in order to arrive at Hayes River before the other boats came. Rowing with might and main for forty-eight hours, they came to the site of the French fort.

The fort had been removed. Jean Groseillers had his own troubles during Radisson's absence. A few days after Radisson's departure in July, 1683, cannon announced the arrival of the annual English ships on Nelson River. Jean at once sent out scouts, who found a tribe of Indians on the way home from trading with the ships that had fired the cannon. The scouts brought the Indians back to the French fort. Young Groseillers admitted the savages only one at a time; but the cunning braves pretended to run back for things they had forgotten in the French house. Suspecting nothing, Jean had permitted his own men to leave the fort. On different pretexts, a dozen warriors had surrounded the young trader. Suddenly the mask was thrown off. Springing up, treacherous as a tiger cat, the chief of the band struck at Groseillers with a dagger. Jean parried the blow, grabbed the redskin by his collar of bears' claws strung on thongs, threw the assassin to the ground almost strangling him, and with one foot on the villain's throat and the sword point at his chest, demanded of the Indians what they meant. The savages would have fled, but French soldiers who had heard the noise dashed to Groseillers' aid. The Indians threw down their weapons and confessed all: the Englishmen of the ship had promised the band a barrel of powder to massacre the French. Jean took his foot from the Indian's throat and kicked him out of the fort. The English outnumbered the French; so Jean removed his fort farther from the bay, among the Indians, where the English could not follow. To keep the warriors about him, he offered to house and feed them for the winter. This protected him from the attacks of the English. In the spring Indians came to the French with pelts. Jean was short of firearms; so he bribed the Indians to trade their peltries to the English for guns, and to retrade the guns to him for other goods. It was a stroke worthy of Radisson himself, and saved the little French fort. The English must have suspected the young trader's straits, for they again paid warriors to attack the French; but Jean had forestalled assault by forming an alliance with the Assiniboines, who came down Hayes River from Lake Winnipeg four hundred strong, and encamped a body-guard around the fort. Affairs were at this stage when Radisson arrived with news that he had transferred his services to the English.

Young Groseillers was amazed.[1] Letters to his mother show that he surrendered his charge with a very ill grace. "Do not forget," Radisson urged him, "the injuries that France has inflicted on your father." Young Groseillers' mother, Marguerite Hayet, was in want at Three Rivers.[2] It was memory of her that now turned the scales with the young man. He would turn over the furs to Radisson for the English Company, if Radisson would take care of the far-away mother at Three Rivers. The

---

[1] See Appendix.

[2] State Papers record payment of money to her because she was in want.

bargain was made, and the two embraced. The surrender of the French furs to the English Company has been represented as Radisson's crowning treachery. Under that odium the great discoverer's name has rested for nearly three centuries ; yet the accusation of theft is without a grain of truth. Radisson and Groseillers were to obtain half the proceeds of the voyage in 1682–1683. Neither the explorers nor Jean Groseillers, who had privately invested £500 in the venture, ever received one sou. The furs at Port Nelson — or Fort Bourbon — belonged to the Frenchmen, to do what they pleased with them. The act of the enthusiast is often tainted with folly. That Radisson turned over twenty thousand beaver pelts to the English, without the slightest assurance that he would be given adequate return, was surely folly ; but it was not theft.

The transfer of all possessions to the English was promptly made. Radisson then arranged a peace treaty between the Indians and the English. That peace treaty has endured between the Indians and the Hudson's Bay Company to this day. A new fort was built, the furs stored in the hold of the vessels, and the crews mustered for the return voyage. Radisson had been given a solemn promise by the Hudson's Bay Company that Jean Groseillers and his comrades should be well treated and reëngaged for the English at £100 a year. Now he learned that the English intended to ship all the French *out* of Hudson Bay and to keep them out. The enthusiast had played his game with more zeal than discretion. The English had what they wanted — furs and fort. In return, Radisson had what had misled him like a will-o'-the-wisp all his life — vague promises. In vain Radisson protested that he had given his promise to the French before they surrendered the fort. The English distrusted foreigners. The Frenchmen had been mustered on the ships to receive last instructions. They were told that they were to be taken to England. No chance was given them to escape. Some of the French had gone inland with the Indians. Of Jean's colony, these alone remained. When Radisson realized the conspiracy, he advised his fellow-countrymen to make no resistance ; for he feared that some of the English bitter against him might seize on the pretext of a scuffle to murder the French. His advice proved wise. He had strong friends at the English court, and atonement was made for the breach of faith to the French.

The ships set sail on the 4th of September and arrived in England on the 23d of October. Without waiting for the coach, Radisson hired a horse and spurred to London in order to give his version first of the quarrel on the bay. The Hudson's Bay Company was delighted with the success of Radisson. He was taken before the directors, given a present of a hundred guineas, and thanked for his services.   He was once more presented to the King and the Duke of York.   The company redeemed its promise to

Hudson Bay Dog Trains laden with Furs arriving at Lower Fort Garry, Red River.   (Courtesy of C. C. Chipman, Commissioner H. B. Company.)

Radisson by employing the Frenchmen of the surrendered fort and offering to engage young Groseillers at £100 a year.[1]

---

[1] Dr. George Bryce, who is really the only scholar who has tried to unravel the mystery of Radisson's last days, supplies new facts about his dealings with the Company to 1710.

For five years the English kept faith with Radisson, and he made annual voyages to the bay; but war broke out with France. New France entered on a brilliant campaign against the English of Hudson Bay. The company's profits fell. Radisson, the Frenchman, was distrusted. France had set a price on his head, and one Martinière went to Port Nelson to seize him, but was unable to cope with the English. At no time did Radisson's salary with the company exceed £100; and now, when war stopped dividends on the small amount of stock which had been given to him, he fell into poverty and debt. In 1692 Sir William Young petitioned the company in his favor; but a man with a price on his head for treason could plainly not return to France.[1] The French were in possession of the bay. Radisson could do no harm to the English. Therefore the company ignored him till he sued them and received payment in full for arrears of salary and dividends on stock which he was not permitted to sell; but £50 a year would not support a man who paid half that amount for rent, and had a wife, four children, and servants to support. In 1700 Radisson applied for the position of warehouse keeper for the company at London. Even this was denied.

The dauntless pathfinder was growing old; and the

[1] Marquis de Denonville ordered the arrest of Radisson wherever he might be found.

old cannot fight and lose and begin again as Radisson had done all his life. State Papers of Paris contain records of a Radisson with Tonty at Detroit![1] Was this his nephew, François Radisson's son, who took the name of the explorer, or Radisson's own son, or the game old warrior himself, come out to die on the frontier as he had lived?

History is silent. Until the year 1710 Radisson drew his allowance of £50 a year from the English Company, then the payments stopped. Did the dauntless life stop too? Oblivion hides all record of his death, as it obscured the brilliant achievements of his life.

There is no need to point out Radisson's faults. They are written on his life without extenuation or excuse, so that all may read. There is less need to eulogize his virtues. They declare themselves in every act of his life. This, only, should be remembered. Like all enthusiasts, Radisson could not have been a hero, if he had not been a bit of a fool. If he had not had his faults, if he had not been as impulsive, as daring, as reckless, as inconstant, as improvident of the morrow, as a savage or a child, he would not have accomplished the exploration of half a continent. Men who weigh consequences are not of the stuff to

[1] Appendix ; see State Papers.

win empires.   Had Radisson haggled as to the means, he would have missed or muddled the end.   He went ahead; and when the way did not open, he went round, or crawled over, or carved his way through.

There was an old saying among retired hunters of Three Rivers that " one learned more in the woods than was ever found in l' petee cat-ee-cheesm."   Radisson's training was of the woods, rather than the curé's catechism; yet who that has been trained to the strictest code may boast of as dauntless faults and noble virtues?   He was not faithful to any country, but he was faithful to his wife and children; and he was " faithful to his highest hope," — that of becoming a discoverer, — which is more than common mortals are to their meanest aspirations.   When statesmen played him a double game, he paid them back in their own coin with compound interest.   Perhaps that is why they hated him so heartily and blackened his memory. But amid all the mad license of savage life, Radisson remained untainted.   Other explorers and statesmen, too, have left a trail of blood to perpetuate their memory;   Radisson never once spilled human blood needlessly, and was beloved by the savages.

Memorial tablets commemorate other discoverers. Radisson needs none.   The Great Northwest is his monument for all time.

PART II

THE SEARCH FOR THE WESTERN SEA: BEING AN
ACCOUNT OF THE DISCOVERY OF THE ROCKY
MOUNTAINS, THE MISSOURI UPLANDS, AND THE
VALLEY OF THE SASKATCHEWAN

CHAPTER VIII

1730–1750

THE SEARCH FOR THE WESTERN SEA[1]

M. de la Vérendrye continues the Exploration of the Great North-
west by establishing a Chain of Fur Posts across the Continent —
Privations of the Explorers and the Massacre of Twenty Followers
— His Sons visit the Mandans and discover the Rockies — The
Valley of the Saskatchewan is next explored, but Jealousy thwarts
the Explorer, and he dies in Poverty

I

1731–1736

A CURIOUS paradox is that the men who have done
the most for North America did not intend to do so.
They set out on the far quest of a crack-brained idealist's dream. They pulled up at a foreshortened
purpose; but the unaccomplished aim did more for
humanity than the idealist's dream.

Columbus set out to find Asia. He discovered
America. Jacques Cartier sought a mythical passage

---

1 The authorities for La Vérendrye's life are, of course, his own reports as found in
the State Papers of the Canadian Archives, Pierre Margry's compilation of these
reports, and the Rev. Father Jones' collection of the *Aulneau Letters*.

to the Orient.   He found a northern empire.   La
Salle thought to reach China.   He succeeded only in
exploring the valley of the Mississippi, but the new
continent so explored has done more for humanity
than Asia from time immemorial.   Of all crack-brained
dreams that led to far-reaching results, none was
wilder than the search for the Western Sea.   Marquette, Jolliet, and La Salle had followed the trail that
Radisson had blazed and explored the valley of the
Mississippi ; but like a will-o'-the-wisp beckoning ever
westward was that undiscovered myth, the Western
Sea, thought to lie like a narrow strait between
America and Japan.

The search began in earnest one sweltering afternoon
on June 8, 1731, at the little stockaded fort on the banks
of the St. Lawrence, where Montreal stands to-day.
Fifty grizzled adventurers — wood runners, *voyageurs*,
Indian interpreters — bareheaded, except for the
colored handkerchief binding back the lank hair,
dressed in fringed buckskin, and chattering with the
exuberant nonchalance of boys out of school, had
finished gumming the splits of their ninety-foot
birch canoes, and now stood in line awaiting the coming of their captain, Sieur Pierre Gaultier de Varennes
de la Vérendrye.   The French soldier with his three
sons, aged respectively eighteen, seventeen, and sixteen,
now essayed to discover the fabled Western Sea, whose

Indians and Hunters spurring to the Fight.

narrow waters were supposed to be between the valley of the "Great Forked River" and the Empire of China.

Certainly, if it were worth while for Peter the Great of Russia to send Vitus Bering coasting the bleak headlands of ice-blocked, misty shores to find the Western Sea, it would—as one of the French governors reported —" be nobler than open war " for the little colony of New France to discover this "sea of the setting sun." The quest was invested with all the rainbow tints of " *la gloire* " ; but the rainbow hopes were founded on the practical basis of profits. Leading merchants of Montreal had advanced goods for trade with the Indians on the way to the Western Sea. Their expectations of profits were probably the same as the man's who buys a mining share for ten cents and looks for dividends of several thousand per cent. And the fur trade at that time was capable of yielding such profits. Traders had gone West with less than $2000 worth of goods in modern money, and returned three years later with a sheer profit of a quarter of a million. Hope of such returns added zest to De la Vérendrye's venture for the discovery of the Western Sea.

Goods done up in packets of a hundred pounds lay at the feet of the *voyageurs* awaiting De la Vérendrye's command. A dozen soldiers in the plumed hats, slashed buskins, the brightly colored doublets of the period, joined the motley company. Priests came out to bless the departing *voyageurs*. Chapel bells rang out their God-speed. To the booming of cannon, and at a word from De la Vérendrye, the gates opened. Falling in line with measured tread, the soldiers marched out from Mount Royal. Behind, in the ambling gait of the moccasined woodsman, came the *voyageurs* and *coureurs* and interpreters, pack-straps across their foreheads, packets on the bent backs, the long birch canoes hoisted to the shoulders of four men, two abreast at each end, heads hidden in the inverted keel.

The path led between the white fret of Lachine Rapids and the dense forests that shrouded the base of Mount Royal. Checkerboard squares of farm patches had been cleared in the woods. La Salle's old thatch-roofed seigniory lay not far back from the water. St. Anne's was the launching place for fleets of canoes that were to ascend the Ottawa. Here, a last look was taken of splits and seams in the birch keels. With invocations of St. Anne in one breath, and invocations of a personage not mentioned in the curé's " petee cat-ee-cheesm " in the next breath, and imprecations that their " souls might be smashed on the end of a picket fence," — the *voyageur's* common oath even to this day, — the boatmen stored goods fore, aft, and athwart till each long canoe sank to the

Fight at the Foot-hills of the Rockies between Crows and Snakes.

gunwale as it was gently pushed out on the water.   A last sign of the cross, and the lithe figures leap light as a mountain cat to their place in the canoes.   There are four benches of paddlers, two abreast, with bowman and steersman, to each canoe.   One can guess that the explorer and his sons and his nephew, Sieur de la Jemmeraie, who was to be second in command, all unhatted as they heard the long last farewell of the bells. Every eye is fastened on the chief bowman's steel-shod pole, held high — there is silence but for the bells — the bowman's pole is lowered — as with one stroke out sweep the paddles in a poetry of motion.   The chimes die away over the water, the chapel spire gleams — it, too, is gone.   Some one strikes up a plaintive ditty, — the *voyageur's* song of the lost lady and the faded roses, or the dying farewell of Cadieux, the hunter, to his comrades, — and the adventurers are launched for the Western Sea.

II

1731–1736

Every mile westward was consecrated by heroism. There was the place where Cadieux, the white hunter, went ashore single-handed to hold the Iroquois at bay, while his comrades escaped by running the rapids; but Cadieux was assailed by a subtler foe than the Iroquois, *la folie des bois*, — the folly of the woods, —

that sends the hunter wandering in endless circles till he dies from hunger; and when his companions returned, Cadieux lay in eternal sleep with a death chant scribbled on bark across his breast. There were the Rapids of the Long Sault where Dollard and seventeen Frenchmen fought seven hundred Iroquois till every white man fell. Not one of all De la Vérendrye's fifty followers but knew that perils as great awaited him.

Streaked foam told the *voyageurs* where they were approaching rapids. Alert as a hawk, the bowman stroked for the shore; and his stroke was answered by all paddles. If the water were high enough to carry the canoes above rocks, and the rapids were not too violent, several of the boatmen leaped out to knees in water, and "tracked" the canoes up stream; but this was unusual with loaded craft. The bowman steadied the beached keel. Each man landed with pack on his back, lighted his pipe, and trotted away over *portages* so dank and slippery that only a moccasined foot could gain hold. On long *portages*, camp-fires were kindled and the kettles slung on the crotched sticks for the evening meal. At night, the *voyageurs* slept under the overturned canoes, or lay on the sand with bare faces to the sky. Morning mist had not risen till all the boats were once more breasting the flood of the Ottawa. For a month the canoe prows met the current when a *portage* lifted the fleet out of the Ottawa into a shallow stream flowing toward Lake Nipissing,

" Each man landed with pack on his back, and trotted away over portages."

and from Lake Nipissing to Lake Huron. The change was a welcome relief. The canoes now rode with the current; and when a wind sprang up astern, blanket sails were hoisted that let the boatmen lie back, paddles athwart.   Going with the stream, the *voyageurs* would " run " — " *sauter les rapides* " — the safest of the cataracts.   Bowman, not steersman, was the pilot of such " runs."   A faint, far swish as of night wind, little forward leaps and swirls of the current, the blur of trees on either bank, were signs to the bowman.   He rose in his place. A thrust of the steel-shod pole at a rock in midstream — the rock raced past ; a throb of the keel to the live waters below

A Cree Indian of the Minnesota Borderlands.

— the bowman crouches back, lightening the prow just as a rider " lifts " his horse to the leap ; a sudden splash — the thing has happened — the canoe has run the rapids or shot the falls.

Pause was made at Lake Huron for favorable weather; and a rear wind would carry the canoes at a bouncing pace clear across to Michilimackinac, at the mouth of Lake Michigan. This was the chief fur post of the lakes at that time. All the boats bound east or west, Sioux and Cree and Iroquois and Fox, traders' and priests' and outlaws'—stopped at Michilimackinac. Vice and brandy and religion were the characteristics of the fort.

This was familiar ground to De la Vérendrye. It was at the lonely fur post of Nepigon, north of Michilimackinac, in the midst of a wilderness forest, that he had eaten his heart out with baffled ambition from 1728 to 1730, when he descended to Montreal to lay before M. de Beauharnois, the governor, plans for the discovery of the Western Sea. Born at Three Rivers in 1686, where the passion for discovery and Radisson's fame were in the very air and traders from the wilderness of the Upper Country wintered, young Pierre Gaultier de Varennes de la Vérendrye, at the ambitious age of fourteen, determined that he would become a discoverer.[1] At eighteen he was fighting in New England, at nineteen in Newfoundland, at twenty-three in Europe at the battle of Malplaquet, where he was carried off the field with nine wounds.

---

[1] The *Pays d'en Haut* or " Up-Country " was the vague name given by the fur traders to the region between the Missouri and the North Pole.

Eager for more distinguished service, he returned to Canada in his twenty-seventh year, only to find himself relegated to an obscure trading post in far Northern wilds.   Then the boyhood ambitions reawakened.   All France and Canada, too, were ringing with projects for the discovery of the Western Sea.   Russia was acting. France knew it.   The great priest Charlevoix had been sent to Canada to investigate plans for the venture, and had recommended an advance westward through the country of the Sioux; but the Sioux [1] swarmed round the little fort at Lake Pepin on the Mississippi like angry wasps.   That way, exploration was plainly barred.   Nothing came of the attempt except a brisk fur trade and a brisker warfare on the part of the Sioux.   At the lonely post of Nepigon, vague Indian tales came to De la Vérendrye of "a great river flowing west" and "a vast, flat country devoid of timber" with "large herds of cattle."   Ochagach, an old Indian, drew maps on birch bark showing rivers that emptied into the Western Sea.   De la Vérendrye's smouldering ambitions kindled.   He hurried to Michilimackinac.   There the traders and Indians told the same story.   Glory seemed suddenly within De la Vérendrye's grasp.   Carried away with the passion for discovery that ruled his age, he took

[1] Throughout this volume the word "Sioux" is used as applying to the entire confederacy, and not to the Minnesota Sioux only.

passage in the canoes bound for Quebec. The Marquis Charles de Beauharnois had become governor. His brother Claude had taken part in the exploration of the Mississippi. The governor favored the project of the Western Sea. Perhaps Russia's activity gave edge to the governor's zest; but he promised De la Vérendrye the court's patronage and prestige. This was not money. France would not advance the enthusiast one sou, but granted him a monopoly of the fur trade in the countries which he might discover. The winter of 1731–1732 was spent by De la Vérendrye as the guest of the governor at Château St. Louis, arranging with merchants to furnish goods for trade; and on May 19 the agreement was signed. By a lucky coincidence, the same winter that M. de la Vérendrye had come down to Quebec, there had arrived from the Mississippi fort, his nephew, Christopher Dufrost, Sieur de la Jemmeraie, who had commanded the Sioux post and been prisoner among the Indians. So M. de la Vérendrye chose Jemmeraie for lieutenant.

And now the explorer was back at Michilimackinac, on the way to the accomplishment of the daring ambition of his life. The trip from Montreal had fatigued the *voyageurs*. Brandy flowed at the lake post freely as at a modern mining camp. The explorer kept military discipline over his men. They received no pay which could be squandered away on liquor. Discontent grew rife. Taking Father Messaiger, the Jesuit, as chaplain, M. de la Vérendrye ordered his grumbling *voyageurs* to their canoes, and, passing through the Straits of the Sault, headed his fleet once more for the Western Sea. Other explorers had preceded him on this part of the route. The Jesuits had coasted the north shore of Lake Superior. So had Radisson. In 1688 De Noyon of Three Rivers had gone as far west as the Lake of the Woods towards what is now Minnesota and Manitoba; and in 1717 De Lanoue had built a fur post at Kaministiquia, near what is now Fort William on Lake Superior. The shore was always perilous to the boatman of frail craft. The harbors were fathoms deep, and the waves thrashed by a cross wind often proved as dangerous as the high sea. It took M. de la Vérendrye's canoemen a month to coast from the Straits of Mackinaw to Kaministiquia, which they reached on the 26th of August, seventy-eight days after they had left Montreal. The same distance is now traversed in two days.

Prospects were not encouraging. The crews were sulky. Kaministiquia was the outermost post in the West. Within a month, the early Northern winter would set in. One hunter can scramble for his winter's food where fifty will certainly starve; and the Indians could not be expected back from the chase

with supplies of furs and food till spring. The canoemen had received no pay. Free as woodland denizens,
they chafed under military command. Boats were
always setting out at this season for the homeland
hamlets of the St. Lawrence; and perhaps other
hunters told De la Vérendrye's men that this Western Sea was a will-o'-the-wisp that would lead for
leagues and leagues over strange lands, through hostile
tribes, to a lonely death in the wilderness. When the
explorer ordered his men once more in line to launch
for the Western Sea, there was outright mutiny.
Soldiers and boatmen refused to go on. The Jesuit
Messaiger threatened and expostulated with the men.
Jemmeraie, who had been among the Sioux, inter-
ceded with the *voyageurs*. A compromise was
effected. Half the boatmen would go ahead with
Jemmeraie if M. de la Vérendrye would remain with
the other half at Lake Superior as a rear guard for
retreat and the supply of provisions. So the explorer
suffered his first check in the advance to the Western
Sea.

III

1732–1736

Equipping four canoes, Lieutenant de la Jemmeraie
and young Jean Ba'tiste de la Vérendrye set out with
thirty men from Kaministiquia, *portaged* through

dense forests over moss and dank rock past the high cataract of the falls, and launched westward to prepare a fort for the reception of their leader in spring. Before winter had closed navigation, Fort St. Pierre — named in honor of the explorer — had been erected on the left bank or Minnesota side of Rainy Lake, and the two young men not only succeeded in holding their mutinous followers, but drove a thriving trade in furs with the Crees.   Perhaps the furs were obtained at too great cost, for ammunition and firearms were the price paid, but the same mistake has been made at a later day for a lesser object than the discovery of the Western Sea.   The spring of 1732 saw the young men back at Lake Superior, going post-haste to Michilimackinac to exchange furs for the goods from Montreal.

On the 8th of June, exactly a year from the day that he had left Montreal, M. de la Vérendrye pushed forward with all his people for Fort St. Pierre.   Five weeks later he was welcomed inside the stockades. Uniformed soldiers were a wonder to the awe-struck Crees, who hung round the gateway with hands over their hushed lips.   Gifts of ammunition won the loyalty of the chiefs.   Not to be lacking in generosity, the Indians collected fifty of their gaudiest canoes and offered to escort the explorer west to the Lake of the Woods.   De la Vérendrye could not miss such an

offer. Though his *voyageurs* were fatigued, he set out
at once. He had reached Fort St. Pierre on July 14.
In August his entire fleet glided over the Lake of the
Woods. The threescore canoes manned by the Cree
boatmen threaded the shadowy defiles and labyrinthine
channels of the Lake of the Woods — or Lake of the
Isles — coasting island after island along the south or

A Group of Cree Indians.

Minnesota shore westward to the opening of the river
at the northwest angle. This was the border of the
Sioux territory. Before the boatmen opened the
channel of an unknown river. Around them were
sheltered harbors, good hunting, and good fishing.
The Crees favored this region for winter camping
ground because they could hide their families from

the Sioux on the sheltered islands of the wooded lake.
Night frosts had painted the forests red. The flacker
of wild-fowl overhead, the skim of ice forming on the
lake, the poignant sting of the north wind — all forewarned winter's approach. Jean de la Vérendrye had
not come up with the supplies from Michilimackinac.
The explorer did not tempt mutiny by going farther.
He ordered a halt and began building a fort that was
to be the centre of operations between Montreal and
the unfound Western Sea. The fort was named St.
Charles in honor of Beauharnois. It was defended by
four rows of thick palisades fifteen feet high. In the
middle of the enclosure stood the living quarters, log
cabins with thatched roofs.

By October the Indians had scattered to their
hunting-grounds like leaves to the wind. The ice
thickened. By November the islands were ice-locked
and snow had drifted waist-high through the forests.
The *voyageurs* could still fish through ice holes for
food; but where was young Jean who was to bring up
provisions from Michilimackinac? The commander
did not voice his fears; and his men were too deep in
the wilds for desertion. One afternoon, a shout
sounded from the silent woods, and out from the
white-edged evergreens stepped a figure on snow-
shoes — Jean de la Vérendrye, leading his boatmen,
with the provisions packed on their backs, from a point

fifty miles away where the ice had caught the canoes. If the supplies had not come, the explorer could neither have advanced nor retreated in spring. It was a risk that De la Vérendrye did not intend to have repeated. Suspecting that his merchant part-ners were dissatisfied, he sent Jemmeraie down to Montreal in 1733 to report and urge the necessity for prompt forwarding of all supplies. With Jemmeraie went the Jesuit Messaiger; but their combined expla-nations failed to satisfy the merchants of Montreal. De la Vérendrye had now been away three years. True, he had constructed two fur posts and sent East two cargoes of furs. His partners were looking for enormous wealth. Disappointed and caring nothing for the Western Sea; perhaps, too, secretly accusing De la Vérendrye of making profits privately, as many a gentleman of fortune did, — the merchants decided to advance provisions only in proportion to earnings. What would become of the fifty men in the Northern wilderness the partners neither asked nor cared.

Young Jean had meanwhile pushed on and built Fort Maurepas on Lake Winnipeg; but his father dared not leave Fort St. Charles without supplies. De la Vérendrye's position was now desperate. He was hopelessly in debt to his men for wages. That did not help discipline. His partners were not only with-holding supplies, but charging up a high rate of interest on the first equipment.   To turn back meant ruin.   To go forward he was powerless.   Leaving Jemmeraie in command, and permitting his eager son to go ahead with a few picked men to Fort Maurepas on Lake Winnipeg, De la Vérendrye took a small canoe and descended with all swiftness to Quebec.   The winter of 1634–1635 was spent with the governor ; and the partners were convinced that they must either go on with the venture or lose all.   They consented to continue supplying goods, but also charging all outlay against the explorer.

Father Aulneau went back with De la Vérendrye as chaplain.   The trip was made at terrible speed, in the hottest season, through stifling forest fires.   Behind, at slower pace, came the provisions.   De la Vérendrye reached the Lake of the Woods in September. Fearing the delay of the goods for trade, and dreading the danger of famine with so many men in one place, De la Vérendrye despatched Jemmeraie to winter with part of the forces at Lake Winnipeg, where Jean and Pierre, the second son, had built Fort Maurepas. The worst fears were realized.   Ice had blocked the Northern rivers by the time the supplies had come to Lake Superior.   Fishing failed.   The hunt was poor. During the winter of 1736 food became scantier at the little forts of St. Pierre, St. Charles, and Maurepas. Rations were reduced from three times to once and

twice a day. By spring De la Vérendrye was put to
all the extremities of famine-stricken traders, his men
subsisting on parchment, moccasin leather, roots, and
their hunting dogs.

He was compelled to wait at St. Charles for the
delayed supplies. While he waited came blow upon
blow: Jean and Pierre arrived from Fort Maurepas
with news that Jemmeraie had died three weeks before
on his way down to aid De la Vérendrye. Wrapped in
a hunter's robe, his body was buried in the sand-bank
of a little Northern stream, La Fourche des Roseaux.
Over the lonely grave the two brothers had erected a
cross. Father and sons took stock of supplies. They
had not enough powder to last another month, and
·already the Indians were coming in with furs and food
to be traded for ammunition. If the Crees had
known the weakness of the white men, short work
might have been made of Fort St. Charles. It never
entered the minds of De la Vérendrye and his sons to
give up. They decided to rush three canoes of twenty
voyageurs to Michilimackinac for food and powder.
Father Aulneau, the young priest, accompanied the
boatmen to attend a religious retreat at Michilimackinac. It had been a hard year for the youthful missionary. The ship that brought him from
France had been plague-stricken. The trip to Fort
St. Charles had been arduous and swift, through

stifling heat; and the year passed in the North was one of famine.

Accompanied by the priest and led by Jean de la Vérendrye, now in his twenty-third year, the *voyageurs* embarked hurriedly on the 8th of June, 1736, five years to a day from the time that they left Montreal — and a fateful day it was — in the search for the Western Sea. The Crees had always been friendly; and when the boatmen landed on a sheltered island twenty miles from Fort St. Charles to camp for the night, no sentry was stationed. The lake lay calm as glass in the hot June night, the camp-fire casting long lines across the water that could be seen for miles. An early start was to be made in the morning and a furious pace to be kept all the way to Lake Superior, and the *voyageurs* were presently sound asleep on the sand. The keenest ears could scarcely have distinguished the soft lapping of muffled paddles; and no one heard the moccasined tread of ambushed Indians reconnoitring. Seventeen Sioux stepped from their canoes, stole from cover to cover, and looked out on the unsuspecting sleepers. Then the Indians as noiselessly slipped back to their canoes to carry word of the discovery to a band of marauders.

Something had occurred at Fort St. Charles without M. de la Verendrye's knowledge. Hilarious with their new possessions of firearms, and perhaps, also,

"The soldiers marched out from Mount Royal."

mad with the brandy of which Father Aulneau had complained, a few mischievous Crees had fired from the fort on wandering Sioux of the prairie.

"Who — fire — on — us?" demanded the outraged Sioux.

"The French," laughed the Crees.

The Sioux at once went back to a band of one hundred and thirty warriors. "Tigers of the plains" the Sioux were called, and now the tigers' blood was up. They set out to slay the first white man seen. By chance, he was one Bourassa, coasting by himself. Taking him captive, they had tied him to burn him, when a slave squaw rushed out, crying: "What would you do? This Frenchman is a friend of the Sioux! He saved my life! If you desire to be avenged, go farther on! You will find a camp of Frenchmen, among whom is the son of the white chief!"

The *voyageur* was at once unbound, and scouts scattered to find the white men. Night had passed before the scouts had carried news of Jean de la Vérendrye's men to the marauding warriors. The ghostly gray of dawn saw the *voyageurs* paddling swiftly through the morning mist from island to island of the Lake of the Woods. Cleaving the mist behind, following solely by the double foam wreaths rippling from the canoe prows, came the silent boats of the Sioux. When sunrise lifted the fog, the pursuers

paused like stealthy cats.   At sunrise Jean de la
Vérendrye landed his crews for breakfast.   Camp-fires
told the Indians where to follow.

A few days later bands of Sautaux came to the
camping ground of the French.   The heads of the
white men lay on a beaver skin.   All had been scalped.
The missionary, Aulneau, was on his knees, as if in
morning prayers.   An arrow projected from his head.
His left hand was on the earth, fallen forward, his
right hand uplifted, invoking Divine aid.   Young
Vérendrye lay face down, his back hacked to pieces,
a spear sunk in his waist, the headless body mockingly
decorated with porcupine quills.   So died one of the
bravest of the young nobility in New France.

The Sautaux erected a cairn of stones over the
bodies of the dead.   All that was known of the massacre was vague Indian gossip.   The Sioux reported
that they had not intended to murder the priest, but a
crazy-brained fanatic had shot the fatal arrow and
broken from restraint, weapon in hand.   Rain-storms
had washed out all marks of the fray.

In September the bodies of the victims were carried
to Fort St. Charles, and interred in the chapel.   Eight
hundred Crees besought M. de la Vérendrye to let
them avenge the murder; but the veteran of Malplaquet exhorted them not to war.   Meanwhile, Fort

St. Charles awaited the coming of supplies from Lake Superior.

IV

1736–1740

A week passed, and on the 17th of June the canoe loads of ammunition and supplies for which the murdered *voyageurs* had been sent arrived at Fort St. Charles. In June the Indian hunters came in with the winter's hunt; and on the 20th thirty Sautaux hurried to Fort St. Charles, to report that they had found the mangled bodies of the massacred Frenchmen on an island seven leagues from the fort. Again La Vérendrye had to choose whether to abandon his cherished dreams, or follow them at the risk of ruin and death. As before, when his men had mutinied, he determined to advance.

Jean, the eldest son, was dead. Pierre and François were with their father. Louis, the youngest, now seventeen years of age, had come up with the supplies. Pierre at once went to Lake Winnipeg, to prepare Fort Maurepas for the reception of all the forces. Winter set in. Snow lay twelve feet deep in the forests now known as the Minnesota Borderlands. On February 8, 1737, in the face of a biting north wind, with the thermometer at forty degrees below zero, M. de la Vérendrye left Fort St. Charles, François carrying the French flag, with ten soldiers, wearing snow-shoes, in line behind, and two or three hundred Crees swathed in furs bringing up a ragged rear. The bright uniforms of the soldiers were patches of red among the snowy everglades. Bivouac was made on beds of pine boughs,— feet to the camp-fire, the night frost snapping like a whiplash, the stars flashing with a steely clearness known only in northern climes. The march was at a swift pace, for three weeks by canoe is short enough time to traverse the Minnesota and Manitoba Borderlands northwest to Lake Winnipeg ; and in seventeen days M. de la Vérendrye was at Fort Maurepas.

Fort Maurepas (in the region of the modern Alexander) lay on a tongue of sand extending into the lake a few miles beyond the entrance of Red River. Tamarack and poplar fringe the shore ; and in windy weather the lake is lashed into a roughness that resembles the flux of ocean tides. I remember once going on a steamer towards the site of Maurepas. The ship drew lightest of draft. While we were anchored the breeze fell, and the ship was stranded as if by ebb tide for twenty-four hours. The action of the wind explained the Indian tales of an ocean tide, which had misled La Vérendrye into expecting to find the Western Sea at this point. He found a magnificent body of fresh water, but not the ocean. The fort was the usual pioneer fur post — a barracks of unbarked logs, chinked up with frozen clay and moss, roofed with branches and snow, occupying the centre of a courtyard, palisaded by slabs of pine logs. M. de la Vérendrye was now in the true realm of the explorer — in territory where no other white man had trod. With a shout his motley

Traders' Boats running the Rapids of the Athabasca River.

forces emerged from the snowy tamaracks, and with a shout from Pierre de la Vérendrye and his tawny followers the explorer was welcomed through the gateway of little Fort Maurepas.

Pierre de la Vérendrye had heard of a region to the south much frequented by the Assiniboine Indians,

who had conducted Radisson to the Sea of the North
fifty years before — the Forks where the Assiniboine
River joins the Red, and the city of Winnipeg stands
to-day.   It was reported that game was plentiful here.
Two hundred tepees of Assiniboines were awaiting the
explorer.   His forces were worn with their marching,
but in a few weeks the glaze of ice above the fathomless
drifts of snow would be too rotten for travel, and not
until June would the riverways be clear for canoes.
But such a scant supply of goods had his partners sent
up that poor De la Vérendrye had nothing to trade
with the waiting Assiniboines.   Sending his sons forward to reconnoitre the Forks of the Assiniboine, — the
modern Winnipeg, — he set out for Montreal as soon
as navigation opened, taking with him fourteen great
canoes of precious furs.

The fourteen canoe loads proved his salvation.   As
long as there were furs and prospects of furs, his partners would back the enterprise of finding the Western
Sea.   The winter of 1738 was spent as the guest of
the governor at Château St. Louis.   The partners
were satisfied, and plucked up hope of their venture.
They would advance provisions in proportion to
earnings.   By September he was back at Fort Maurepas on Lake Winnipeg, pushing for the undiscovered
bourne of the Western Sea.   Leaving orders for trade
with the chief clerk at Maurepas, De la Vérendrye

picked out his most intrepid men ; and in September of 1738, for the first time in history, white men glided up the ochre-colored, muddy current of the Red for the Forks of the Assiniboine. Ten Cree wigwams and two war chiefs awaited De la Vérendrye on the low flats of what are now known as South Winnipeg. Not the fabled Western Sea, but an illimitable ocean of rolling prairie — the long russet grass rising and falling to the wind like waves to the run of invisible feet — stretched out before the eager eyes of the explorer. Northward lay the autumn-tinged brushwood of Red River. South, shimmering in the purple mists of Indian summer, was Red River Valley. Westward the sun hung like a red shield, close to the horizon, over vast reaches of prairie billowing to the sky-line in the tide of a boundless ocean. Such was the discovery of the Canadian Northwest.

Doubtless the weary gaze of the tired *voyageurs* turned longingly westward. Where was the Western Sea? Did it lie just beyond the horizon where skyline and prairie met, or did the trail of their quest run on — on — on — endlessly? The Assiniboine flows into the Red, the Red into Lake Winnipeg, the Lake into Hudson Bay. Plainly, Assiniboine Valley was not the way to the Western Sea. But what lay just beyond this Assiniboine Valley? An old Cree chief warned the boatmen that the Assiniboine River was very low and would wreck the canoes; but he also told vague yarns of "great waters beyond the mountains of the setting sun," where white men dwelt, and

The Ragged Sky-line of the Mountains.

the waves came in a tide, and the waters were salt. The Western Sea where the Spaniards dwelt had long been known.   It was a Western Sea to the north, that would connect Louisiana and Canada, that De la Véren-

arye sought.   The Indian fables, without doubt, referred
to a sea beyond the Assiniboine River, and thither
would De la Vérendrye go at any cost.   Some sort of
barracks or shelter was knocked up on the south side
of the Assiniboine opposite the flats.   It was subsequently known as Fort Rouge, after the color of the
adjacent river, and was the foundation of Winnipeg.
Leaving men to trade at Fort Rouge, De la Vérendrye
set out on September 26, 1738, for the height of land
that must lie beyond the sources of the Assiniboine.   De
la Vérendrye was now like a man hounded by his own
Frankenstein.   A thousand leagues—every one marked
by disaster and failure and sinking hopes — lay behind
him.   A thousand leagues of wilderness lay before
him.   He had only a handful of men.   The Assiniboine Indians were of dubious friendliness.   The
white men were scarce of food.   In a few weeks they
would be exposed to the terrible rigors of Northern
winter.   Yet they set their faces toward the west, types
of the pioneers who have carved empire out of wilderness.

The Assiniboine was winding and low, with many
sand bars.   On the wooded banks deer and buffalo
grazed in such countless multitudes that the boatmen
took them for great herds of cattle.   Flocks of wild
geese darkened the sky overhead.   As the boats
wound up the shallows of the river, ducks rose in

myriad flocks. Prairie wolves skulked away from the river bank, and the sand-hill cranes were so unused to human presence that they scarcely rose as the *voyageurs* poled past. While the boatmen poled, the soldiers marched in military order across country, so avoiding the bends of the river. Daily, Crees and Assiniboines of the plains joined the white men. A week after leaving the Forks or Fort Rouge, De la Vérendrye came to the Portage of the Prairie, leading north to Lake Manitoba and from the lake to Hudson Bay. Clearly, northward was not the way to the Western Sea; but the Assiniboines told of a people to the southwest — the Mandans — who knew a people who lived on the Western Sea. As soon as his baggage came up, De la Vérendrye ordered the construction of a fort — called De la Reine — on the banks of the Assiniboine. This was to be the forwarding post for the Western Sea. To the Mandans living on the Missouri, who knew a people living on salt water, De la Vérendrye now directed his course.

On the morning of October 18 drums beat to arms. Additional men had come up from the other forts. Fifty-two soldiers and *voyageurs* now stood in line. Arms were inspected. To each man were given powder, balls, axe, and kettle. Pierre and François de la Vérendrye hoisted the French flag. For the first time a bugle call sounded over the prairie. At the word, out stepped the little band of white men, marking time for the Western Sea. The course lay west-southwest, up the Souris River, through wooded ravines now stripped of foliage, past alkali sloughs ice-edged by frost, over rolling cliffs russet and bare, where gopher and badger and owl and roving buffalo were

Hungry Hall, 1870; near the site of the Vérendrye Fort in Rainy River Region.

the only signs of life. On the 21st of October two hundred Assiniboine warriors joined the marching white men. In the sheltered ravines buffalo grazed by the hundreds of thousands, and the march was delayed by frequent buffalo hunts to gather pemmican — pounded marrow and fat of the buffalo — which was much esteemed by the Mandans. Within a month so many Assiniboines had joined the French that the company numbered more than six hundred warriors, who were ample protection against the Sioux; and the Sioux were the deadly terror of all tribes of the plains. But M. de la Vérendrye was expected to present ammunition to his Assiniboine friends.

Four outrunners went speeding to the Missouri to notify the Mandans of the advancing warriors. The *coureurs* carried presents of pemmican. To prevent surprise, the Assiniboines marched under the sheltered slopes of the hills and observed military order. In front rode the warriors, dressed in garnished buckskin and armed with spears and arrows. Behind, on foot, came the old and the lame. To the rear was another guard of warriors. Lagging in ragged lines far back came a ragamuffin brigade, the women, children, and dogs — squaws astride cayuses lean as barrel hoops, children in moss bags on their mothers' backs, and horses and dogs alike harnessed with the *travaille* — two sticks tied into a triangle, with the shafts fastened to a cinch on horse or dog. The joined end of the shafts dragged on the ground, and between them hung the baggage, surmounted by papoose, or pet owl, or the half-tamed pup of a prairie-wolf, or even a wild-eyed young squaw with hair flying to the wind. At night camp was made in a circle formed of the hobbled

horses.   Outside, the dogs scoured in pursuit of
coyotes.   The women and children took refuge in the
centre, and the warriors slept near their picketed
horses.   By the middle of November the motley caval-
cade had crossed the height of land between the Assiniboine River and the Missouri, and was heading fcr
the Mandan villages.   Mandan *coureurs* came out
to welcome the visitors, pompously presenting De la
Vérendrye with corn in the ear and tobacco.   At this
stage, the explorer discovered that his bag of presents
for his hosts had been stolen by the Assiniboines ; but
he presented the Mandans with what ammunition he
could spare, and gave them plenty of pemmican which
his hunters had cured.   The two tribes drove a brisk
trade in furs, which the northern Indians offered, and
painted plumes, which the Mandans displayed to the
envy of Assiniboine warriors.

On the 3d of December, De la Vérendrye's sons
stepped before the ragged host of six hundred savages
with the French flag hoisted.   The explorer himself
was lifted to the shoulders of the Mandan *coureurs*.
A gun was fired and the strange procession set out for
the Mandan villages.   In this fashion white men first
took possession of the Upper Missouri.   Some miles
from the lodges a band of old chiefs met De la Vérendrye and gravely handed him a grand calumet of pipe-
stone ornamented with eagle feathers.   This typified

Q

peace.   De la Vérendrye ordered his fifty French followers to draw up in line.   The sons placed the
French flag four paces to the fore.   The Assiniboine
warriors took possession in stately Indian silence to
the right and left of the whites.   At a signal three
thundering volleys of musketry were fired.   The
Mandans fell back, prostrated with fear and wonder.
The command " forward " was given, and the Mandan village was entered in state at four in the afternoon
of December 3, 1738.

The village was in much the same condition as a
hundred years later when visited by Prince Maximilian and by the artist Catlin.   It consisted of
circular huts, with thatched roofs, on which perched the
gaping women and children.   Around the village of
huts ran a moat or ditch, which was guarded in time
of war with the Sioux.   Flags flew from the centre
poles of each hut; but the flags were the scalps of
enemies slain.   In the centre of the village was a
larger hut.   This was the " medicine lodge," or council
hall, of the chiefs, used only for ceremonies of religion
and war and treaties of peace.   Thither De la Vérendrye
was conducted.   Here the Mandan chiefs sat on
buffalo robes in a circle round the fire, smoking the
calumet, which was handed to the white man.   The
explorer then told the Indians of his search for the
Western Sea.   Of a Western Sea they could tell him

nothing definite. They knew a people far west who grew corn and tobacco and who lived on the shores of water that was bitter for drinking. The people were white. They dressed in armor and lived in houses of stone. Their country was full of mountains. More of the Western Sea, De la Vérendrye could not learn.

Meanwhile, six hundred Assiniboine visitors were a tax on the hospitality of the Mandans, who at once spread a rumor of a Sioux raid. This gave speed to the Assiniboines' departure. Among the Assiniboines who ran off in precipitate fright was De la Vérendrye's interpreter. It was useless to wait longer. The French were short of provisions, and the Missouri Indians could not be expected to support fifty white men. Though it was the bitter cold of midwinter, De la Vérendrye departed for Fort de la Reine. Two Frenchmen were left to learn the Missouri dialects. A French flag in a leaden box with the arms of France inscribed was presented to the Mandan chief; and De la Vérendrye marched from the village on the 8th of December. Scarcely had he left, when he fell terribly ill; but for the pathfinder of the wilderness there is neither halt nor retreat. M. de la Vérendrye's ragged army tramped wearily on, half blinded by snow glare and buffeted by prairie blizzards, huddling in snowdrifts from the wind at night and uncertain of their compass over the white wastes by day. There is nothing so deadly silent and utterly destitute of life as the prairie in midwinter. Moose and buffalo had sought the shelter of wooded ravines. Here a fox track ran over the snow. There a coyote skulked from cover, to lope away the next instant for brush-wood or hollow, and snow-buntings or whiskey-jacks might have followed the marchers for pickings of waste; but east, west, north, and south was nothing but the wide, white wastes of drifted snow. On Christmas Eve of 1738 low curling smoke above the prairie told the wan-derers that they were near-ing the Indian camps of the Assiniboines; and by nightfall of February 10, 1739, they were under the shelter of Fort de la Reine. " I have never been so wretched from illness and fatigue in all my life as on that journey," reported De la Vérendrye. As usual, provisions were scarce at the fort. Fifty people had to be fed. Buffalo and deer meat saved the French from starvation till spring.

A Monarch of the Plains.

All that De la Vérendrye had accomplished on this trip was to learn that salt water existed west-south-west. Anxious to know more of the Northwest, he sent his sons to the banks of a great northern river. This was the Saskatchewan. In their search of the Northwest, they constructed two more trading posts, Fort Dauphin near Lake Manitoba, and Bourbon on the Saskatchewan. Winter quarters were built at the forks of the river, which afterwards became the site of Fort Poskoyac. This spring not a canoe load of food came up from Montreal. Papers had been served for the seizure of all De la Vérendrye's forts, goods, property, and chattels to meet the claims of his creditors. Desperate, but not deterred from his quest, De la Vérendrye set out to contest the lawsuits in Montreal.

V

1740–1750

Which way to turn now for the Western Sea that eluded their quest like a will-o'-the-wisp was the question confronting Pierre, François, and Louis de la Vérendrye during the explorer's absence in Montreal. They had followed the great Saskatchewan westward to its forks. No river was found in this region flowing in the direction of the Western Sea. They had been in the country of the Missouri; but neither did any river there flow to a Western Sea. Yet the Mandans told of salt water far to the west. Thither they would turn the baffling search.

The two men left among the Mandans to learn the language had returned to the Assiniboine River with more news of tribes from "the setting sun" who dwelt on salt water.   Pierre de la Vérendrye went down to the Missouri with the two interpreters ; but the Mandans refused to supply guides that year, and the young Frenchman came back to winter on the Assiniboine.   Here he made every preparation for another attempt to find the Western Sea by way of the Missouri.   On April 29, 1742, the two brothers, Pierre and François, left the Assiniboine with the two interpreters.   Their course led along the trail that for two hundred years was to be a famous highway between the Missouri and Hudson Bay.   Heading southwest, they followed the Souris River to the watershed of the Missouri, and in three weeks were once more the guests of the smoky Mandan lodges.   Round the inside walls of each circular hut ran berth beds of buffalo skin with trophies of the chase, — hide-shields and weapons of war, fastened to the posts that separated berth from berth.   A common fire, with a family meat pot hanging above, occupied the centre of the lodge. In one of these lodges the two brothers and their men were quartered.   The summer passed feasting with the

Mandans and smoking the calumet of peace; but all was in vain. The Missouri Indians were arrant cowards in the matter of war. The terror of their existence was the Sioux. The Mandans would not venture through Sioux territory to accompany the brothers in the search for the Western Sea. At last

Fur Traders' Boats towed down the Saskatchewan in the Summer of 1900.

two guides were obtained, who promised to conduct the French to a neighboring tribe that might know of the Western Sea.

The party set out on horseback, travelling swiftly southwest and along the valley of the Little Missouri toward the Black Hills. Here their course turned sharply west toward the Powder River country, past the southern bounds of the Yellowstone.   For three weeks they saw no sign of human existence.   Deer and antelope bounded over the parched alkali uplands. Prairie dogs perched on top of their earth mounds, to watch the lonely riders pass; and all night the far howl of grayish forms on the offing of the starlit prairie told of prowling coyotes.   On the 11th of August the brothers camped on the Powder Hills. Mounting to the crest of a cliff, they scanned far and wide for signs of the Indians whom the Mandans knew.   The valleys were desolate.   Kindling a signal-fire to attract any tribes that might be roaming, they built a hut and waited.   A month passed.   There was no answering signal.   One of the Mandan guides took himself off in fright.   On the fifth week a thin line of smoke rose against the distant sky.   The remaining Mandans went to reconnoitre and found a camp of Beaux Hommes, or Crows, who received the French well.   Obtaining fresh guides from the Crows and dismissing the Mandans, the brothers again headed westward.   The Crows guided them to the Horse Indians, who in turn took the French to their next western neighbors, the Bows.   The Bows were preparing to war on the Snakes, a mountain tribe to the west.   Tepees dotted the valley.   Women were pounding the buffalo meat into pemmican for the raiders. The young braves spent the night with war-song and

war-dance, to work themselves into a frenzy of bravado.
The Bows were to march west ; so the French joined
the warriors, gradually turning northwest toward
what is now Helena.

It was winter. The hills were powdered with snow
that obliterated all traces of the fleeing Snakes. The
way became more mountainous and dangerous.. Iced
sloughs gave place to swift torrents and cataracts. On
New Year's day, 1743, there rose through the gray
haze to the fore the ragged sky-line of the Bighorn
Mountains. Women and children were now left in a
sheltered valley, the warriors advancing unimpeded.
François de la Vérendrye remained at the camp to
guard the baggage. Pierre went on with the raiders.
In two weeks they were at the foot of the main
range of the northern Rockies. Against the sky the
snowy heights rose — an impassable barrier between
the plains and the Western Sea. What lay beyond —
the Beyond that had been luring them on and on,
from river to river and land to land, for more than
ten years ? Surely on the other side of those lofty
summits one might look down on the long-sought
Western Sea. Never suspecting that another thousand miles of wilderness and mountain fastness lay
between him and his quest, young De la Vérendrye
wanted to cross the Great Divide. Destiny decreed
otherwise. The raid of the Bows against the Snakes

ended in a fiasco.   No Snakes were to be found at
their usual winter hunt.   Had they decamped to massacre the Bow women and children left in the valley
to the rear ?   The Bows fled back to their wives in a
panic; so De la Vérendrye could not climb the mountains that barred the way to the sea.   The retreat was
made in the teeth of a howling mountain blizzard,
and the warriors reached the rendezvous more dead
than alive.   No Snake Indians were seen at all.   The
Bows marched homeward along the valley of the Upper
Missouri through the country of the Sioux, with whom
they were allied.   On the banks of the river the
brothers buried a leaden plate with the royal arms
of France imprinted.   At the end of July, 1743, they
were once more back on the Assiniboine River.   For
thirteen years they had followed a hopeless quest.
Instead of a Western Sea, they had found a sea of
prairie, a sea of mountains, and two great rivers, the
Saskatchewan and the Missouri.

VI

1743–1750

But the explorer, who had done so much to extend
French domain in the West, was a ruined man.   To
the accusations of his creditors were added the jealous
calumnies of fur traders eager to exploit the new

country.   The eldest son, with tireless energy, had
gone up the Saskatchewan to Fort Poskoyac when he
was recalled to take a position in the army at Montreal.   In 1746 De la Vérendrye himself was summoned
to Quebec and his command given to M. de Noyelles.
The game being played by jealous rivals was plain.
De la Vérendrye was to be kept out of the West while
tools of the Quebec traders spied out the fur trade
of the Assiniboine and the Missouri.   Immediately on
receiving freedom from military duty, young Chevalier
de la Vérendrye set out for Manitoba.   On the way
he met his father's successor, M. de Noyelles, coming
home crestfallen.   The supplanter had failed to control the Indians.   In one year half the forts of the
chain leading to the Western Sea had been destroyed.
These Chevalier de la Vérendrye restored as he passed
westward.

Governor Beauharnois had always refused to believe
the charges of private peculation against M. de la
Vérendrye.   Governor de la Galissonnière was equally
favorable to the explorer ; and De la Vérendrye was
decorated with the Order of the Cross of St. Louis,
and given permission to continue his explorations.
The winter of 1749 was passed preparing supplies
for the posts of the West; but a life of hardship and
disappointment had undermined the constitution of
the dauntless pathfinder.   On the 6th of December,

while busy with plans for his hazardous and thankless quest, he died suddenly at Montreal.

Rival fur traders scrambled for the spoils of the Manitoba and Missouri territory like dogs for a bone. De la Jonquière had become governor. Allied with him was the infamous Bigot, the intendant, and those two saw in the Western fur trade an opportunity to

"Tepees dotted the valley."

enrich themselves.   The rights of De la Vérendrye's sons to succeed their father were entirely disregarded. Legardeur de Saint-Pierre was appointed commander of the Western Sea.   The very goods forwarded by De la Vérendrye were confiscated.

But Saint-Pierre had enough trouble from his appointment.   His lieutenant, M. de Niverville, almost lost his life among hostiles on the way down the

Saskatchewan after building Fort Lajonquière at the foothills of the Rockies, where Calgary now stands. Saint-Pierre had headquarters in Manitoba on the Assiniboine, and one afternoon in midwinter, when his men were out hunting, he saw his fort suddenly fill with armed Assiniboines bent on massacre. They jostled him aside, broke into the armory, and helped themselves to weapons. Saint-Pierre had only one recourse. Seizing a firebrand, he tore the cover off a keg of powder and threatened to blow the Indians to perdition. The marauders dashed from the fort, and Saint-Pierre shot the bolts of gate and sally-port. When the white hunters returned, they quickly gathered their possessions together and abandoned Fort de la Reine. Four days later the fort lay in ashes. So ended the dream of enthusiasts to find a way overland to the Western Sea.

PART III

1769-1782

SEARCH FOR THE NORTHWEST PASSAGE LEADS
SAMUEL HEARNE TO THE ARCTIC CIRCLE AND
ATHABASCA REGION

CHAPTER IX

1769–1782

SAMUEL HEARNE

The Adventures of Hearne in his Search for the Coppermine River and the Northwest Passage — Hilarious Life of Wassail led by Governor Norton — The Massacre of the Eskimo by Hearne's Indians North of the Arctic Circle — Discovery of the ~habasca Country — Hearne becomes Resident Governor of the Huds(1's Bay Company, but is captured by the French — Frightful Death of Norton and Suicide of Matonabbee

FOR a hundred years after receiving its charter to exploit the furs of the North, the Hudson's Bay Company slumbered on the edge of a frozen sea.

Its fur posts were scattered round the desolate shores of the Northern bay like beads on a string; but the languid Company never attempted to penetrate the unknown lands beyond the coast. It was unnecessary. The Indians came to the Company. The company did not need to go to the Indians. Just as surely as spring cleared the rivers of ice and set the unlocked torrents rushing to the sea, there floated down-stream Indian dugout and birch canoe, loaded

R 241

with wealth of peltries for the fur posts of the English Company. So the English sat snugly secure inside their stockades, lords of the wilderness, and drove a thriving trade with folded hands. For a penny knife, they bought a beaver skin; and the skin sold in Europe for two or three shillings. The trade of the old Company was not brisk; but it paid.

An Eskimo Belle. Note the apron of ermine and sable.

It was the prod of keen French traders that stirred the slumbering giant. In his search for the Western Sea, De la Vérendrye had pushed west by way of the Great Lakes to the Missouri and the Rocky Mountains and the Saskatchewan. Henceforth, not so many furs came down-stream to the English Company on the bay. De la Vérendrye had been followed by hosts of free-lances — *coureurs* and *voyageurs* — who spread through the wilderness from the Missouri to the Athabasca, intercepting the fleets of furs that formerly went to Hudson Bay. The English Company rubbed its eyes; and rivals at home began to ask what had been done

in return for the charter. France had never ceased
seeking the mythical Western Sea that was supposed to lie just beyond the Mississippi; and when
French buccaneers destroyed the English Company's
forts on the bay, the English ambassador at Paris
exacted such an enormous bill of damages that the
Hudson Bay traders were enabled to build a stronger
fortress up at Prince of Wales on the mouth of
Churchill River than the French themselves possessed at Quebec on the St. Lawrence. What —
asked the rivals of the Company in London — had
been done in return for such national protection?
France had discovered and explored a whole new world
north of the Missouri. What had the English done?
Where did the Western Sea of which Spain had possession in the South lie towards the North? What
lay between the Hudson Bay and that Western Sea?
Was there a Northwest passage by water through this
region to Asia? If not, was there an undiscovered
world in the North, like Louisiana in the South?
There was talk of revoking the charter. Then the
Company awakened from its long sleep with a mighty
stir.

The annual boats that came out to Hudson Bay in
the summer of 1769 anchored on the offing, six miles
from the gray walls of Fort Prince of Wales, and
roared out a salute of cannon becoming the importance

of ships that bore almost revolutionary commissions.
The fort cannon on the walls of Churchill River
thundered their answer. A pinnace came scudding
over the waves from the ships. A gig boat launched
out from the fort to welcome the messengers. Where
the two met halfway, packets of letters were handed
to Moses Norton, governor at Fort Prince of
Wales, commanding him to despatch his most intrepid explorers for the discovery of unknown rivers,
strange lands, rumored copper mines, and the mythical
Northwest Passage that was supposed to lead directly
to China.

The fort lay on a spit of sand running out into the
bay at the mouth of Churchill River. It was three
hundred yards long by three hundred yards wide,
with four bastions, in three of which were stores and
wells of water. The fourth bastion contained the
powder-magazine. The walls were thirty feet wide at
the bottom and twenty feet wide at the top, of ham-
mer-dressed stone, mounted with forty great cannon.
A commodious stone house, furnished with all the
luxuries of the chase, stood in the centre of the courtyard. This was the residence of the governor.
Offices, warehouses, barracks, and hunters' lodges were
banked round the inner walls of the fort. The garrison consisted of thirty-nine common soldiers and a
few officers. In addition, there hung about the fort

the usual habitués of a Northern fur post, — young clerks from England, who had come out for a year's experience in the wilds; underpaid artisans, striving to mend their fortunes by illicit trade; hunters and *coureurs* and *voyageurs*, living like Indians but with a strain of white blood that forever distinguished them from their comrades; stately Indian sachems, stalking about the fort with whiffs of contempt from their long calumets for all this white-man luxury; and a ragamuffin brigade, — squaws, youngsters, and beggars, — who subsisted by picking up food from the waste heap of the fort.

The commission to despatch explorers to the inland country proved the sensation of a century at the fort. Round the long mess-room table gathered officers and traders, intent on the birch-bark maps drawn by old Indian chiefs of an unknown interior, where a " Far-Off-Metal River " flowed down to the Northwest Passage. Huge log fires blazed on the stone hearths at each end of the mess room. Smoky lanterns and pine fagots, dipped in tallow and stuck in iron clamps, shed a fitful light from rafters that girded ceiling and walls. On the floor of flagstones lay enormous skins of the chase — polar bear, Arctic wolf, and grizzly. Heads of musk-ox, caribou, and deer decorated the great timber girders. Draped across the walls were Company flags — an English ensign with the letters " H. B. C." painted in white on a red background, or in red on a white background.

At the head of the table sat one of the most remarkable scoundrels known in the annals of the Company, Moses Norton, governor of Fort Prince of Wales, a full-blooded Indian, who had been sent to England for nine years to be educated and had returned to the fort to resume all the vices and none of the virtues of white man and red. Clean-skinned, copper-colored, lithe and wiry as a tiger cat, with the long, lank, oily black hair of his race, Norton bore himself with all the airs of a European princelet and dressed himself in the beaded buckskins of a savage. Before him the Indians cringed as before one of their demon gods, and on the same principle. Bad gods could do the Indians harm. Good gods wouldn't. Therefore, the Indians propitiated the bad gods ; and of all Indian demons Norton was the worst. The black arts of mediæval poisoning were known to him, and he never scrupled to use them against an enemy. The Indians thought him possessed of the power of the evil eye ; but his power was that of arsenic or laudanum dropped in the food of an unsuspecting enemy. Two of his wives, with all of whom he was inordinately jealous, had died of poison. Against white men who might offend him he used more open means, — the triangle, the whipping post, the branding

iron. Needless to say that a man who wielded such
power swelled the Company's profits and stood high
in favor with the directors. At his right hand lay an
enormous bunch of keys. These he carried with him
by day and kept under his pillow by night. They
were the keys to the apartments of his many wives,
for like all Indians Norton believed in a plurality of
wives, and the life of no Indian was safe who refused
to contribute a daughter to the harem. The two
master passions of the governor were jealousy and
tyranny ; and while he lived like a Turkish despot
himself, he ruled his fort with a rod of iron and left
the brand of his wrath on the person of soldier or
officer who offered indignity to the Indian race. It
was a common thing for Norton to poison an Indian
who refused to permit a daughter to join the collection of wives ; then to flog the back off a soldier who
casually spoke to one of the wives in the courtyard ;
and in the evening spend the entire supper hour
preaching sermons on virtue to his men. By a
curious freak, Marie, his daughter, now a child of
nine, inherited from her father the gentle qualities of
the English life in which he had passed his youth.
She shunned the native women and was often to be
seen hanging on her father's arm, as officers and
governor smoked their pipes over the mess-room
table.

Near Norton sat another famous Indian, Matonabbee, the son of a slave woman at the fort, who had

Samuel Hearne.

grown up to become a great ambassador to the native
tribes for the English traders.   Measuring more than

six feet, straight as a lance, supple as a wrestler, thin, wiry, alert, restless with the instinct of the wild creatures, Matonabbee was now in the prime of his manhood, chief of the Chipewyans at the fort, and master of life and death to all in his tribe. It was Matonabbee whom the English traders sent up the Saskatchewan to invite the tribes of the Athabasca down to the bay. The Athabascans listened to the message of peace with a treacherous smile. At midnight assassins stole to his tent, overpowered his slave, and dragged the captive out. Leaping to his feet, Matonabbee shouted defiance, hurled his assailants aside like so many straws, pursued the raiders to their tents, single-handed released his slave, and marched out unscathed. That was the way Matonabbee had won the Athabascans for the Hudson's Bay Company.

Officers of the garrison, bluff sea-captains, spinning yarns of iceberg and floe, soldiers and traders, made up the rest of the company. Among the white men was one eager face, — that of Samuel Hearne, who was to explore the interior and now scanned the birchbark drawings to learn the way to the "Far-off-Metal River."

By November 6 all was in readiness for the departure of the explorer. Two Indian guides, who knew the way to the North, were assigned to Hearne;

two European servants went with him to look after the provisions; and two Indian hunters joined the company. In the gray mist of Northern dawn, with the stars still pricking through the frosty air, seven salutes of cannon awakened the echoes of the frozen

Eskimo using Double-bladed Paddle.

sea. The gates of the fort flung open, creaking with the frost rust, and Hearne came out, followed by his little company, the dog bells of the long toboggan sleighs setting up a merry jingling as the huskies broke from a trot to a gallop over the snow-fields for the North. Heading west-northwest, the band travelled swiftly with all the enthusiasm of untested courage. North winds cut their faces like whip-lashes. The first night out there was not enough snow to make a wind-break of the drifts; so the sleighs were piled on edge to windward, dogs and men lying heterogeneously in their shelter. When morning came, one of the Indian guides had deserted. The way became barer. Frozen swamps across which the storm wind swept with hurricane force were succeeded by high, rocky barrens devoid of game, unsheltered, with barely enough stunted shrubbery for the whittling of chips that cooked the morning and night meals. In a month the travellers had not accomplished ten miles a day. Where deer were found the Indians halted to gorge themselves with feasts. Where game was scarce they lay in camp, depending on the white hunters. Within three weeks rations had dwindled to one partridge a day for the entire company. The Indians seemed to think that Hearne's white servants had secret store of food on the sleighs. The savages refused to hunt. Then Hearne suspected some ulterior design. It was to drive him back to the fort by famine. Henceforth, he noticed on the march that the Indians always preceded the whites and secured any game before his men could fire a shot. One night toward the end of November the savages plundered the sleighs. Hearne awakened in amazement to see the company marching off, laden with guns, ammunition, and hatchets. He called. Their answer was laughter that set the woods ringing. Hearne was now two hundred miles from the fort, without either ammunition or food. There was nothing to do but turn back. The weather was fair. By snaring partridges, the white men obtained enough game to sustain them till they reached the fort on the 11th of December.

The question now was whether to wait till spring or set out in the teeth of midwinter. If Hearne left the fort in spring, he could not possibly reach the Arctic Circle till the following winter; and with the North buried under drifts of snow, he could not learn where lay the Northwest Passage. If he left the fort in winter in order to reach the Arctic in summer, he must expose his guides to the risks of cold and starvation. The Indians told of high, rocky barrens, across which no canoes could be carried. They advised snow-shoe travel. Obtaining three Chipewyans and two Crees as guides, and taking no white servants, Hearne once more set out, on February 23, 1770, for the " Far-Away-Metal River." This time there was no cannonading. The guns were buried under snow-drifts twenty feet deep, and the snow-shoes of the travellers glided over the fort walls to the echoing cheers of soldiers and governor standing on the ramparts. The company travelled light, depending on

chance game for food. All wood that could be used
for fire lay hidden deep under snow. At wide inter-
vals over the white wastes mushroom cones of snow
told where a stunted tree projected the antlered
branches of topmost bough through the depths of
drift; but for the most part camp was made by digging through the shallowest snow with snow-shoes to
the bottom of moss, which served the double purpose
of fuel for the night kettle and bed for travellers. In
the hollow a wigwam was erected, with the door to the
south, away from the north wind. Snared rabbits and
partridges supplied the food. The way lay as before —
west-northwest — along a chain of frozen lakes and
rivers connecting Hudson Bay with the Arctic Ocean.
By April the marchers were on the margin of a desolate
wilderness — the Indian region of " Little Sticks," —
known to white men as the Barren Lands, where
dwarf trees project above the billowing wastes of snow
like dismantled masts on the far offing of a lonely sea.
Game became scarcer. Neither the round footprint
of the hare nor the frost tracery of the northern grouse
marked the snowy reaches of unbroken white. Caribou had retreated to the sheltered woods of the interior; and a cleverer hunter than man had scoured the
wide wastes of game. Only the wolf pack roamed the
Barren Lands. It was unsafe to go on without food.
Hearne kept in camp till the coming of the goose month

— April — when birds of passage wended their way north. For three days rations consisted of snow water and pipes of tobacco. The Indians endured the privations with stoical indifference, daily marching out on a bootless quest for game. On the third night Hearne was alone in his tent. Twilight deepened to night, night to morning. Still no hunters returned. Had he been deserted? Not a sound broke the waste silence but the baying of the wolf pack. Weak from hunger, Hearne fell asleep. Before daylight he was awakened by a shout; and his Indians shambled over the drifts laden with haunches of half a dozen deer. That relieved want till the coming of the geese. In May Hearne struck across the Barren Lands. By June the rotting snow clogged the snow-shoes. Dog trains drew heavy, and food was again scarce. For a week the travellers found nothing to eat but cranberries. Half the company was ill from hunger when a mangy old musk-ox, shedding his fur and lean as barrel hoops, came scrambling over the rocks, sure of foot as a mountain goat. A single shot brought him down. In spite of the musky odor of which the coarse flesh reeked, every morsel of the ox was instantly devoured. Sometimes during their long fasts they would encounter a solitary Indian wandering over the rocky barren. If he had arms, gun, or arrow, and carried skins of the chase, he was welcomed to

camp, no matter how scant the fare.   Otherwise he
was shunned as an outcast, never to be touched or
addressed by a human being; for only one thing
could have fed an Indian on the Barren Lands who
could show no trophies of the chase, and that was the
flesh of some human creature weaker than himself.
The outcast was a cannibal, condemned by an unwritten law to wander alone through the wastes.

Snow had barely cleared from the Barren Lands
when Hearne witnessed the great traverse of the
caribou herds, marching in countless multitudes with
a clicking of horns and hoofs from west to east for the
summer.   Indians from all parts of the North had
placed themselves at rivers across the line of march to
spear the caribou as they swam ; and Hearne was joined
by a company of six hundred savages.   Summer had
dried the moss.   That gave abundance of fuel.   Caribou were plentiful.   That supplied the hunters with
pemmican.   Hearne decided to pass the following
winter with the Indians ; but he was one white man
among hundreds of savages.   Nightly his ammunition
was plundered.   One of his survey instruments was
broken in a wind storm.   Others were stolen.   It
was useless to go on without instruments to take
observations of the Arctic Circle; so for a second
time Hearne was compelled to turn back to Fort
Prince of Wales.   Terrible storms impeded the return

march. His dog was frozen in the traces. Tent poles were used for fire-wood; and the northern lights served as the only compass. On midday of November 25, 1770, after eight months' absence, in which he had not found the " Far-Off-Metal River," Hearne reached shelter inside the fort walls.

Beating through the gales of sleet and snow on the homeward march, Hearne had careened into a majestic figure half shrouded by the storm. The explorer halted before a fur-muffled form, six feet in its moccasins, erect as a mast pole, haughty as a king; and the gauntleted hand of the Indian chief went up to his forehead in sign of peace. It was Matonabbee, the ambassador of the Hudson's Bay Company to the Athabascans, now returning to Fort Prince of Wales, followed by a long line of slave women driving their dog sleighs. The two travellers hailed each other through the storm like ships at sea. That night they camped together on the lee side of the dog sleighs, piled high as a wind-break; and Matonabbee, the famous courser of the Northern wastes, gave Hearne wise advice. Women should be taken on a long journey, the Indian chief said; for travel must be swift through the deadly cold of the barrens. Men must travel light of hand, trusting to chance game for food. Women were needed to snare rabbits, catch partridges, bring in game shot by the braves, and attend to the camping. And then in a burst of enthusiasm, perhaps warmed by Hearne's fine tobacco, Matonabbee, who had found the way to the Athabasca, offered to conduct the white man to the " Far-Off-Metal River " of the Arctic Circle. The chief was the greatest pathfinder of the Northern tribes. His offer was the chance of a lifetime. Hearne could hardly restrain his eagerness till he reached the fort. Leaving Matonabbee to follow with the slave women, the explorer hurried to Fort Prince of Wales, laid the plan before Governor Norton, and in less than two weeks from the day of his return was ready to depart for the unknown river that was to lead to the Northwest Passage.

The weather was dazzlingly clear, with that burnished brightness of polished steel known only where unbroken sunlight meets unbroken snow glare. On the 7th of December, 1770, Hearne left the fort, led by Matonabbee and followed by the slave Indians with the dog sleighs. One of Matonabbee's wives lay ill; but that did not hinder the iron pathfinder. The woman was wrapped in robes and drawn on a dog sleigh. There was neither pause nor hesitation. If the woman recovered, good. If she died, they would bury her under a cairn of stones as they travelled. Matonabbee struck directly west-northwest for some *caches* of provisions which he had left hidden on the trail. The place was found; but the *caches* had been rifled clean

of food. That did not stop Matonabbee. Nor did
he show the slightest symptoms of anger. He simply
hastened their pace the more for their hunger, recog-
nizing the unwritten law of the wilderness — that starving hunters who had rifled the *cache* had a right to food
wherever they found it. Day after day, stoical as men
of bronze, the marchers reeled off the long white miles
over the snowy wastes, pausing only for night sleep
with evening and morning meals. Here nibbled twigs
were found; there the stamping ground of a deer shelter; elsewhere the small, cleft foot-mark like the ace
of hearts. But the signs were all old. No deer were
seen. Even the black marble eye that betrays the
white hare on the snow, and the fluffy bird track of
the feather-footed northern grouse, grew rarer; and
the slave women came in every morning empty-handed
from untouched snares. In spite of hunger and cold,
Matonabbee remained good-natured, imperturbable,
hard as a man of bronze, coursing with the winged speed
of snow-shoes from morning till night without pause,
going to a bed of rock moss on a meal of snow water
and rising eager as an arrow to leave the bow-string for
the next day's march. For three days before Christmas
the entire company had no food but snow. Christmas
was celebrated by starvation. Hearne could not in-
dulge in the despair of the civilized man's self-pity
when his faithful guides went on without complaint.

Eskimo Family, taken by Light of Midnight Sun. — C. W. Mathers.

By January the company had entered the Barren Lands. The Barren Lands were bare but for an occasional oasis of trees like an island of refuge in a shelterless sea. In the clumps of dwarf shrubs, the Indians found signs that meant relief from famine — tufts of hair rubbed off on tree trunks, fallen antlers, and countless heart-shaped tracks barely puncturing the snow but for the sharp outer edge. The caribou were on their yearly traverse east to west for the shelter of the inland woods. The Indians at once pitched camp. Scouts went scouring to find which way the caribou herds were coming. Pounds of snares were constructed of shrubs and saplings stuck up in palisades with scarecrows on the pickets round a V-shaped enclosure. The best hunters took their station at the angle of the V, armed with loaded muskets and long, lank, and iron-pointed arrows. Women and children lined the palisades to scare back high jumpers or strays of the caribou herd. Then scouts and dogs beat up the rear of the fleeing herd, driving the caribou straight for the pound. By a curious provision of nature, the male caribou sheds its antlers just as he leaves the Barren Lands for the wooded interior, where the horns would impede flight through brush, and he only leaves the woods for the bare open when the horns are grown enough to fight the annual battle to protect the herd from the wolf pack ravenous with spring hunger.

For one caribou caught in the pound by Hearne's Indians, a hundred of the herd escaped; for the caribou crossed the Barrens in tens of thousands, and Matonabbee's braves obtained enough venison for the trip to the " Far-Off-Metal River."

The farther north they travelled the scanter became the growth of pine and poplar and willow. Snow still lay heavy in April; but Matonabbee ordered a halt while there was still large enough wood to construct dugouts to carry provisions down the river. The boats were built large and heavy in front, light behind. This was to resist the ice jam of Northern currents. The caribou hunt had brought other Indians to the Barren Lands. Matonabbee was joined by two hundred warriors. Though the tribes puffed the calumet of peace together, they drew their war hatchets when they saw the smoke of an alien tribe's fire rise against the northern sky. A suspicion that he hardly dared to acknowledge flashed through Hearne's mind. Eleven thousand beaver pelts were yearly brought down to the fort from the unknown river. How did the Chipewyans obtain these pelts from the Eskimo? What was the real reason of the Indian eagerness to conduct the white man to the " Far-Off-Metal River "? The white man was not taken into the confidence of the Indian council; but he could not fail to draw his own conclusions.

Scouts were sent cautiously forward to trail the path of the aliens who had lighted the far moss fire. Women and children were ordered to head about for a rendezvous southwest on Lake Athabasca. Carrying only the lightest supplies, the braves set out swiftly for the North on June 1. Mist and rain hung so heavily over the desolate moors that the travellers could not see twenty feet ahead. In places the rocks were glazed with ice and scored with runnels of water. Half the warriors here lost heart and turned back. The others led by Hearne and Matonabbee crossed the iced precipices on hands and knees, with gun stocks strapped to backs or held in teeth. On the 21st of June the sun did not set. Hearne had crossed the Arctic Circle. The sun hung on the southern horizon all night long. Henceforth the travellers marched without tents. During rain or snow storm, they took refuge under rocks or in caves. Provisions turned mouldy with wet. The moss was too soaked for fire. Snow fell so heavily in drifting storms that Hearne often awakened in the morning to find himself almost immured in the cave where they had sought shelter. Ice lay solid on the lakes in July. Once, clambering up steep, bare heights, the travellers met a herd of a hundred musk-oxen scrambling over the rocks with the agility of squirrels, the spreading, agile hoof giving grip that lifted the hulking forms over all obstacles.

Down the bleak, bare heights there poured cataract and mountain torrent, plainly leading to some near river bed; but the thick gray fog lay on the land like a blanket.   At last a thunder-storm cleared the air ; and Hearne saw bleak moors sloping north, bare of all growth but the trunks of burnt trees, with barren heights of rock and vast, desolate swamps, where the wild-fowl flocked in myriads.

Fort Garry, Winnipeg, a Century Ago.

All count of day and night was now lost, for the sun did not set. Sometime between midnight and morning of July 12, 1771, with the sun as bright as noon, the lakes converged to a single river-bed a hundred yards wide, narrowing to a waterfall that roared over the rocks in three cataracts. This, then, was the " Far-Off-Metal River."   Plainly, it was a dis-appointing discovery, this Coppermine River.   It did not lead to China. It did not point the way to a

Northwest Passage. In his disappointment, Hearne learned what every other discoverer in North America had learned — that the Great Northwest was something more than a bridge between Europe and Asia, that it was a world in itself with its own destiny.[1]

But Hearne had no time to brood over disappointment. The conduct of his rascally companions could no longer be misunderstood. Hunters came in with game; but when the hungry slaves would have lighted a moss fire to cook the meat, the forbidding hand of a chief went up. No fires were to be lighted. The Indians advanced with whispers, dodging from stone to stone like raiders in ambush. Spies went forward on tiptoe. Then far down-stream below the cataracts Hearne descried the domed tent-tops of an Eskimo band sound asleep; for it was midnight, though the sun was at high noon. When Hearne looked back to his companions, he found himself deserted. The Indians were already wading the river for the west bank, where the Eskimo had camped. Hearne overtook his guides stripping themselves of everything that might impede flight or give hand-hold to an enemy, and daubing their skin with war-paint. Hearne begged Matonabbee to restrain the murderous warriors. The great chief smiled with silent contempt. He was too

---

[1] I have purposely avoided bringing up the dispute as to a mistake of some few degrees made by Hearne in his calculations — the point really being finical.

true a disciple of a doctrine which Indians practised hundreds of years before white men had avowed it — the survival of the fit, the extermination of the weak, for any qualms of pity towards a victim whose death would contribute profit. Wearing only moccasins and bucklers of hardened hide, armed with muskets, lances, and tomahawks, the Indians jostled Hearne out of their way, stole forward from stone to stone to within a gun length of the Eskimo, then with a wild war shout flung themselves on the unsuspecting sleepers.

The Eskimo were taken unprepared. They staggered from their tents, still dazed in sleep, to be mowed down by a crashing of firearms which they had never before heard. The poor creatures fled in frantic terror, to be met only by lance point and gun butt. A young girl fell coiling at Hearne's feet like a wounded snake. A well-aimed lance had pinioned the living form to earth. She caught Hearne round the knees, imploring him with dumb entreaty; but the white man was pushed back with jeers. Sobbing with horror, Hearne begged the Indians to put their victim out of pain. The rocks rang with the mockery of the torturers. She was speared to death before Hearne's eyes. On that scene of indescribable horror the white man could no longer bear to look. He turned toward the river, and there was a spectacle like a nightmare. Some of the Eskimo were escaping by leaping to their hide boats and with lightning strokes of the double-bladed paddles dashing down the current to the far bank of the river ; but sitting motionless as stone was an old, old woman — probably a witch of the tribe — red-eyed as if she were blind, deaf to all the noise about her, unconscious of all her danger, fishing for salmon below the falls. There was a shout from the raiders ; the old woman did not even look up to face her fate ; and she too fell a victim to that thirst for blood which is as insatiable in the redskin as in the wolf pack. Odd commentary in our modern philosophies — this white-man explorer, unnerved, unmanned, weeping with pity, this champion of the weak, jostled aside by bloodthirsty, triumphant savages, represented the race that was to jostle the Indian from the face of the New World. Something more than a triumphant, aggressive Strength was needed to the permanency of a race ; and that something more was represented by poor, weak, vacillating Hearne, weeping like a woman.

Horror of the massacre robbed Hearne of all an explorer's exultation. A day afterward, on July 17, he stood on the shores of the Arctic Ocean, — the first white man to reach it overland in America. Ice extended from the mouth of the river as far as eye could see. Not a sign of land broke the endless reaches of cold steel, where the snow lay, and icy green, where pools of the ocean cast their reflection on the sky of the far horizon. At one in the morning, with the sun hanging above the river to the south, Hearne formally took possession of the Arctic re-

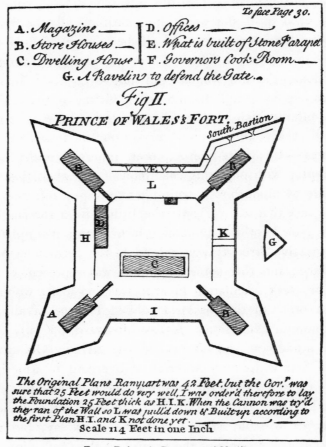

A. Magazine ——— D. Offices. ———
B. Store Houses ——— E. What is built of Stone Parapet
C. Dwelling House. F. Governors Cook Room. ———
G. A Ravelin to defend the Gate.

Fig II.

PRINCE OF WALES'S FORT.

South Bastion

The Original Plan Rampart was 42 Feet but the Gov.ʳ was sure that 25 Feet would do very well, I was order'd therefore to lay the Foundation 25 Feet thick as H.I.K. When the Cannon was try'd they ran of the Wall so L was pull'd down & Built up according to the first Plan H.I. and K not done yet. ———

Scale 114 Feet in one Inch.

From Robson's Drawing, 1733–47.

gions for the Hudson's Bay Company. The same
Company rules those regions to-day. Not an eye had
been closed for three days and nights. Throwing
themselves down on the wet shore, the entire band
now slept for six hours. The hunters awakened to
find a musk-ox nosing over the mossed rocks. A
shot sent it tumbling over the cliffs. Whether it was
that the moss was too wet for fuel to cook the meat,
or the massacre had brutalized the men into beasts of
prey, the Indians fell on the carcass and devoured it
raw.[1]

The retreat from the Arctic was made with all
swiftness, keeping close to the Coppermine River.
For thirty miles from the sea not a tree was to be
seen. The river was sinuous and narrow, hemmed in
by walls of solid rock, down which streamed cascades
and mountain torrents. On both sides of the high
bank extended endless reaches of swamps and barrens.
Twenty miles from the sea Hearne found the copper
mines from which the Indians made their weapons.
His guides were to join their families in the Athabasca
country of the southwest, and thither Matonabbee now

[1] I am sorry to say that in pioneer border warfares I have heard of white men acting
in a precisely similar beastly manner after some brutal conflict. To be frank, I know
of one case in the early days of Minnesota fur trade, where the irate fur trader killed
and devoured his weak companion, not from famine, but sheer frenzy of brutalized
passion. Such naked light does wilderness life shed over our drawing-room philosophies
of the triumphantly strong being the highest type of manhood.

led the way at such a terrible pace that moccasins were worn to shreds and toe-nails torn from the feet of the marchers; and woe to the man who fell behind, for the wolf pack prowled on the rear.

When the smoke of moss fires told of the wives' camp, the Indians halted to take the sweat bath of purification for the cleansing of all blood guilt from the massacre. Heated stones were thrown into a small pool. In this each Indian bathed himself, invoking his deity for freedom from all punishment for the deaths of the slain.[1] By August the Indians had joined their wives. By October they were on Lake Athabasca, which had already frozen. Here one of the wives, in the last stages of consumption, could go no farther. For a band short of food to halt on the march meant death to all. The Northern wilderness has its grim unwritten law, inexorable and merciless as death. For those who fall by the way there is no pity. A whole tribe may not be exposed to death for the sake of one person. Civilized nations follow the same principle in their quarantine. Giving the squaw food and a tent, the Indians left her to meet her last enemy, whether death came by starvation or cold or the wolf pack. Again and again the abandoned

[1] Again the wilderness plunges us back to the primordial : if man be but the supreme beast of prey, whence this consciousness of blood guilt in these unschooled children of the wilds ?

squaw came up with the marchers, weeping and begging their pity, only to fall from weakness. But the
wilderness has no pity ; and so they left her.

Christmas of 1771 was passed on Athabasca Lake,
the northern lights rustling overhead with the crackling
of a flag. There was food in plenty ; for the Athabasca was rich in buffalo meadows and beaver dams
and moose yards. On the lake shore Hearne found
a little cabin, in which dwelt a solitary woman of the
Dog Rib tribe who for eight months had not seen a
soul. Her band had been massacred. She alone
escaped and had lived here in hiding for almost a
year. In spring the Indians of the lake carried their
furs to the forts of Hudson Bay. With the Athabascans went Hearne, reaching Fort Prince of Wales on
June 30, 1772, after eighteen months' absence.

He had discovered Coppermine River, the Arctic
Ocean, and the Athabasca country, — a region in all
as large as half European Russia.

For his achievements Hearne received prompt pro-
motion. Within a year of his return to the fort,
Governor Norton, the Indian bully, fell deadly ill.
In the agony of death throes, he called for his wives.
The great keys to the apartments of the women were
taken from his pillow, and the wives were brought in.
Norton lay convulsed with pain. One of the younger
women began to sob. An officer of the garrison took

her hand to comfort her grief. Norton's rolling eyes caught sight of the innocent conference between the officer and the young wife. With a roar the dying bully hurled himself up in bed: —

"I'll burn you alive! I'll burn you alive," he shrieked. With oaths on his lips he fell back dead.

Fort Prince of Wales (Churchill), from Hearne's Account, 1799 Edition.

Samuel Hearne became governor of the fort. For ten years nothing disturbed the calm of his rule. Marie, Norton's daughter, still lived in the shelter of the fort; the wives found consolation in other husbands; and Matonabbee continued the ambassador of the company to strange tribes. One afternoon of August, 1782, the sleepy calm of the fort was upset by the sentry dashing in breathlessly with news that three great vessels of war with full-blown sails and carrying many guns were ploughing straight for Prince of Wales. At sundown the ships swung at anchor six miles from the fort. From their masts fluttered a foreign flag — the French ensign. Gig boat and pinnace began sounding the harbor. Hearne had less than forty men to defend the fort. In the morning four hundred French troopers lined up on Churchill

Beaver Coin of Hudson's Bay Company, melted from Old Tea Chests, one Coin representing one Beaver.

River, and the admiral, La Perouse, sent a messenger with demand of surrender. Hearne did not feel justified in exposing his men to the attack of three warships carrying from seventy to a hundred guns apiece, and to assault by land of four hundred troopers. He surrendered without a blow.

The furs were quickly transferred to the French ships, and the soldiers were turned loose to loot the fort. The Indians fled, among them Moses Norton's gentle daughter, now in her twenty-second year. She

could not revert to the loathsome habits of savage
life; she dared not go to the fort filled with lawless
foreign soldiers; and she perished of starvation outside the walls. Matonabbee had been absent when the
French came. He returned to find the fort where he
had spent his life in ruins. The English whom he
thought invincible were defeated and prisoners of war.
Hearne, whom the dauntless old chief had led through
untold perils, was a captive. Matonabbee's proud
spirit was broken. The grief was greater than he
could bear. All that living stood for had been lost.
Drawing off from observation, Matonabbee blew his
brains out.

PART IV

1780–1793

FIRST ACROSS THE ROCKIES — HOW MACKENZIE
CROSSED THE NORTHERN ROCKIES AND LEWIS
AND CLARK WERE FIRST TO CROSS FROM MIS-
SOURI TO COLUMBIA

CHAPTER X

1780–1793

FIRST ACROSS THE ROCKIES

How Mackenzie found the Great River named after him and then
pushed across the Mountains to the Pacific, forever settling the
question of a Northwest Passage

THERE is an old saying that if a man has the right
mettle in him, you may stick him a thousand leagues
in the wilderness on a barren rock and he will plant
pennies and grow dollar bills.   In other words, no
matter where or how, success will succeed.   No class
illustrates this better than a type that has almost
passed away — the old fur traders who were lords of
the wilderness.   Cut off from all comfort, from all
encouragement, from all restraint, what set of men
ever had fewer incentives to go up, more temptations
to go down?   Yet from the fur traders sprang the pioneer heroes of America.   When young Donald Smith
came out — a raw lad — to America, he was packed off
to eighteen years' exile on the desert coast of Labrador.
Donald Smith came out of the wilderness to become

the Lord Strathcona of to-day.   Sir Alexander Mackenzie's life presents even more dramatic contrasts. A clerk in a counting-house at Montreal one year, the next finds him at Detroit setting out for the backwoods of Michigan to barter with Indians for furs.

Then he is off with a fleet of canoes forty strong for the Upper Country of forest and wilderness beyond the Great Lakes, where he fights such a desperate battle with rivals that one of his companions is murdered, a second lamed, a third wounded.   In all this Alexander Mackenzie was successful while still in the prime of his manhood, — not more than thirty years of age ; and the reward of

Alexander Mackenzie, from a Painting of the Explorer.

his success was to be exiled to the sub-arctics of the Athabasca, six weeks' travel from another fur post, — not a likely field to play the hero.   Yet Mackenzie emerged from the polar wilderness bearing a name that ranks with Columbus and Cartier and La Salle.

Far north of the Missouri beyond the borderlands flows the Saskatchewan.   As far north again, beyond

the Saskatchewan, flows another great river, the Athabasca, into Athabasca Lake, on whose blue shores
to the north lies a little white-washed fort of some
twenty log houses, large barn-like stores, a Catholic
chapel, an Episcopal mission, and a biggish residence of
pretence for the chief trader. This is Fort Chipewyan.
At certain seasons Indian tepees dot the surrounding
plains; and bronze-faced savages, clad in the ill-fitting
garments of white people, shamble about the stores,
or sit haunched round the shady sides of the log
houses, smoking long-stemmed pipes. These are the
Chipewyans come in from their hunting-grounds; but
for the most part the fort seems chiefly populated by
regiments of husky dogs, shaggy-coated, with the sharp
nose of the fox, which spend the long winters in harness
coasting the white wilderness, and pass the summers
basking lazily all day long except when the bell rings
for fish time, when half a hundred huskies scramble
wildly for the first meat thrown.

A century ago Chipewyan was much the same as
to-day, except that it lay on the south side of the lake.
Mails came only once in two years instead of monthly,
and rival traders were engaged in the merry game of
slitting each other's throats. All together, it wasn't
exactly the place for ambition to dream; but ambition
was there in the person of Alexander Mackenzie, the
young fur trader, dreaming what he hardly dared hope.

Business men fight shy of dreamers; so Mackenzie told his dreams to no one but his cousin Roderick, whom he pledged to secrecy. For fifty years the

Eskimo trading his Pipe, carved from Walrus Tusk, for the Value of Three Beaver Skins.

British government had offered a reward of £20,000 to any one who should discover a Northwest Passage between the Atlantic and the Pacific. The hope of such a passageway had led many navigators on bootless voyages; and here was Mackenzie with the same bee in his bonnet. To the north of Chipewyan he saw a mighty river, more than a mile wide in places, walled in by great ramparts, and flowing to unknown seas. To the west he saw another river rolling through the far mountains. Where did this river come from, and where did both rivers go? Mackenzie was not the man to leave vital questions unanswered. He determined to find out; but difficulties lay in the way. He couldn't leave the Athabascan posts. That was overcome by getting his cousin Roderick to take charge. The Northwest Fur Company, which had succeeded the French fur traders of Quebec and Montreal when Canada passed from the hands of the French to the English, wouldn't assume any cost or risk for exploring unknown seas. This was more niggardly than the Hudson's Bay Company, which had paid all cost of outlay for its explorers; but Mackenzie assumed risk and cost himself. Then the Indians hesitated to act as guides; so Mackenzie hired guides when he could, seized them by compulsion when he couldn't hire them, and went ahead without guides when they escaped.

May — the frog moon — and June — the bird's egg moon — were the festive seasons at Fort Chipewyan on Lake Athabasca. Indian hunters came tramping in from the Barren Lands with toboggan loads of pelts drawn by half-wild husky dogs. Woody Crees and Slaves and Chipewyans paddled across the lake in canoes laden to the gunwales with furs. A world of white skin tepees sprang up like mushrooms round the fur post. By June the traders had collected the furs, sorted and shipped them in flotillas of keel boat, barge, and canoe, east to Lake Superior and Montreal. On the evening of June 2, 1789, Alexander Mackenzie, chief trader, had finished the year's trade and sent the furs to the Eastern warehouses of the Northwest Company, on Lake Superior, at Fort William, not far from where Radisson had first explored, and La Vérendrye followed. Indians lingered round the fort of the Northern lake engaged in mad *boissons*, or drinking matches, that used up a winter's earnings in the spree of a single week. Along the shore lay upturned canoes, keels red against the blue of the lake, and everywhere in the dark burned the red fires of the boatmen melting resin to gum the seams of the canoes; for the canoes were to be launched on a long voyage the next day. Mackenzie was going to float down with the current of the Athabasca or Grand River, and find out where that great river emptied in the North.

The crew must have spent the night in a last wild spree; for it was nine in the morning before all hands were ready to embark. In Mackenzie's large birch canoe went four Canadian *voyageurs*, their Indian wives, and a German. In other canoes were the Indian hunters and interpreters, led by " English Chief," who had often been to Hudson Bay. Few provisions were taken. The men were to hunt, the women to cook and keep the *voyageurs* supplied with moccasins, which wore out at the rate of one pair a day for each man. Traders bound for Slave Lake followed behind. Only fifty miles were made the first day. Henceforth Mackenzie embarked his men at three and four in the morning.

Quill and Bead Work on Buckskin, Mackenzie River Indians.

The mouth of Peace River was passed a mile broad as it pours down from the west, and the boatmen *portaged* six rapids the third day, one of the canoes, steered by a squaw more intent on her sewing than the paddles, going over the falls with a smash that shivered the bark to kindling-wood. The woman escaped, as the current caught the canoe, by leaping into the water and swimming ashore with the aid of a line. Ice four feet thick clung to the walls of the rampart shores, and this increased the danger of landing for a *portage*, the Indians whining out their complaints in exactly the tone of the wailing north wind that had cradled their lives — " Eduiy, eduiy! — It is hard, white man, it is hard ! " And harder the way became. For nine nights fog lay so heavily on the river that not a star was seen. This was followed by driving rain and wind. Mackenzie hoisted a three-foot sail and cut over the water before the wind with the hiss of a boiling kettle. Though the sail did the work of the paddles, it gave the *voyageurs* no respite. Cramped and rain-soaked, they had to bail out water to keep the canoe afloat. In this fashion the boats entered Slave Lake, a large body of water with one horn pointing west, the other east. Out of both horns led unknown rivers. Which way should Mackenzie go? Low-lying marshlands — beaver meadows where the wattled houses of the beaver had stopped up the current of streams till moss overgrew the swamps and the land became quaking muskeg — lay along the shores of the lake. There were islands in deep water, where caribou had taken refuge, travelling over ice in winter for the calves to be safe in summer from wolf pack and bear. Mackenzie hired a guide from the Slave Indians to pilot the canoes over the lake; but the man proved useless. Days were wasted poking through mist and rushes trying to find an outlet to the Grand River of the North. Finally, English Chief lost his temper and threatened to kill the Slave Indian unless he succeeded in taking the canoes out of the lake. The waters presently narrowed to half a mile; the current began to race with a hiss; sails were hoisted on fishing-poles; and Mackenzie found himself out of the

Fort William, Headquarters Northwest Company, Lake Superior.

rushes on the Grand River to the west of Slave Lake.

Here pause was made at a camp of Dog Ribs, who took the bottom from the courage of Mackenzie's comrades by gruesome predictions that old age would come upon the *voyageurs* before they reached salt water. There were impassable falls ahead. The river flowed through a land of famine peopled by a

monstrous race of hostiles who massacred all Indians
from the South.   The effect of these cheerful prophe-
cies was that the Slave Lake guide refused to go on.
English Chief bodily put the recalcitrant into a canoe
and forced him ahead at the end of a paddle.   Snow-
capped mountains loomed to the west.   The river
from Bear Lake was passed, greenish of hue like the
sea, and the Slave Lake guide now feigned such illness that watch was kept day and night to prevent his
escape.   The river now began to wind, with lofty
ramparts on each side ; and once, at a sharp bend in
the current, Mackenzie looked back to see Slave Lake
Indians following to aid the guide in escaping.   After
that one of the white men slept with the fellow each
night to prevent desertion ; but during the confusion
of a terrific thunder-storm, when tents and cooking
utensils were hurled about their heads, the Slave
succeeded in giving his watchers the slip.   Mackenzie
promptly stopped at an encampment of strange
Indians, and failing to obtain another guide by persua-
sion, seized and hoisted a protesting savage into the
big canoe, and signalled the unwilling captive to point
the way.   The Indians of the river were indifferent, if
not friendly ; but once Mackenzie discovered a band
hiding their women and children as soon as the boatmen came in view.   The unwilling guide was forced
ashore, as interpreter, and gifts pacified all fear.   But

the incident left its impression on Mackenzie's comrades. They had now been away from Chipewyan for forty days. If it took much longer to go back, ice would imprison them in the polar wilderness. Snow lay drifted in the valleys, and scarcely any game was seen but fox and grouse. The river was widening almost to the dimensions of a lake, and when this was whipped by a north wind the canoes were in peril enough. The four Canadians besought Mackenzie to return. To return Mackenzie had not the slightest intention; but he would not tempt mutiny. He promised that if he did not find the sea within seven days, he would go back.

That night the sun hung so high above the southern horizon that the men rose by mistake to embark at twelve o'clock. They did not realize that they were in the region of midnight sun; but Mackenzie knew and rejoiced, for he must be near the sea. The next day he was not surprised to find a deserted Eskimo village. At that sight the enthusiasm of the others took fire. They were keen to reach the sea, and imagined that they smelt salt water. In spite of the lakelike expanse of the river, the current was swift, and the canoes went ahead at the rate of sixty and seventy miles a day — if it could be called day when there was no night. Between the 13th and 14th of July the *voyageurs* suddenly awakened to find themselves and their baggage floating in rising water.   What had happened to the lake?   Their hearts took a leap; for it was no lake.   It was the tide.   They had found the sea.

How hilariously jubilant were Mackenzie's men, one may guess from the fact that they chased whales all the next day in their canoes.   The whales dived below, fortunately; for one blow of a finback or sulphur bottom would have played skittles with the canoes. Coming back from the whale hunt, triumphant as if they had caught a dozen finbacks, the men erected a post, engraving on it the date, July 14, 1789, and the names of all present.

It had taken six weeks to reach the Arctic.   It took eight to return to Chipewyan, for the course was against stream, in many places tracking the canoes by a tow-line.   The beaver meadows along the shore impeded the march.   Many a time the quaking moss gave way, and the men sank to mid-waist in water. While skirting close ashore, Mackenzie discovered the banks of the river to be on fire.   The fire was a natural tar bed, which the Indians said had been burning for centuries and which burns to-day as when Mackenzie found it.   On September 12, with a high sail up and a driving wind, the canoes cut across Lake Athabasca and reached the beach of Chipewyan at three in the afternoon, after one hundred and two

Running a Rapid on Mackenzie River.

days' absence.   Mackenzie had not found the Northwest Passage.   He had proved there was no Northwest Passage, and discovered the Mississippi of the
north — Mackenzie River.

Mackenzie spent the long winter at Fort Chipewyan;
but just as soon as the rivers cleared of ice, he took
passage in the east-bound canoes and hurried down to
the Grand Portage or Fort William on Lake Superior,
the headquarters of the Northwest Company, where
he reported his discovery of Mackenzie River.   His
report was received with utter indifference.   The company had other matters to think about.   It was
girding itself for the life-and-death struggle with its
rival, the Hudson's Bay Company.   " My expedition
was hardly spoken of, but that is what I expected," he
writes to his cousin.   But chagrin did not deter purpose.   He asked the directors' permission to explore
that other broad stream — Peace River — rolling down
from the mountains.   His request was granted.
Winter saw him on furlough in England, studying
astronomy and surveying for the next expedition.
Here he heard much of the Western Sea — the Pacific
— that fired his eagerness.   The voyages of Cook and
Hanna and Meares were on everybody's lips.   Spain
and England and Russia were each pushing for first
possession of the northwest coast.   Mackenzie
hurried back to his Company's fort on the banks of

Peace River, where he spent a restless winter waiting for navigation to open. Doubts of his own ambitions began to trouble him. What if Peace River did not lead to the west coast at all? What if he were behind some other discoverer sent out by the Spaniards or the Russians? " I have been so vexed of late that I cannot sit down to anything steadily," he confesses in a letter to his cousin. Such a tissue-paper wall separates the aims of the real hero from those of the fool, that almost every ambitious man must pass through these periods of self-doubt before reaching the goal of his hopes. But despondency did not benumb Mackenzie into apathy, as it has weaker men.

By April he had shipped the year's furs from the forks of Peace River to Chipewyan. By May his season's work was done. He was ready to go up Peace River. A birch canoe thirty feet long, lined with lightest of cedar, was built. In this were stored pemmican and powder. Alexander Mackay, a clerk of the company, was chosen as first assistant. Six Canadian *voyageurs* — two of whom had accompanied Mackenzie to the Arctic — and two Indian hunters made up the party of ten who stepped into the canoes at seven in the evening of May 9, 1793.

Peace River tore down from the mountains flooded with spring thaw. The crew soon realized that paddles must be bent against the current of a veritable mill-race; but it was safer going against, than with, such a current, for unknown dangers could be seen from below instead of above, where suction would whirl a canoe on the rocks. Keen air foretold the nearing mountains. In less than a week snow-capped peaks had crowded the canoe in a narrow cañon below a tumbling cascade where the river was one wild sheet of tossing foam as far as eye could see. The difficulty was to land; for precipices rose on each side in a wall, down which rolled enormous boulders and land-slides of loose earth. To *portage* goods up these walls was impossible. Fastening an eighty-foot tow-line to the bow, Mackenzie leaped to the declivity, axe in hand, cut foothold along the face of the steep cliff to a place where he could jump to level rock, and then, turning, signalled through the roar of the rapids for his men to come on. The *voyageurs* were paralyzed with fear. They stripped themselves ready to swim if they missed the jump, then one by one vaulted from foothold to foothold where Mackenzie had cut till they came to the final jump across water. Here Mackenzie caught each on his shoulders as the *voyageurs* leaped. The tow-line was then passed round trees growing on the edge of the precipice, and the canoe tracked up the raging cascade. The waves almost lashed the frail craft to pieces. Once a wave caught her sideways; the tow-line snapped like a pistol shot,

U

for just one instant the canoe hung poised, and then the back-wash of an enormous boulder drove her bow foremost ashore, where the *voyageurs* regained the tow-line.

The men had not bargained on this kind of work. They bluntly declared that it was absurd trying to go

Slave Lake Indians.

up cañons with such cascades. Mackenzie paid no heed to the murmurings. He got his crew to the top of the hill, spread out the best of a regale — including tea sweetened with sugar — and while the men were stimulating courage by a feast, he went ahead to reconnoitre the gorge. Windfalls of enormous spruce trees, with a thickness twice the height of a man, lay on a steep declivity of sliding rock. Up this climbed Mackenzie, clothes torn to tatters by devil's club (a thorn bush with spines like needles), boots hacked to pieces by the sharp rocks, and feet gashed with cuts. The prospect was not bright. As far as he could see the river was one succession of cataracts fifty feet wide walled in by stupendous precipices, down which rolled great boulders, shattering to pebbles as they fell. The men were right. No canoe could go up that stream. Mackenzie came back, set his men to repairing the canoe and making axe handles, to avoid the idleness that breeds mutiny, and sent Mackay ahead to see how far the rapids extended. Mackay reported that the *portage* would be nine miles over the mountain.

Leading the way, axe in hand, Mackenzie began felling trees so that the trunks formed an outer railing to prevent a fall down the precipice. Up this trail they warped the canoe by pulling the tow-line round stumps, five men going in advance to cut the way, five hauling and pushing the canoe. In one day progress was three miles. By five in the afternoon the men were so exhausted that they went to bed — if bare ground with sky overhead could be called bed. One thing alone encouraged them: as they rose higher up the mountain side, they saw that the green edges of the glaciers and the eternal snows projected

over the precipices.   They were nearing the summit
— they must surely soon cross the Divide.   The air
grew colder.   For three days the choppers worked in
their blanket coats.   When they finally got the canoe
down to the river-bed, it was to see another range of
impassable mountains barring the way westward.   All
that kept Mackenzie's men from turning back was
that awful *portage* of nine miles.   Nothing ahead
could be worse than what lay behind ; so they embarked, following the south branch where the river
forked.   The stream was swift as a cascade.   Half the
crew walked to lighten the canoe and prevent grazing
on the rocky bottoms.

Once, at dusk, when walkers and paddlers happened to have camped on opposite shores, the marchers came dashing across stream, wading neck-high, with
news that they had heard the firearms of Indian
raiders.   Fires were put out, muskets loaded, and
each man took his station at the foot of a tree, where
all passed a sleepless night.   No hostiles appeared.
The noise was probably falling avalanches.   And once
when Mackenzie and Mackay had gone ahead with
the Indian interpreters, they came back to find that
the canoe had disappeared.   In vain they kindled
fires, fired guns, set branches adrift on the swift current as a signal — no response came from the *voyageurs*.
The boatmen evidently did not wish to be found.

What Mackenzie's suspicions were one may guess. It would be easier for the crew to float back down Peace River than pull against this terrific current with more *portages* over mountains.   The Indians became so alarmed that they wanted to build a raft forthwith and float back to Chipewyan.   The abandoned party had not tasted a bite of food for twenty-four hours. They had not even seen a grouse, and in their powder horns were only a few rounds of ammunition.   Separating, Mackenzie and his Indian went up-stream, Mackay and his went down-stream, each agreeing to signal the other by gunshots if either found the canoe.   Barefooted and drenched in a terrific thunderstorm, Mackenzie wandered on till darkness shrouded the forest.   He had just lain down on a soaking couch of spruce boughs when the ricochetting echo of a gun set the boulders crashing down the precipices. Hurrying down-stream, he found Mackay at the canoe.   The crew pretended that a leakage about the keel had caused delay; but the canoe did not substantiate the excuse.   Mackenzie said nothing; but he never again allowed the crew out of his sight on the east side of the mountains.

So far there had been no sign of Indians among the mountains; and now the canoe was gliding along calm waters when savages suddenly sprang out of a thicket, brandishing spears.   The crew became panic-stricken; but Mackenzie stepped fearlessly ashore, offered the hostiles presents, shook hands, and made his camp with them. The savages told him that he was nearing a *portage* across the Divide. One of them went with Mackenzie the next day as guide. The river narrowed to a small tarn — the source of Peace River; and a short *portage* over rocky ground brought the canoe to a second tarn emptying into a river that, to Mackenzie's disappointment, did not flow west, but south. He had crossed the Divide, the first white man to cross the continent in the North; but how could he know whether to follow this stream? It might lead east to the Saskatchewan. As a matter of fact, he was on the sources of the Fraser, that winds for countless leagues south through the mountains before turning westward for the Pacific.

Full of doubt and misgivings, uncertain whether he had crossed the Divide at all, Mackenzie ordered the canoe down this river. Snowy peaks were on every side. Glaciers lay along the mountain tarns, icy green from the silt of the glacier grinding over rock; and the river was hemmed in by shadowy cañons with roaring cascades that compelled frequent *portage*. Mackenzie wanted to walk ahead, in order to lighten the canoe and look out for danger; but fear had got in the marrow of his men. They thought that he was trying to avoid risks to which he was exposing them; and they compelled him to embark, vowing, if they were to perish, he was to perish with them.

To quiet their fears, Mackenzie embarked with them. Barely had they pushed out when the canoe was caught by a sucking undercurrent which the paddlers could not stem — a terrific rip told them that the canoe had struck — the rapids whirled her sideways and away she went down-stream — the men jumped out, but the current carried them to such deep water that they were clinging to the gunwales as best they could when, with another rip, the stern was torn clean out of the canoe. The blow sent her swirling — another rock battered the bow out — the keel flattened like a raft held together only by the bars. Branches hung overhead. The bowman made a frantic grab at these to stop the rush of the canoe — he was hoisted clear from his seat and dropped ashore Mackenzie jumped out up to his waist in ice-water. The steersman had yelled for each to save himself; but Mackenzie shouted out a countermand for every man to hold on to the gunwales. In this fashion they were all dragged several hundred yards till a whirl sent the wreck into a shallow eddy. The men got their feet on bottom, and the wreckage was hauled ashore. During the entire crisis the Indians sat on top of the canoe, howling with terror.

All the bullets had been lost. A few were recovered. Powder was spread out to dry ; and the men flatly refused to go one foot farther. Mackenzie listened to the revolt without a word. He got their clothes dry and their benumbed limbs warmed over a roaring fire. He fed them till their spirits had risen. Then he quietly remarked that the experience would teach them how to run rapids in the future. Men of the North — to turn back ? Such a thing had never been known in the history of the Northwest Fur Company. It would disgrace them forever. Think of the honor of conquering disaster. Then he vowed that he would go ahead, whether the men accompanied him or not. Then he set them to patching the canoe with oil-cloth and bits of bark ; but large sheets of birch bark are rare in the Rockies ; and the patched canoe weighed so heavily that the men could scarcely carry it. It took them fourteen hours to make the three-mile *portage* of these rapids. The Indian from the mountain tribe had lost heart. Mackenzie and Mackay watched him by turns at night ; but the fellow got away under cover of darkness, the crew conniving at the escape in order to compel Mackenzie to turn back. Finally the river wound into a large stream on the west side of the main range of the Rockies. Mackenzie had crossed the Divide.

For a week after crossing the Divide, the canoe

followed the course of the river southward. This was
not what Mackenzie expected. He sought a stream
flowing directly westward, and was keenly alert for sign
of Indian encampment where he might learn the short-
est way to the Western Sea. Once the smoke of a
camp-fire rose through the bordering forest; but no
sooner had Mackenzie's interpreters approached than
the savages fired volley after volley of arrows and
swiftly decamped, leaving no trace of a trail. There
was nothing to do but continue down the devious
course of the uncertain river. The current was swift
and the outlook cut off by the towering mountains;
but in a bend of the river they came on an Indian
canoe drawn ashore. A savage was just emerging
from a side stream when Mackenzie's men came in
view. With a wild whoop, the fellow made off for
the woods; and in a trice the narrow river was lined
with naked warriors, brandishing spears and displaying
the most outrageous hostility. When Mackenzie
attempted to land, arrows hissed past the canoe, which
they might have punctured and sunk. Determined to
learn the way westward from these Indians, Mackenzie
tried strategy. He ordered his men to float some distance from the savages. Then he landed alone on the
shore opposite the hostiles, having sent one of his
interpreters by a detour through the woods to lie in
ambush with fusee ready for instant action. Throwing

aside weapons, Mackenzie displayed tempting trinkets. The warriors conferred, hesitated, jumped in the canoes, and came, backing stern foremost, toward Mackenzie. He threw out presents. They came ashore and were presently sitting by his side.

From them he learned the river he was following ran for " many moons " through the " shining mountains " before it reached the " midday sun." It was barred by fearful rapids ; but by retracing the way back up the river, the white men could leave the canoe at a carrying place and go overland to the salt water in eleven days. From other tribes down the same river, Mackenzie gathered similar facts. He knew that the stream was misleading him ; but a retrograde movement up such a current would discourage his men. He had only one month's provisions left. His ammunition had dwindled to one hundred and fifty bullets and thirty pounds of shot. Instead of folding his hands in despondency, Mackenzie resolved to set the future at defiance and go on. From the Indians he obtained promise of a man to guide him back. Then he frankly laid all the difficulties before his followers, declaring that he was going on alone and they need not continue unless they voluntarily decided to do so. His dogged courage was contagious. The speech was received with huzzas, and the canoe was headed upstream.

The Indian guide was to join Mackenzie higher up-stream; but the reappearance of the white men when they had said they would not be back for " many moons" roused the suspicions of the savages. The shores were lined with warriors who would receive no explanation that Mackenzie tried to give in sign language. The canoe began to leak so badly that the boatmen had to spend half the time bailing out water; and the *voyageurs* dared not venture ashore for resin. Along the river cliff was a little three-cornered hut of thatched clay. Here Mackenzie took refuge, awaiting the return of the savage who had promised to act as guide. The three walls protected the rear, but the front of the hut was exposed to the warriors across the river; and the whites dared not kindle a fire that might serve as a target. Two nights were passed in this hazardous shelter, Mackay and Mackenzie alternately lying in their cloaks on the wet rocks, keeping watch. At midnight of the third day's siege, a rustling came from the woods to the rear and the boatmen's dog set up a furious barking. The men were so frightened that they three times loaded the canoe to desert their leader, but something in the fearless confidence of the explorer deterred them. As daylight sifted through the forest, Mackenzie descried a vague object creeping through the underbrush. A less fearless man would have fired and lost all. Mackenzie dashed out to find the cause of alarm an old blind man, almost in convulsions from fear. He had been driven from this river hut. Mackenzie quieted his terror with food. By signs the old man explained that the Indians had suspected treachery when the whites returned so soon; and by signs Mackenzie requested him to guide the canoe back up the river to the carrying place; but the old creature went off in such a palsy of fear that he had to be lifted bodily into the canoe. The situation was saved. The hostiles could not fire without wounding one of their own people; and the old man could explain the real reason for Mackenzie's return. Rations had been reduced to two meals a day. The men were still sulking from the perils of the siege when the canoe struck a stump that knocked a hole in the keel, "which," reports Mackenzie, laconically, "gave them all an opportunity to let loose their discontent without reserve." Camp after camp they passed, which the old man's explanations pacified, till they at length came to the carrying place. Here, to the surprise and delight of all, the guide awaited them.

On July 4, provisions were _cached_, the canoe abandoned, and a start made overland westward, each man carrying ninety pounds of provisions besides musket and pistols. And this burden was borne on the rations of two scant meals a day. The way was ridgy, steep, and obstructed by windfalls. At cloud-line, the rocks were slippery as glass from moisture, and Mackenzie led the way, beating the drip from the branches as they marched. The record was twelve miles the first day. When it rained, the shelter was a piece of oil-cloth held up in an extemporized tent, the men crouching to sleep as best they could. The

Good Hope, Mackenzie River. Hudson's Bay Company Fort.

way was well beaten and camp was frequently made for the night with strange Indians, from whom fresh guides were hired; but when he did not camp with the natives, Mackenzie watched his guide by sleeping with him. Though the fellow was malodorous from fish oil and infested with vermin, Mackenzie would spread his cloak in such a way that escape was impossible without awakening himself. No sentry was kept at night. All hands were too deadly tired from the day's climb. Once, in the impenetrable gloom of the midnight forest, Mackenzie was awakened by a plaintive chant in a kind of unearthly music. A tribe was engaged in religious devotions to some woodland deity. Totem poles of cedar, carved with the heads of animals emblematic of family clans, told Mackenzie that he was nearing the coast tribes. Barefooted, with ankles swollen and clothes torn to shreds, they had crossed the last range of mountains within two weeks of leaving the inland river. They now embarked with some natives for the sea.

One can guess how Mackenzie's heart thrilled as they swept down the swift river — six miles an hour — past fishing weirs and Indian camps, till at last, far out between the mountains, he descried the narrow arm of the blue, limitless sea. The canoe leaked like a sieve; but what did that matter? At eight o'clock on the morning of Saturday, July 20, the river carried them to a wide lagoon, lapped by a tide, with the seaweed waving for miles along the shore. Morning fog still lay on the far-billowing ocean. Sea otters tumbled over the slimy rocks with discordant cries. Gulls darted overhead; and past the canoe dived the great floundering grampus. There was no mistaking.

This was the sea — the Western Sea, that for three hundred years had baffled all search overland, and led the world's greatest explorers on a chase of a will-o'-the-wisp. What Cartier and La Salle and La Vérendrye failed to do, Mackenzie had accomplished.

But Mackenzie's position was not to be envied. Ten starving men on a barbarous coast had exactly twenty pounds of pemmican, fifteen of rice, six of flour. Of ammunition there was scarcely any. Between home and their leaky canoe lay half a continent of wilderness and mountains. The next day was spent coasting the cove for a place to take observations. Canoes of savages met the white men, and one impudent fellow kept whining out that he had once been shot at by men of Mackenzie's color. Mackenzie took refuge for the night on an isolated rock which was barely large enough for his party to gain a foothold. The savages hung about pestering the boatmen for gifts. Two white men kept guard, while the rest slept. On Monday, when Mackenzie was setting up his instruments, his young Indian guide came, foaming at the mouth from terror, with news that the coast tribes were to attack the white men by hurling spears at the unsheltered rock. The boatmen lost their heads and were for instant flight, anywhere, everywhere, in a leaky canoe that would have foundered a mile out at sea. Mackenzie did not stir, but ordered fusees primed and the canoe gummed. Mixing up a pot of vermilion, he painted in large letters on the face of the rock where they had passed the night: —

" Alexander Mackenzie, from Canada, by land, the twenty-second of July, one thousand seven hundred and ninety-three."

The canoe was then headed eastward for the homeward trip. Only once was the explorer in great danger on his return. It was just as the canoe was leaving tide-water for the river. The young Indian guide led him full tilt into the village of hostiles that had besieged the rock. Mackenzie was alone, his men following with the baggage. Barely had he reached the woods when two savages sprang out, with daggers in hand ready to strike. Quick as a flash, Mackenzie quietly raised his gun. They dropped back; but he was surrounded by a horde led by the impudent chief of the attack on the rock the first night on the sea. One warrior grasped Mackenzie from behind. In the scuffle hat and cloak came off; but Mackenzie shook himself free, got his sword out, and succeeded in holding the shouting rabble at bay till his men came. Then such was his rage at the indignity that he ordered his followers in line with loaded fusees, marched to the village, demanded the return of the hat and cloak, and obtained a peace-offering of fish as well. The Indians knew the power of firearms, and fell at his feet in contrition. Mackenzie named this camp Rascal Village.

At another time his men lost heart so completely over the difficulties ahead that they threw everything they were carrying into the river. Mackenzie patiently sat on a stone till they had recovered from their panic. Then he reasoned and coaxed and dragooned them into the spirit of courage that at last brought them safely over mountain and through cañon to Peace River. On August 24, a sharp bend in the river showed them the little home fort which they had left four months before. The joy of the *voyageurs* fairly exploded. They beat their paddles on the canoe, fired off all the ammunition that remained, waved flags, and set the cliffs ringing with shouts.

Mackenzie spent the following winter at Chipewyan, despondent and lonely. " What a situation, starving and alone! " he writes to his cousin. The hard life was beginning to wear down the dauntless spirit. " I spend the greater part of my time in vague speculations. . . . In fact my mind was never at ease, nor could I bend it to my wishes. Though I am not superstitious, my dreams cause me great annoyance. I scarcely close my eyes without finding myself in company with the dead."

x

The following winter Mackenzie left the West never to return. The story of his travels was published early ·in the nineteenth century, and he was knighted by the English king. The remainder of his life was spent quietly on an estate in Scotland, where he died in 1820.

The Mouth of the Mackenzie by the Light of the Midnight Sun.
—C. W. Mathers.

CHAPTER XI

1803–1806

LEWIS AND CLARK

The First White Men to ascend the Missouri to its Sources and descend the Columbia to the Pacific — Exciting Adventures on the Cañons of the Missouri, the Discovery of the Great Falls and the Yellowstone — Lewis' Escape from Hostiles

THE spring of 1904 witnessed the centennial celebration of an area as large as half the kingdoms of Europe, that has the unique distinction of having transferred its allegiance to three different flags within twenty-four hours.

At the opening of the nineteenth century Spain had ceded all the region vaguely known as Louisiana back to France, and France had sold the territory to the United States; but post-horse and stage of those old days travelled slowly. News of Spain's cession and France's sale reached Louisiana almost simultaneously. On March 9, 1804, the Spanish grandees of St. Louis took down their flag and, to the delight of Louisiana, for form's sake erected French colors. On

March 10, the French flag was lowered for the emblem that has floated over the Great West ever since — the stars and stripes. How vast was the new territory acquired, the eastern states had not the slighest conception. As early as 1792 Captain Gray, of the ship *Columbia*, from Boston, had blundered into the harbor of a vast river flowing into the Pacific. What lay between this river and that other great river on the eastern side of the mountains — the Missouri? Jefferson had arranged with John Ledyard of Connecticut, who had been with Captain Cook on the Pacific, to explore the northwest coast of America by crossing Russia overland; but Russia had similar designs for herself, and stopped Ledyard on the way. In 1803 President Jefferson asked Congress for an appropriation to explore the Northwest by way of the Missouri. Now that the wealth of the West is beyond the estimate of any figure, it seems almost inconceivable that there were people little-minded enough to haggle over the price paid for Louisiana — $15,000,000 — and to object to the appropriation required for its exploration — $2500; but fortunately the world goes ahead in spite of hagglers.

May of 1804 saw Captain Meriwether Lewis, formerly secretary to President Jefferson, and Captain William Clark of Virginia launch out from Wood River opposite St. Louis, where they had kept their men encamped all winter on the east side of the Mississippi, waiting until the formal transfer of Louisiana for the long journey of exploration to the sources of the Missouri and the Columbia. Their escort consisted of twenty soldiers, eleven *voyageurs*, and nine frontiersmen. The

Captain Meriwether Lewis.

main craft was a keel boat fifty-five feet long, of light draft, with square-rigged sail and twenty-two oars, and tow-line fastened to the mast pole to track the boat upstream through rapids. An American flag floated from the prow, and behind the flag the universal types of progress everywhere — goods for trade and a swivel-gun. Horses were led alongshore for hunting, and two pirogues — sharp at prow, broad at stern, like a flat-iron or a turtle — glided to the fore of the keel boat.

Captain William Clark.

The Missouri was at flood tide, turbid with crumbling clay banks and great trees torn out by the roots, from which keel boat and pirogues sheered safely off. For the first time in history the Missouri resounded to the Fourth of July guns; and round camp-fire the men danced to the strains of a *voyageur's* fiddle.

Usually, among forty men is one traitor, and Liberte must desert on pretence of running back for a knife; but perhaps the fellow took fright from the wild yarns told by the lonely-eyed, shaggy-browed, ragged trappers who came floating down the Platte, down the Osage, down the Missouri, with canoe loads of furs for St. Louis. These men foregathered with the *voyageurs* and told only too true stories of the dangers ahead. Fires kindled on the banks of the river called neighboring Indians to council. Council Bluffs commemorates one conference, of which there were many with Iowas and Omahas and Ricarees and Sioux. Pause was made on the south side of the Missouri to visit the high mound where Blackbird, chief of the Omahas, was buried astride his war horse that his spirit might forever watch the French *voyageurs* passing up and down the river.

By October the explorers were sixteen hundred miles north of St. Louis, at the Mandan villages near where Bismarck stands to-day. The Mandans welcomed the white men; but the neighboring tribes of Ricarees were insolent. "Had I these white warriors on the upper plains," boasted a chief to Charles Mackenzie, one of the Northwest Fur Company men from Canada, "my young men on horseback would finish them as they would so many wolves; for there are only two sensible men among them, the worker of iron [blacksmith] and the mender of guns." Four Canadian traders had already been massacred by this chief. Captain Lewis knew that his company must winter on the east side of the mountains, and there were a dozen traders — Hudson Bay and Nor'westers — on the ground practising all the unscrupulous tricks of rivals, Nor'westers driving off Hudson Bay horses, Hudson Bay men driving off Nor'westers', to defeat trade; so Captain Lewis at once had a fort constructed. It was triangular in shape, the two converging walls consisting of barracks with a loopholed bastion at the apex, the base being a high wall of strong pickets where sentry kept constant guard. Hitherto Captain Lewis had been able to secure the services of French trappers as interpreters with the Indians; but the next year he was going where there were no trappers; and now he luckily engaged an old Nor'wester, Chaboneau, whose Indian wife, Sacajawea, was a captive from the Snake tribe of the Rockies.[1] On Christmas morning, the stars and stripes were hoisted above Fort Mandan; and all that night the men danced hilariously. On New

[1] Mention of this man is to be found in Northwest Company manuscripts, lately sold in the Masson collection of documents to the Canadian Archives and McGill College Library. It was also my good fortune — while this book was going to print — to see the entire family collection of Clark's letters, owned by Mrs. Julia Clark Voorhis of New York. Among these letters is one to Chaboneau from Clark. In spite of the cordial relations between the Nor'westers and Lewis and Clark, these fur traders cannot conceal their fear that this trip presages the end of the fur trade.

Years of 1805, the white men visited the Mandan lodges, and one *voyageur* danced " on his head " to the uproarious applause of the savages.   All winter the men joined in the buffalo hunts, laying up store of pemmican.   In February, work was begun on the small boats for the ascent of the Missouri.   By the end of March, the river had cleared of ice, and a dozen men were sent back to St. Louis.

At five, in the afternoon of April 7, six canoes and two pirogues were pushed out on the Missouri.   Sails were hoisted; a cheer from the Canadian traders and Indians standing on the shore — and the boats glided up the Missouri with flags flying from foremost prow. Hitherto Lewis and Clark had passed over travelled ground.   Now they had set sail for the Unknown. Within a week they had passed the Little Missouri, the height of land that divides the waters of the Missouri from those of the Saskatchewan, and the great Yellowstone River, first found by wandering French trappers and now for the first time explored.   The current of the Missouri grew swifter, the banks steeper, and the use of the tow-line more frequent.   The voyage was no more the holiday trip that it had been all the way from St. Louis.   Hunters were kept on the banks to forage for game, and once four of them came so suddenly on an open-mouthed, ferocious old bear that he had turned hunter and they hunted before guns

could be loaded; and the men saved themselves only
by jumping twenty feet over the bank into the river.

For miles the boats had to be tracked up-stream by
the tow-line. The shore was so steep that it offered
no foothold. Men and stones slithered heterogene-

Tracking Up-stream.

ously down the sliding gravel into the water. Moccasins wore out faster than they could be sewed; and
the men's feet were cut by prickly-pear and rock as if
by knives. On Sunday, May 26, when Captain
Lewis was marching to lighten the canoes, he had
just climbed to the summit of a high, broken cliff when

there burst on his glad eyes a first glimpse of the far, white " Shining Mountains " of which the Indians told, the Rockies, snowy and dazzling in the morning sun. One can guess how the weather-bronzed, ragged man paused to gaze on the glimmering summits. Only one other explorer had ever been so far west in this region — young De la Vérendrye, fifty years before ; but the Frenchman had been compelled to turn back without crossing the mountains, and the two Americans were to assail and conquer what had proved an impassable barrier. The Missouri had become too deep for poles, too swift for paddles ; and the banks were so precipitous that the men were often poised at dizzy heights above the river, dragging the tow-line round the edge of rock and crumbly cliff. Captain Lewis was leading the way one day, crawling along the face of a rock wall, when he slipped. Only a quick thrust of his spontoon into the cliff saved him from falling almost a hundred feet. He had just struck it with terrific force into the rock, where it gave him firm handhold, when he heard a voice cry, " Good God, Captain, what shall I do ? "

Windsor, a frontiersman, had slipped to the very verge of the rock, where he lay face down with right arm and leg completely over the precipice, his left hand vainly grabbing empty air for grip of anything that would hold him back. Captain Lewis was horrified, but kept his presence of mind; for the man's life hung by a thread. A move, a turn, the slightest start of alarm to disturb Windsor's balance — and he was lost.

Typical Mountain Trapper.

Steadying his voice, Captain Lewis shouted back, "You're in little danger. Stick your knife in the cliff to hoist yourself up."

With the leverage of the knife, Windsor succeeded in lifting himself back to the narrow ledge. Then

The Discovery of the Great Falls.

taking off his moccasins, he crawled along the cliff to broader foothold. Lewis sent word for the crews to wade the margin of the river instead of attempting this pass — which they did, though shore water was breast high and ice cold.

The Missouri had now become so narrow that it was hard to tell which was the main river and which a tributary; so Captain Lewis and four men went in advance to find the true course. Leaving camp at sunrise, Captain Lewis was crossing a high, bare plain, when he heard the most musical of all wilderness sounds — the far rushing that is the voice of many waters. Far above the prairie there shimmered in the morning sun a gigantic plume of spray. Surely this was the Great Falls of which the Indians told. Lewis and his men broke into a run across the open for seven miles, the rush of waters increasing to a deafening roar, the plume of spray to clouds of foam. Cliffs two hundred feet high shut off the view. Down these scrambled Lewis, not daring to look away from his feet till safely at bottom, when he faced about to see the river compressed by sheer cliffs over which hurled a white cataract in one smooth sheet eighty feet high. The spray tossed up in a thousand bizarre shapes of wind-driven clouds. Captain Lewis drew the long sigh of the thing accomplished. He had found the Great Falls of the Missouri.

Seating himself on the rock, he awaited his hunters. That night they camped under a tree near the falls. Morning showed that the river was one succession of falls and rapids for eighteen miles. Here was indeed a stoppage to the progress of the boats. Sending back word to Captain Clark of the discovery of the falls, Lewis had ascended the course of the cascades to a high hill when he suddenly encountered a herd of a thousand buffalo. It was near supper-time. Quick as thought, Lewis fired. What was his amazement to see a huge bear leap from the furze to pounce on the wounded quarry; and what was Bruin's amazement to see the unusual spectacle of a thing as small as a man marching out to contest possession of that quarry? Man and bear reared up to look at each other. Bear had been master in these regions from time immemorial. Man or beast — which was to be master now? Lewis had aimed his weapon to fire again, when he recollected that it was not loaded; and the bear was coming on too fast for time to recharge. Captain Lewis was a brave man and a dignified man; but the plain was bare of tree or brush, and the only safety was inglorious flight. But if he had to retreat, the captain determined that he *would* retreat only at a walk. The rip of tearing claws sounded from behind, and Lewis looked over his shoulder to see the bear at a hulking gallop, open-mouthed, — and off they went,

Fighting a Grizzly.

explorer and exploited, in a sprinting match of eighty yards, when the grunting roar of pursuer told pursued that the bear was gaining. Turning short, Lewis plunged into the river to mid-waist and faced about with his spontoon at the bear's nose. A sudden turn is an old trick with all Indian hunters; the bear floundered back on his haunches, reconsidered the sport of hunting this new animal, man, and whirled right about for the dead buffalo.

It took the crews from the 15th to the 25th of June to *portage* past the Great Falls. Cottonwood trees yielded carriage wheels two feet in diameter, and the masts of the pirogues made axletrees. On these wagonettes the canoes were dragged across the *portage*. It was hard, hot work. Grizzlies prowled round the camp at night, wakening the exhausted workers. The men actually fell asleep on their feet as they toiled, and spent half the night double-soling their torn moccasins, for the cactus already had most of the men limping from festered feet. Yet not one word of complaint was uttered; and once, when the men were camped on a green along the *portage*, a *voyageur* got out his fiddle, and the sore feet danced, which was more wholesome than moping or poulticing. The boldness of the grizzlies was now explained. Antelope and buffalo were carried over the falls. The bears prowled below for the carrion.

After failure to construct good hide boats, two other craft, twenty-five and thirty-three feet long, were knocked together, and the crews launched above the

Packer carrying Goods across *Portage*.

rapids for the far Shining Mountains that lured like a mariner's beacon. Night and day, when the sun was hot, came the boom-boom as of artillery from the mountains. The *voyageurs* thought this the explosion of stones, but soon learned to recognize the sound of avalanche and land-slide. The river became narrower, deeper, swifter, as the explorers approached the mountains. For five miles rocks rose on each side twelve hundred feet high, sheer as a wall. Into this shadowy cañon, silent as death, crept the boats of the white men, vainly straining their eyes for glimpse of egress from the watery defile. A word, a laugh, the snatch of a *voyageur's* ditty, came back with elfin echo, as if spirits hung above the dizzy heights spying on the intruders. Springs and tenuous, wind-blown falls like water threads trickled down each side of the lofty rocks. The water was so deep that poles did not touch bottom, and there was not the width of a foot-hold between water and wall for camping ground. Flags were unfurled from the prows of the boats to warn marauding Indians on the height above that the *voyageurs* were white men, not enemies. Darkness fell on the cañon with the great hushed silence of the mountains; and still the boats must go on and on in the darkness, for there was no anchorage. Finally, above a small island in the middle of the river, was found a tiny camping ground with pine-drift enough for fire-wood. Here they landed in the pitchy dark. They had entered the Gates of the Rockies on the 19th of July. In the morning bighorn and mountain goat were seen scrambling along the ledges above the water. On the 25th the Three Forks of the Missouri were reached. Here the Indian woman, Saca-jawea, recognized the ground and practically became the guide of the party, advising the two explorers to follow the south fork or the Jefferson, as that was the stream which her tribe followed when crossing the mountains to the plains.

It now became absolutely necessary to find moun-

Y

tain Indians who would supply horses and guide the white men across the Divide. In the hope of finding the Indian trail, Captain Lewis landed with two men and preceded the boats. He had not gone five miles when to his sheer delight he saw a Snake Indian on horseback. Ordering his men to keep back, he advanced within a mile of the horseman and three times spread his blanket on the ground as a signal of friend-

Spying on an Enemy's Fort.

ship. The horseman sat motionless as bronze. Captain Lewis went forward, with trinkets held out to tempt a parley, and was within a few hundred yards when the savage wheeled and dashed off. Lewis' men had disobeyed orders and frightened the fellow by advancing. Deeply chagrined, Lewis hoisted an American flag as sign of friendship and continued his march. Tracks of horses were followed across a bog, along what was plainly an Indian road, till the sources of the Mis-

souri became so narrow that one of the men put a foot
on each side and thanked God that he had lived to
bestride the Missouri.   Stooping, all drank from
the crystal spring whose waters they had traced for
three thousand miles from St. Louis.   Following a
steep declivity, they were presently crossing the course
of a stream that flowed west and must lead to some
branch of the Columbia.

Suddenly, on the cliff in front, Captain Lewis discovered two squaws, an Indian, and some dogs.   Un-
furling his flag, he advanced.   The Indians paused,
then dashed for the woods.   Lewis tried to tie some
presents round the dogs' necks as a peace-offering,
but the curs made off after their master.   The white
men had not proceeded a mile before they came to
three squaws, who never moved but bowed their heads
to the ground for the expected blow that would make
them captives.   Throwing down weapons, Lewis
pulled up his sleeve to show that he was white.   Presents allayed all fear, and the squaws had led him two
miles toward their camp when sixty warriors came
galloping at full speed with arrows levelled.   The
squaws rushed forward, vociferating and showing their
presents.   Three chiefs at once dismounted, and fell on
Captain Lewis with such greasy embraces of welcome
that he was glad to end the ceremony.   Pipes were
smoked, presents distributed, and the white men con-

ducted to a great leathern lodge, where Lewis announced his mission and prepared the Indians for the coming of the main force in the boats.

The Snakes scarcely knew whether to believe the white man's tale. The Indian camp was short of pro-

Indian Camp at Foothills of Rockies.

visions, and Lewis urged the warriors to come back up the trail to meet the advancing boats. The braves hesitated. Cameahwait, the chief, harangued till a dozen warriors mounted their horses and set out, Lewis and his men each riding behind an Indian. Captain Clark could advance only slowly, and the Indians with Lewis grew suspicious as they entered the rocky defiles without meeting the explorers' party. Half the Snakes turned back. Among those that went on were three women. To demonstrate good faith, Lewis again mounted a horse behind an Indian, though the bare-back riding over rough ground at a mad pace was almost jolting his bones apart. A spy came back breathless with news for the hungry warriors that one of the white hunters had killed a deer, and the whole company lashed to a breakneck gallop that nearly finished Lewis, who could only cling for dear life to the Indian's waist. The poor wretches were so ravenous that they fell on the dead deer and devoured it raw. It was here that Lewis expected the boats. They were not to be seen. The Indians grew more distrustful. The chief at once put fur collars, after the fashion of Indian dress, round the white men's shoulders. As this was plainly a trick to conceal the whites in case of treachery on their part, Lewis at once took off his hat and placed it on the chief's head. Then he hurried the Indians along, lest they should lose courage completely. To his mortification, Captain Clark did not appear. To revive the Indians' courage, the white men then passed their guns across to the Snakes, signalling willingness to suffer death if the Indians discovered treachery. That night all the Indians hid in the woods but five, who slept on guard round the whites. If anything had stopped Clark's advance, Lewis was lost. Though neither knew it, Lewis and Clark were only four miles apart. Clark, Chaboneau, the guide, and Sacajawea, the Indian woman, were walking on the shore early in the morning, when the squaw began to dance with signs of the most extravagant joy. Looking ahead, Clark saw one of Lewis' men, disguised as an Indian, leading a company of Snake warriors that the squaw had recognized as her own people, from whom she had been wrested when a child. The Indians broke into songs of delight, and Sacajawea, dashing through the crowd, threw her arms round an Indian woman, sobbing and laughing and exhibiting all the hysterical delight of a demented creature. Sacajawea and the woman had been playmates in childhood and had been captured in the same war; but the Snake woman had escaped, while Sacajawea became a slave and married the French guide.

Meanwhile, Captain Clark was being welcomed by Lewis and the chief, Cameahwait. Sacajawea was called to interpret. Cameahwait rose to speak. The poor squaw flung herself on him with cries of delight. In the chief of the Snakes she had recognized her brother. Laced coats, medals, flags, and trinkets were presented to the Snakes; but though willing enough to act as guides, the Indians discouraged the explorers about going on in boats. The western stream was broken for leagues by terrible rapids walled in with impassable precipices. Boats were abandoned and horses bought from the Snakes. The white men set their faces northwestward, the southern trail, usually followed by the Snakes, leading too much in the direction of the Spanish settlements. Game grew so scarce that by September the men were without food and a colt was killed for meat.

By October the company was reduced to a diet of dog; but the last Divide had been crossed. Horses were left with an Indian chief of the Flatheads, and the explorers glided down the Clearwater, leading to the Columbia, in five canoes and one pilot boat. Great was the joy in camp on November 8, 1805; for the boats had passed the last *portage* of the Columbia. When heavy fog rose, there burst on the eager gaze of the *voyageurs* the shining expanse of the Pacific. The shouts of the jubilant *voyageurs* mingled with the roar of ocean breakers. Like Alexander Mackenzie of the far North a decade before, Lewis and Clark had reached the long-sought Western Sea. They had been first up the Missouri, first across the middle Rockies, and first down the Columbia to the Pacific.

Seven huts, known as Fort Clatsop, were knocked up on the south side of the Columbia's harbor for winter quarters; and a wretched winter the little fort spent, beleaguered not by hostiles, but by such inclement damp that all the men were ill before spring and their very leather suits rotted from their backs. Many a time, coasting the sea, were they benighted. Spreading mats on the sand, they slept in the drenching rain. Unused to ocean waters, the inland *voyageurs* became deadly seasick. Once, when all were encamped on the shore, an enormous tidal wave broke over the camp with a smashing of log-drift that almost crushed the boats. Nez Perces and Flatheads had assisted the white men after the Snake guides had turned back. Clatsops and Chinooks were now their neighbors. Christmas and New Year of 1806 were celebrated by a discharge of firearms. No boats chanced to touch at the Columbia during the winter. The time was passed laying up store of elk meat and leather; for the company was not only starving, but nearly naked. The Pacific had been reached on November 14, 1805. Fort Clatsop was evacuated on the afternoon of March 23, 1806.

The goods left to trade for food and horses when Lewis and Clark departed from the coast inland had dwindled to what could have been tied in two handkerchiefs; but necessity proved the mother of invention, and the men cut the brass buttons from their tattered clothes and vended brass trinkets to the Indians. The

On Guard.

medicine-chest was also sacrificed, every Indian tribe besieging the two captains for eye-water, fly-blisters, and other patent wares. The poverty of the white man roused the insolence of the natives on the return over the mountains. Rocks were rolled down on the boatmen at the worst *portages* by aggressive Indians; and once, when the hungry *voyageurs* were at a meal of dog meat, an Indian impudently flung a live pup straight at Captain Lewis' plate. In a trice the pup was back in the fellow's face; Lewis had seized a weapon; and the crestfallen aggressor had taken ignominiously to his heels. When they had crossed the mountains, the forces divided into three parties, two to go east by the Yellowstone, one under Lewis by the main Missouri.

Somewhere up the height of land that divides the southern waters of the Saskatchewan from the northern waters of the Missouri, the tracks of Minnetaree warriors were found. These were the most murderous raiders of the plains. Over a swell of the prairie Lewis was startled to see a band of thirty horses, half of them saddled. The Indians were plainly on the war-path, for no women were in camp; so Lewis took out his flag and advanced unfalteringly. An Indian came forward. Lewis and the chief shook hands, but Lewis now had no presents to pacify hostiles. Camping with the Minnetarees for the night as if he feared nothing, Lewis nevertheless took good

care to keep close watch on all movements. He
smoked the pipe of peace with them as late as he
dared ; and when he retired to sleep, he had ordered
Fields and the other two white men to be on guard.
At sunrise the Indians crowded round the fire, where

Indians of the Up-country or *Pays d'en Haut.*

Fields had for the moment carelessly laid his rifle.
Simultaneously, the warriors dashed at the weapons of
the sleeping white men, while other Indians made off
with the explorers' horses. With a shout, Fields gave
the alarm, and pursuing the thieves, grappled with the

Indian who had stolen his rifle.   In the scuffle the Indian was stabbed to the heart.   Drewyer succeeded in wresting back his gun, and Lewis dashed out with his pistol, shouting for the Indians to leave the horses. The raiders were mounting to go off at full speed. The white men pursued on foot.   Twelve horses fell behind; but just as the Indians dashed for .hiding behind a cliff, Lewis' strength gave out.   He warned them if they did not stop he would shoot.   An Indian turned to fire with one of the stolen weapons, and instantly Lewis' pistol rang true.   The fellow rolled to earth mortally wounded; but Lewis felt the whiz of a bullet past his own head.   Having captured more horses than they had lost, the white men at once mounted and rode for their lives through river and slough, sixty miles without halt; for the Minnetarees would assuredly rally a larger band of warriors to their aid.   A pause of an hour to refresh the horses and a wilder ride by moonlight put forty more miles between Captain Lewis and danger.   At daylight the men were so sore from the mad pace for twenty-four hours that they could scarcely stand; but safety depended on speed and on they went again till they reached the main Missouri, where by singularly good luck some of the other *voyageurs* had arrived.

The entire forces were reunited below the Yellowstone on August 12th.   Traders on the way up the

Missouri from St. Louis brought first news of the outer world, and the discoverers were not a little amused to learn that they had been given up for dead. At the Mandans, Colter, one of the frontiersmen, asked leave to go back to the wilds; and Chaboneau, with his dauntless wife, bade the white men farewell. On September 20th settlers on the river bank above St. Louis were surprised to see thirty ragged men, with faces bronzed like leather, passing down the river. Then some one remembered who these worn *voyageurs* were, and cheers of welcome made the cliffs of the Missouri ring. On September 23d, at midday, the boats drew quietly up to the river front of St. Louis. Lewis and Clark, the greatest pathfinders of the United States, had returned from the discovery of a new world as large as half Europe, without losing a single man but Sergeant Floyd, who had died from natural causes a few months after leaving St. Louis. What Radisson had begun in 1659–1660, what De la Vérendrye had attempted when he found the way barred by the Rockies—was completed by Lewis and Clark in 1805. It was the last act in that drama of heroes who carved empire out of wilderness; and all alike possessed the same hero-qualities — courage and endurance that were indomitable, the strength that is generated in life-and-death grapple with naked primordial reality, and that reckless daring which defies life and death. Those were hero-days; and they produced hero-types, who flung themselves against the impossible — and conquered it. What they conquered we have inherited. It is the Great Northwest.

APPENDIX

For the very excellent translations of the almost untranslatable transcripts taken from the Marine Archives of Paris, and forwarded to me by the Canadian Archives, I am indebted to Mr. R. Roy, of the Marine Department, Ottawa, the eminent authority on French Canadian genealogical matters.

Some of the topics in the Appendices are of such a controversial nature — the whereabouts of the Mascoutins, for instance — that at my request Mr. Roy made the translation absolutely literal no matter how incongruous the wording. To those who say Radisson was not on the Missouri I commend Appendix E, where the tribes of the West are described.

APPENDIX A

Copy of Letter written to M. Comporté by M. Chouart, at London, the 29th April, 1685

Sir,

I have received the two letters with which you have honored me ; I have even received one inclosed that I have not given, for reasons that I will tell you, God willing, in a few days.

I have received your instructions contained in the one and the other, as to the way I should act, and I should not have failed to execute all that you order me for the service of our Master, if I had been at full liberty so to do ; you must have no doubt about it, because my inclination and my duty agree perfectly well. All the advantages that I am offered did not for a moment cause me to waver, but, in short, sir, I could not go to Paris, and I shall be happy to go and meet you by the route you travel. I shall be well pleased to find landed the people you state will be there; in case they may have the commission you speak of in your two letters, have it accompanied if you please with a memorandum of what I shall have to do for the service of our Master. I know of a case whereby I am sufficiently taught that it is not safe to undertake too many things, however advantageous they may be, nor undertaking too little. I am convinced, sir, that having orders, I will carry them out at the risk of my life, and I flatter myself that you do not doubt it.

There is much likelihood that the men you sent last year are lost.

I should like, sir, to be at the place you desire me to go; be assured I will perish, or be there as soon as I possibly can; it is saying enough. I do not answer to the rest of your letter, it is sufficient that I am addressing a sensible man, who, knowing my heart, will not doubt that I will keep my word with him, as I believe he will do all he can for my interests.

I am, with much anxiety to see you, sir, your most humble and most obedient servant,

(signed) CHOUART.

I will leave here only on the 25th of next month.

APPENDIX B

COPY OF LETTER WRITTEN BY M. CHOUART TO MRS. DES GROSEILLERS, HIS MOTHER

AT LONDON, 11TH APRIL, 1685.

MY VERY DEAR MOTHER,

I learn by the letter you have written me, of the 2nd November last, that my father has returned from France without obtaining anything at that Court, which made you think of leaving Quebec; my sentiment would be that you abandon this idea as I am strongly determined to go and be by you at the first opportunity I get, which shall be, God willing, as soon as I have taken means to that effect when I have returned from the North.

I hope to start on this voyage in a month or six weeks at the latest;

I cannot determine on what date I could be near you ; my father may know what difficulties there are. However, I hope to surmount them, and there is nothing I would not do to that end.

The money I left with my cousin is intended to buy you a house, as I have had always in mind to do, had not my father opposed it, but now I will do it so as to give you a chance to get on, and always see you in the country where I will live.

I have been made, here, proposals of marriage, to which I have not listened, not being here under the rule of my king nor near my parents, and I would have left this kingdom had I been given the liberty to do so, but they hold back on me my pay and the price of my merchandise, and I cannot sail away as orders have been given to arrest me in case I should prepare to leave.

What you fear in reference to my money should not give you any uneasiness on account of the English. I will cause it to be pretty well known that I never intended to follow the English. I have been sur- prised and forced by my uncle's subterfuges to risk this voyage being unable to escape the English vessels where my uncle made me go with- out disclosing his plan, which he has worked out in bringing me here, but I will not disclose mine either : to abandon this nation. I am willing that my cousin should pay you the income on my money, until I return home. M. the earl of Denonville, your governor, will see to my mother's affairs, as they who render service to the country will not be forsaken as in the past, and being generous as he is, loyal and zealous for his country, he will inform the Court what there is to be done for the benefit of our nation.

I am, my dear mother, to my father and to you,

most obedient servant,

(signed) CHOUART.

And below is written : —

MOTHER,

I pray you to see on my behalf M. du Lude, and assure him of my very humble services. I will have the honor of seeing him as soon as I can. Please do the same with M. Peray and all our good friends.

z

APPENDIX C

COUNCIL

Held at fort Pontchartrain, in lake Erie strait, 8th June, 1704.

By the indians Kiskacous, Ottawa, Sinagot of the Sable Nation, Hurons, Saulteurs (Sault Indians), Amikoique (Amikoués), Mississaugas, Nipissings, Miamis and Wolves, in the presence of M. de Lamothe-Cadillac, commanding at the said fort; de Tonty, captain of a detachment of Marines; the rev F. Constantin, Recollet missionary at the said post; Messrs Desnoyers and Radisson, principal clerks of the Company of the Colony, and of all the French, soldiers as well as *voyageurs*.

The one named FORTY SOLS, (40 half-penny), indian chief of the Huron nation speaks as much on behalf of the said nation as of all those present at the meeting.

The French having come, he said : —
"We ask that all the French be present at this Council so that they hear and know what we will say to you.

"We are well on this land, it is very good, and we are much pleased with it; listen well, father, we pray you.

"Mrs de Tonty went away last year; she did not return; we see you going away to-day, father, with your wife, your children and all the Frenchwomen as well as that of M. Radisson, who is going down with you; that reveals to us that you abandon us.

"We are angry for good and ill-disposed if the women go away. We pray you to pay attention to this because we could not stop you nor your young men: we demand that Radisson remains, or at least, that he returns promptly.

By a Necklace (Wampum)

"We will escort your wife and the other Frenchwomen who intend to go down to Montreal. Now, mind well what we are asking you.

"We readily see that the Governor is a liar, as he does not keep to what he has promised us; as he has lied to us we will lie to him also, and we will listen no more to his word.

"What brings that man here (speaking of M. Desnoyers)? We do not know him and do not understand him; we are ill-disposed. It is two years since you have been gathering in our peltries, part of which has been taken down; we will allow nothing to leave until the French come up with goods.

By another Necklace

"Father, we pray you to send back that man (speaking of M. Desnoyers), because if he remains here, we do not answer for his safety; our people have told us that he despises our peltries and only wanted beaver; where does he want us to get it. We absolutely want him to go; nothing will leave the house where the trading is done and where the peltries and bundles are, until the French arrive here with merchandise and they be allowed to trade. When we came here, the Governor did not tell us that the merchants would be masters over the merchandise; he lied to us; we ask that all the Frenchmen trade here; we pray you to write and tell him what we are saying, and if he does not listen to us, we will also refuse to accept his word.

"The land is not yours, it is ours, and we will leave it to go where we like without anybody finding fault. We regret having allowed the surgeon to leave as we apprehend he will not come back.

"We pray you will cause to remain Gauvereau the blacksmith and gunsmith.

"I have nothing more to say, I have spoken for all the nations here present."

M. de Lamothe had a question put to the Ottawa and the other nations, if that was their sentiment; they all answered: Yes, and that they were of one and the same mind. He told them that, seeing they had taken time to think over what they had just said, he would consider as to what he had to answer them, and, put them off to the morrow, after having accepted their necklace.

(Not signed.)

COUNCIL

Held at fort Pontchartrain, in lake Erie strait, the 9th June, 1704.

By the indians Kiskacous; Ottawas; Sinagotres, the Sable nation; Hurons; Sauteux (Sault Ste Marie indians); Amikoique (Beaver nation); Mississaugas; Miamis and Wolves in the presence of M. de Lamothe-Cadillac, commanding at the said fort; de Tonty, captain of a detachment of Marines; the rev F. Constantin, Recollet missionary at the said post, Messrs Desnoyers and Radisson, principal clerks of the Company of the Colony, and of all the French, soldiers as well as *voyageurs*.

M. de Lamothe addressed all the said nations : —

"As you requested me to pay attention to your words, please listen, the same, to-day.

"I was aware that Mdme. de Tonty's trip to Montreal last year had given you umbrage, because she did not come back ; and the cause of it is her pregnancy.

"I knew also that my wife's setting out for Montreal as also the other Frenchwomen was causing you uneasiness, because you believed I was going to abandon you. It is true she was going away, but it was not for ever. I showed her your necklace ; that her children would miss her very much and that they begged of her to stay. When she heard of your grief, she accepted your necklace and she will stay for some time, because she does not like to refuse her children ; the other Frenchwomen will remain also.

"You spoke ill of the Governor when you said he was a liar. If anyone told you that he was forsaking you, I will be pleased if you will tell me who it is. As for me I have no knowledge of it.

"M. Desnoyers was present when you offered your necklace, and like me he heard your statement. He told me you were wrong to complain about him because he would not take your peltries and that he wanted beaver only ; you are complaining inopportunely seeing that he has not done any trading. You should tell me who made those reports. But as you are not glad to see him, he has decided to go back, and as I am going down to Montreal on good business, he will accompany me, and also M. Radisson, because the Governor wants him, and he must obey, and we will arrange so that we come back together.

"You have asked me to write down your speech to the Governor. I will be the bearer of it. I have not the authority to have the French to trade here ; it is a matter that M. the Governor will settle with M. the Intendant.

"The Governor did not lie to you because he did not notify you the first year, that the merchants would be masters of the merchandise, because it was the King who sent it here then and I could dispose of it ; since then, an order came from the King in favor of the merchants.

"This land is mine, because I am the first one who lighted a fire thereon, and you all took some to light yours.

"I am very glad that you like this land, and that you find it is good.

"It is of no consequence that the surgeon left, because when one goes another comes, and the same applies for the gunsmith.

"I have no more to tell you. Here is some tobacco that you may all smoke together, and that it may give you wisdom until I return and the Governor sends you his word. Attend to your mother during my absence, and see that she does not want for provisions, for if you do not take care of her, on my return I will not give you a drink of brandy.

"M. de Tonty replaces me ; I pray you to be on good terms with him."

FORTY SOLS, chief of the Hurons, spoke for all the indians : —

"We remember well, father, of what we said yesterday because you repeat it to-day. We thank you for having listened to us and granted all we asked you. We thank the women for not going away, because their remaining is as if you remained. From to-morrow we will stimulate our young men to go after provisions for our mother.

"It is three years ago, when in Montreal at the general meeting our chiefs died, the governor told us to have courage, that he was sorry for us, that he saw we were very far to come and get goods in Montreal, and he invited us to come and settle around you, and that he would send us merchandise at the same price as in Montreal. This worked well for two years, but goods rose up too much in price the third year.

"The first year you came, we were very happy, but now we are naked, not even having a bad shirt to put on our back. We would be pleased by the establishment of several stores here, because if we were refused in one, we could go to another.

"We are very glad of M. Desnoyers' going back because we do not know him and we fear some of our young men may be ill-disposed.

"We were under the impression the Governor had sold us to the merchants since they are the masters of the commerce.

"It is true that we took of your fire to light ours but we have waited two years without anything coming this way so that your land is ours. I told the same thing to the Governor last year in Montreal.

"Have courage, father, we will pray God for you during your voyage so that you may bring back good news."

(Not signed.)

APPENDIX D

AT QUEBEC, THE 25TH OCTOBER, 1735.

GENTLEMEN,

CIE DES INDES

(Indies Co'y)

Renders account to the said company of the death of Mr. Radisson, receiver at Montreal, of the nomination ad interim of Mr. Gamelin to fill the vacancy of receiver, of account to render by Mr. Duplessis, heir of Mr. Radisson to reëstablish price of summer beaver as before ordinance of the 4th January, 1733.

I have received the letter you did me the honor to send me of the 9th March last.

M. Radisson, your receiver at Montreal, died there the 14th of June, and immediately M. Gamelin, merchant, to whom Messrs La Gorgendière and Daine had given three years ago, had commissioned to look after your interests in default or in case of death of M. Radisson, applied to M. Michel, my sub-delegate to affix the seals on all your effects, which was done according to the account rendered you by Messrs. La Gorgendière and Daine.

It was necessary to fill the vacancy. I have appointed temporarily in virtue of the authority, you gave, gentlemen, the same M. Gamelin; I thought I could not have your interests in better hands, as much for his honesty than his intelligence in regulating his sales and his receipts. Independently of the knowledge he has of the different qualities of beaver, I have had the honor to speak to you on this subject in my preceding letters and to say that the only obstacle I find to giving him the office of receiver at Montreal was his quality of merchant outfitter for the upper country, which might render him suspicious to you because of the returns he gets in beaver. Although I have a pretty good opinion of him to believe his loyalty proof against any particular interest, you shall see, gentlemen, by the copy of the commission I have given him, which is sent you, that it is on condition either directly or indirectly to do no traffic in the upper country, and to confine himself either to marine trade or other inland commerce, to which he has agreed, but nevertheless has represented to me that being engaged as a partner with M. Lamarque, another merchant, for the working out of the post named "the Western Sea" and that of the Sioux ; this partnership only terminating in 1737 ; that he was looking around to sell his share, but, if this thing was impossible requesting me to kindly allow him to continue until that term, past which he would cease all commerce in the upper country. I agreed to this arrangement on account of his good qualities, and this will not turn to any account of consequence ; whatever, selection you may make, gentlemen, you will not find a better one in this country.

M. de La Gorgendière having offered me his son to act as clerk to M. Gamelin and comptroller in the Montreal office, for the auditing to be made, without increasing on that score the expenditure of your administration, I have consented on these conditions ; M. Gamelin to give him 800 livres (shillings) on the commission of one per cent the company allow the receiver at Montreal, and

M. Daine has assured me he was satisfied with his work.

I will not entertain, you, messieurs, with the discussion of the account to be rendered by M. Duplessis, M. Radisson's heir, to your agent, who claims he owes 5 to 6000 livres. Those discussions did not take place in my presence.

Most of the beaver shipped this year were put up in bundles, and shortage in cotton cloth for packing prevented shipment of the whole.

The disturbances which have occurred for some years in the upper country have effectively prevented the indians from hunting; the post of the Bay which abounds ordinarily with beaver, produced nothing; those of Detroit and Michilimakinac, only furnished very little. Happily the post of the Sioux and of the Western Sea produced near to 100,000 which swelled up the receipt; otherwise it would have been very middling.

The party commanded by M. Desnoyelles against the indians Sakis and Foxes was not as successful as expected on account of the desertion and retreat of 100 Hurons and Iroquois who left him when at the Kakanons (Kiskanons of Michilimakinac?) without his being able to hold them, so that this officer found himself after a long tramp at those indians' fort, not only inferior in numbers but also much in want of provisions. He was under the necessity of returning after a rather sharp skirmish which took place between some of his men and the enemy. We lost two Frenchmen and one of our indians; the Foxes and Sakis lost 21 men, either killed, wounded or captured.

If the Sakis come back to the Bay, as they

pledged themselves to M. Desnoyelles we are in hopes here that peace will again flourish and consequently the trade of the upper country.

I have seen, gentlemen, what you were pleased to say as to reduction in price on the summer-beaver. I had been assured by reliable persons that this reduction might become very injurious to your commerce. I have learned that some of this kind of beaver were carried to the English who pay two livres (shillings) for one and at a higher price than you pay over your counters. It was from what you wrote me in 1732, that the hatters could make no use of that beaver, that at your request I published an ordinance of the 4th January, 1733, reducing the price of summer-beaver either green (gras) or dry (sec) to ten pence a pound, on condition that it should be burned. There could be nothing suspicious in that. But since you now deem that that reduction may be harmful, as I have also had in mind to invite the indians and even the French under this pretence to take the good as well as the bad beaver to the English ; I will restore the price of the summer-beaver as it was before my ordinance. I will not be at a loss for a cause : it is not in your interest to give a lower price. You run your commerce, gentlemen, with too much good faith to give rise to suspicion that you wished for a reduction in price to 10 pence for this kind of beaver, and having it burned only to procure it yourself at that price and not burn it. Besides, the quantity received is too small a matter to deserve consideration.

M. the marquis de Beauharnois and I have received the orders of the King with reference to

Beaver hats half worked made in the country.

beaver hats half worked made in Canada. His Majesty has ordered us to break up the workmen's benches and to prevent any manufacture of hats. We have made some representations on this subject, to those made to us, namely by a man named   , hatter, and your receiver at Quebec. It is true that the making of beaver hats half worked and other for export to France could turn out of consequence in ruining your privilege and the hat establishments in France. These are the only inconveniences, to my mind, to be feared, as I do not look upon such, the making of hats for the use of residents of the country. So that we have satisfied ourselves, until further orders, to forbid the going, out of the colony, of all kind of hats, as you will see by the ordinance we have published together, M. the General and I. If we had been more strict, the three hatters established in this colony, who know no other business than their trade, the man   amongst others, who follow that calling from father to son, would have been reduced to begging.

The quantity of hats they will manufacture when export is stopped, cannot be of any injury to the manufactures of the kingdom and be but of small matter to your commerce. Moreover, I am aware that these hatters employ the worst kind of beaver, which they get very cheap, and your stores at Paris are that much rid of them.

Defects in list of cloth sent.

The cloths you sent this year are of better quality than the precedding shipment. Messrs La Gorgendière, Daine and Gamelin have observed on defects which happen in the lists; they told me they would inform you.

Remittance of 300 livres (shillings) to the Baron de Longueuil.

I have the honor to thank you, gentlemen, for the remittance of 300 livres you were pleased to grant to M. the Baron of Longueuil, on my recommendation.

It is very difficult to prevent the indians going to Chouaguen; the brandy that the English give out freely is an invincible attraction.

I have heard, the same as you, that some Frenchmen disguised as indians had been there; if I can discover some one, you may be sure that I will deal promptly with them. You may have heard that the man LENOIR, resident of Montreal, having gone to England three years ago without leave, I have kept him in prison till he had settled the fine he was condemned to pay, and which I transferred to the hospitals. I add that a part of the interest you have in the indians not going to Chouaguen, I have another on account of the trading carried on for the benefit of the King at Niagara and at fort Frontenac which that English post has ruined. By all means you may rely on my attention to break up English trade. I fear I may not succeed in this so long as the brandy traffic, although moderate, will find adversaries among those who govern consciences.

Foreign trade; Beaver at trade at Labrador.

I will do my best to prevent the beaver which is traded at Labrador and the other posts in the lower part of the River to be smuggled to France by ships from Bayonne, St Malo and Marseille. This will be difficult as we cannot have at those posts any inspector. I will try, however, to give an ordinance so as to prevent that, which may intimidate some of those who carry on that commerce.

It is true that the commandants of the upper country posts have relaxed in the sending of the declarations made or to be made by the *voyageurs* as to the quantity and quality of the bundles of beaver they take down to Montreal. M. the General and I have renewed the necessary orders on this subject so that the commandants shall conform to them.

M. Michel, my subdelegate at Montreal has received the bounty of 500 livres you have requested your agent to pay to him ; he hopes that you will be pleased to have it continued next year. I have the honor to pray you to do so, and even augment it, if possible. I can assure you, gentlemen that he lends himself on all occasions to all that may concern your commerce. As for myself, I am very flattered by the opinion you entertain that I have at heart your interests. I always feel a true satisfaction in renewing you these assurances.

I am, respectfully,

GENTLEMEN, M. de La Gorgendière has delivered to me on your behalf, a bale of Moka coffee. I am very sensible, gentlemen, to this token of friendship on your part.

I have the honor to thank you, and to assure you that I am very truly and respectfully, etc.

(signed) HOCQUART.

APPENDIX E

MEMORANDUM RE CANADA

(No locality) 1697

All the discoveries in America were only made step by step and little by little, especially those of lands held by the French in that part of the North.

It being certain that during the reign of king Francis I, several of his subjects, amateurs of shipping and of discoveries, in imitation of the Portuguese and the Spaniards, made the voyage, where they found the great cod bank. The quality of birds frequenting this sea where they always find food, caused them to heave the lead, and bottom was found and the said great bank.

He got an opinion on the nearest lands, and other curious persons desired to go farther, and discovered Cape Breton, Virginia and Florida. Some even inhabited and took possession of the divers places, abandoned since, through misunderstanding of the commanders and their poor skill in knowing how to keep on good terms with the indians of those countries, who, good natured all at the beginning, could not suffer the rigor with which it was wanted to subjugate them, so that after a short occupation, they left to return to Europe. And since, the Spaniards and the English successfully have taken possession of the land and all the coasts that the said English have kept until this day to much advantage, so that Frenchmen who have returned since have been obliged to settle at Cape Breton and Acadia.

About the year 1540, the said Cape Breton was fortified by Jacques Cartier, captain of St Malo, who afterward entered the river St. Lawrence up to 7 or 8 leagues above Quebec, where desiring to know more, the season also being too far advanced he stopped off to winter at a small river which bears his name and which forms the boundary of M. de Bécancourt's land whom he knew ; he made sociable a number of indians who came aboard his ship and brought back beaver pretty abundantly.

Since, he made another voyage with Saintonge men which did not prevent several other ships to go after the said beaver ; men from Dieppe, Brittany and La Rochelle, some with a passport and others by fraud and piracy, especially the latter, the Civil war having carried away persons out of dutifulness, the Admiralty and the Marine being then held in very little consideration, which lasted a long time.

However, I believe for having heard it said, that the lands after new discoveries were given since to M. Chabot or to M. Ventadour, where a certain gentleman from Saintonge named M. du Champlain, had very free admittance and who may have mingled with those of his country who had navigated with Cartier and had given him a longing to see that of which he had only heard speak.

He was a proper man for such a scheme ; a great courage, wisdom, sensible, pious, fair and of great experience ; a robust body which would render him indefatigable and capable to resist hunger, cold and heat.

This gentleman then solicited permission to come to Canada and obtained it. His small estate and his friends supplied him with a medium sized vessel for the passage. This new commandant or governor pitied much the indians and had the satisfaction at his arrival to see that he was much feared and loved by them. He took memoranda through his interpreter of their wars, their mode of living and of their interests. At that time they were numerous and proud of the great advantages they had over the Iroquois, their enemy. With this information he recrossed to France ; gave an account of his voyage, and was so charmed with the land, the climate and of the good which would result from a permanent establishment that he persuaded his wife to accompany him. His example induced missionaries of St François and some parisian families to follow him. He was granted a commission or governor's provisions to take his living from the country.

He erected a palissade fort at the place now occupied by the fort St Louis of Quebec.

To please the indians he went with them and three Frenchmen only, warring in the Iroquois country, which has no doubt given rise to our quarrel with this nation.

The Commerce was then in the hands of the Rochelois (?) who supplied some provisions to the said M. de Champlain, a man without interest and disposed to be content with little.

He returns to France in the interests of the country and took back Madam his wife who died in a Ursuline convent, at Saintes, I believe, and he at Quebec, after having worked hard there, with little help because of the misfortunes of France.

M. the Cardinal of Richelieu have inspired France with confidence by the humiliation of the Rochelois (?) wanted to take care of the marine and formed at that time, about 1626 or 1627 what was then called the "Society of One Hundred," in which joined persons of all qualifications, and also merchants from Dieppe and Rouen. Dieppe was then reputed for good navigators and for navigation.

The said M. the Cardinal got granted to the said company the islands of St Christophe, newly discovered and all the lands of Canada. The Company composed of divers states did not take long to disjoin, and of this great Company several were formed by themselves, the ones concerning themselves about the Isles and the others about Canada, where they were also divided up in a Company of Miscou, which is an island of the Bay in the lower part of the River, where all the indians meet, and a Company of Tadoussac or Quebec.

The Basques, Rochelois, Bretons, and Normans, who during the disorders of the war had commenced secretly on the River, crossed their commerce much by the continuation of their runs without passport. Sometimes on pretext of cod or whale fishing, notwithstanding the interdiction of decrees, the gain made them risk everything, as the two sides of the river were all settled and many more came down from inland.

Those Companies for being badly served on account of inexperience and through poor economy, as will happen at the beginning of all affairs, were put to large expenses.

The English had already seized on Boston abandoned by the French after their new discovery ; beaver and elk peltry were much sought after and at a very high price in Europe ; they could be had for a needle, a hawk-bell or a tin looking-glass, a marked copper coin. Our possession was there very well-off. The English who made war to us in France, also made it in Canada, and began to take the fleet about Ile Percée, as it was ascending to Quebec.

As four or five vessels came every year loaded with goods for the indians, it was at that time quantity of peas, plums, raisins, figs and others and provisions for M. de Champlain; a garrison of 15 or 20 men; a store in the lower town where the clerks of the Company lived with 10 or 12 families already used to the country. This succor failing, much hardship was endured in a country which then produced nothing by itself, so that the English presenting themselves the next year with their fleet, surrender was obligatory; the governor and the Recollets crossed over to France and the families were treated honestly enough.

Happily in 1628 or 1629, France made it up with England and the treaty gave back Canada to the French, when M. de Champlain, returned and died some years later.

Those of the Company of 100, who were persons of dignity and consideration, living in Paris, thought fit to leave the care and benefits of commerce for Canada with the Rouen and Dieppe merchants, with whom joined a few from Paris. They were charged with the payment of the governor's appointments, to furnish him with provisions and subsistence and to keep up the garrisons of Quebec and Three-Rivers where there was also a post on account of the large number of indians calling; to furnish the things necessary for the war; to pay themselves off the product and give account of the surplus to the directors of the Company who had an office at Paris.

It has been said that Dieppe and Rouen benefitted and that Paris suffered and was disgusted.

To M. de Champlain succeeded M. de Montmagny, very wise and very dignified; knight of Malta; relative of M. de Poinsy, who commanded at the Island of St Christophe where the said M. de Montmagny died after leaving Canada after a sojourn of 14 or 15 years, loved and cherished by the French and the natives — we say the

2 A

French, although the complaints made against him by the principals were the cause of his sorrow and he resigned voluntarily.

It is to be remarked that all the commerce was done at Rouen to go out through Dieppe on the hearsay and the fine connections that the Jesuit Fathers who had taken the Recollets' place, took great care to have printed and distributed every year.

Canada was in vogue and several families from Normandy and the Perche took sail to come and reside in it; there were nobles, the most of them poor, we might say, who found out from the first, that M. de Montmagny was too disinterested to be willing to consider the change they desired for their advantage. They intrigued against him five or six families without the participation of the others, got leave from him to go to France to ask for favors and there had one of themselves as governor; obtained liberty in the beaver trade, which until then had been strictly forbidden to the inhabitants who had been reserved the fruits of the country to advance the culture of the land such as pease, indian corn, and wheat bread. That was the first title of the inhabitants to trade with the indians.

To arrive at that end they promised to pay annually 1000 beaver to the Paris office for its seignorial right which it did not receive through its attention and management of its affairs.

They got permission to form a Board from their principal men, to transact with the governor all matters in the country for peace, for war, the settlement of accounts of their society or little republic, and also sitting on cases concerning interests of private individuals.

It was then that to keep up this sham republic or society, a tax of one-fourth was imposed on the export of beaver.

By these means the authority of the Company and its store were ruined and the whole was turning to the advantage of those four or six families, the others, either poor or slighted by the authority of M. D'Ailleboust, their governor.

On this footing it was not hard for them to find large credit at La Rochelle, because loans were made in the name of the Community, although it consisted only of these four or six families;

which from their being poor found themselves in large managements
enlarged their household, ran into expense, that of their vessels and
shipments was excessive and the wealth derived from the beaver was
to pay all.

Their bad management altered their credit and brought them to
agree, after several years' enjoyment so as not to pay La Rochelle, to
take their ships to Hâvre-de-Grâce, where, on arrival they sold
to Messrs Lick and Tabac ; this perfidy which they excused because
of the large interest taken from them, alarmed La Rochelle who complained to Paris, and after much pressing a trustee was appointed to
give bonds in the name of the society for large sums yet due to the city
of La Rochelle.

Their vessels all bore off to Normandy ; they took on their cargoes there in part, and part at La Rochelle, the trade having been
allowed those two places, because Rouen and Dieppe had several persons on the roll of the Company and obligation was due La Rochelle
for having loaned property.

The governor and the families addressed reproaches to each other,
and the King being pleased to listen to them, had the kindness to appoint from the body of the company persons of first dignity to give
attention to what was going on in this colony, who were called Commissioners ; they were Messrs de Morangis, de la Marguerid, Vertha-
mont and Chame, and since, Messrs de Lamoignon, de Boucherat
and de Lauzon, the latter also of the body of the Company offered to
pass over to this country to arrange the difficulties, and he asked for its
government, which was accorded him.

He embarked at La Rochelle because of the obligation of the creditors of that city to treat him gently ; Rouen did not care much. He
was a literary man ; he made friends with the R. F. Jesuits, and
created a new council in virtue of the powers he had brought, rebuke
the one and the other place, even the inhabitants, in forbidding them
to barter in what was called the limits of Tadoussac, which he bounded
for a particular lease as a security for his payment and of what has
always since been called the offices of the country or the state of the

33,000 livres ; the emoluments of the Councillors, the garrison, the Jesuits, the Parish, the Ursulines, the Hote-Dieu, etc.

The pretext given was that the Iroquois having burned and ruined the Hurons or Ottawa, the tax of one-fourth did not produce enough to meet those demands, and because Tadoussac also was not sufficient to meet all the expenditure contemplated to give war to the Iroquois, he it was also who began in not paying the thousand weight in beaver owing for seignorial right to the Company who was irritated and blamed his conduct, and after the lapse of some years his friends write him they could not longer shield him he anticipated his recall in returning to France, where he has since served as sub-dean of the Council, residing at the cloister of Notre-Dame with his son, canon at the said church.

I only saw him two years in Canada where he was hardly liked, by reason of the little care he took to keep up his rank, without servant, living on pork and peas like an artisan or a peasant.

However, having decided to go back, for a second time he threw open the Tadoussac trade, by an order of his Council.

M. de Lamoignon, the first president, got named to replace him, M. D'Argenson, young man of 30 to 32 years steady as could be, who remained four or five years to the satisfaction of everybody ; he kept up the Council as it is intended for the security of his emoluments and of the garrison, selected twelve of the most notable persons to whom he gave the faculty of trading at Tadoussac and all the sureties to be wished for the administration and maintenance.

He had the misfortune to fall out with the Jesuit Fathers, and they, with messieurs de Mont Royal, of St Sulpice who had sent Mr the abbey de Queysac, in the hope of making a bishop of him ; the former wishing to have one of their nomination presented to the Queen-mother of the reigning King, whom God preserve, M. de Laval, to-day elder and first bishop, who, very rigid, not only backed the Jesuits against the governor in all difficulties but specially in the matter of the liquor traffic with the indians. Although (D'Argenson) a much God-fearing-man he had his private opinions, and this offended him ; he asked M. de Lamoignon for his recall, which was done in 1661, when M. d'Avaugour came out.

It was in 1660 that the Office in Paris, at the request of the governor, of the Local council and on the advice of Messrs de Lamoignon, Chame and other commissioners made an agreement with the Rouen merchants to supply the inhabitants with all goods they would require with 60% profit on dry goods and 100% on liquors, freight paid.

It was pretended that the country was not safely secured by ships of private parties, and that when they arrived alone by unforeseen accidents, they happened unexpectedly, to the ruin of the country ; as well as the beaver fallen to a low price and which was restored only at the marriage of the king should keep up.

The creditors then pressing payment of their claims, a decree ordered that of the 60%, 10% should be taken for the payment of debts which were fixed at 10,000 livres at the rate of the consumption of the time and of which the Company of Normandy took charge.

The country was favorable enough to this treaty because they were well served, but when the treaty arrived at first, the bishop who was jealous because he had not been consulted and that some little gratification had been given to facilitate matters had it opposed by some of the inhabitants and by M. D'Avaugour, governor in the place of the said D'Argenson.

The Society of Normandy consented to the breaking off of the treaty on receiving a minute account and being paid some compensation, as to which they had no satisfaction because of the changes, for M. D'Avaugour, like the others, fell out with the Bishop who went to France and had him revoked, presenting in his stead M. de Mézy, a Norman gentleman who did nothing better than to overdo all the difficulties arising on the question of the Bishop and the Governor's powers.

The beaver dropped down, as soon, to a low price, and there was a difference by half when the King in 1664 formed the Company of the West Indies, which alone, to the exclusion of all others, had to supply the country with merchandise and receive also all the beaver ; in 1669, came M. de Tracy, de Courcelles and Talon ; the latter did not want any Company and employed all kinds of ways to ruin the one he found established. He gave to understand to M. Colbert that this country was too big to be bounded ; that there should come out of it fleets and armies ; his plans appeared too broad, still he met with no contradiction at first, on the contrary he was lauded, which moved him to establish a large trade and put out that of the company, which through bad success in its affairs at the Isles, was relaxing enough of itself in all sorts of undertakings.

M. Talon desiring to bring together the government and the superintendence was spending on a large scale to make friends and therefore there was not a merchant when the Company quit who could transact any business in his presence ; he gets his goods free of dues, freight and insurance ; he also refused to pay the import tax on his wines, liquors and tobacco.

Finally his friends or enemies told him aloud that it was of profits of his commerce that the King would be enriched.

They fell out, M. de Courcelles and he ; their misunderstanding forced the first to ask for his discharge. M. de Frontenac, who succeeded him also complained and I believe he returned to France without his congé whence he never came back although he had promised so to all his friends.

You are aware as well as and perhaps better than I of the disputes of M. de Frontenac and M. du Chesneau.

And that is all I have been told for my satisfaction of what occurred previous to 1655 when I came here to attend to the affairs of the Rouen Company.

I have also learned at the time of my arrival that properly speaking, though there were a very large number of indians, known under divers names, which they bear with reference to certain action that their chiefs had performed or with reference to lakes, rivers, lands or mountains which they inhabit, or sometimes to animals stocking their rivers and forests, nevertheless they could all be comprised under two mother languages, to wit : the Huron and the Algonquin.

At that period, I was told, the Huron was the most spread over men and territory, and at present, I believe, that the Algonquin can well be compared to it.

To note, that all the indians of the Algonquin language are stationed and occupy land that we call land of the North on account of the River which divides the country into two parts, and where they all live by fishing and hunting.

As well as the indians of the Huron language who inhabit land to the South, where they till the land and winter wheat, horse-beans, pease, and other similar seeds to subsist; they are sedentary and the Algonquin follow fish and game.

However, this nation has always passed for the noblest, proudest and hardest to manage when prosperous. When the French came here the true Algonquin owned land from Tadoussac to Quebec, and I have always thought they were issued from the Saguenay. It was a tradition that they had expelled the Iroquois from the said place of Quebec and neighborhood where they once lived; we were shown the sites of their villages and towns covered by trees of a fresh growth, and now that the lands are of value through cultivation, the farmers find thereon tools, axes and knives as they were used to make them.

We must believe that the said Algonquin were really masters over the said Iroquois, because they obliged them to move away so far.

Nobody could tell me anything certain about the origin of their war but it was of a more cruel nature between these two nations than between the said Iroquois and Hurons, who have the same language or nearly so.

It is only known that the Iroquois commenced first to burn, importuned by their enemies who came to break their heads whilst at work in their wilderness; they imagined that such cruel treatment would give them relaxation, and since, all the nations of this continent have used fire, with the exception of the Abenakis and other tribes of Virginia.

These Iroquois having had the best of the fight and reduced the Algonquins since our discovery of this country, principally because their pride giving us apprehension about their large number, they would not arm themselves until a long time after the Dutch had armed the Iroquois, made war and ruined all the other nations who were not nearly so warlike as the Algonquin, and after the war, diseases came on that killed those remaining ; some have scattered in the woods, but in comparison to what I have seen on my arrival, one might say that there are no more men in this country outside of the fastnesses of the forests recently discovered.

The Hurons before their defeat by the Iroquois had, through the hope of their conversion obliged the Jesuits to establish with them a strong mission, and as from time to time it was necessary to carry to them necessities of life, the governors began to allow some of their servants to run up there every three or four years, from where they brought that good green (gras) Huron beaver that the hatters eek for so much.

Sometimes this was kept up ; sometimes no one offered for the voyage there being then so little greediness it is true that the Iroquois were so feared ; M. de Lauson was the only one to send two individuals in 1656 who each secured 14 to 15,000 livres and came back with an indian fleet worth 100,000 crowns. However, M. D'Argenson who succeeded him and was five years in the country sent nobody neither did Messrs Avaugour and de Mézy.

It was consequently after the arrival of M. Talon that under pretext of discovery, and of finding copper mines, he alone became director of those voyages, for he obliged M. de Courcelles to sign him congés which he got worked, but on a dispute between the workers he handled some himself, of which I remember.

You know the number and the regulations given under the first administration of M. the Earl of Frontenac.

It is certain that it is the holders of congés who look after and bring down the beaver, and, can it be said that it is wrong to have an abundance of goods.

The French and the indians have come down this year ; the receipts of the office must total up 200 millions or thereabouts, which judging from your letter, will surprise those gentlemen very much. The clerks have rejected it as much as they liked ; I am told that they admitted somewhere about six thousands of muscovy ; during our administration there were 28 or 30 thousands received, which is a large difference without taking into account other qualities, and all this does not give the French much trouble, and at the most for the year we were not informed. I have given my sentiments to the meeting, and in particular to M. de Frontenac and to M. de Champigny.

We should be agreeable to our Prince's wishes who is doing so much good to this country : his tenants who must supply him in such troubled times, lose, and it is proper that people in Canada contribute something to compensate them by freely agreeing to a pretty rich receipt on their commodity but what resource in regard to the indian so interested that everything moves with him, through necessity ; they are asked and sought after to receive English goods, infinitely better than ours, at a cost half as low and to pay their beaver very high.

This commercial communication gives them peace with their enemies and liberty to hunt, and consequently to live in abundance instead of their living at present with great hardship. Should we not say that it requires a great affection not to break away in the face of such strong attractions ; if we lose them once we lose them for ever, that it is certain, and from friends they become our enemies ; thus we lose not only the beaver but the colony, and absolutely no more cattle, no more grains, no more fishing.

The colony with all the forces of the Kingdom cannot resist the indians when they have the English or other Europeans to supply them with ammunitions of war, which leads me to the query : what is the beaver worth to the English that they seek to get it by all means ?

If also the rumors set agoing are true the farmers-general would not sell a considerable part to the Danes at a very high price, should they not have had somebody in their employ who understands and knows that article well ; it appears to me that the thing is worth while.

All the same, people are asking why they want to sell so dear, what costs them so little, for taking one and the other, that going out this year should not cost them more than 50 s (sous), the entries, Tadoussac, and the tax of one fourth, does it not pay the lease with profit. This is in everybody's mind, and everyone looks at it as he fancies.

I was of opinion to arrange the receipts on a basis that these gentlemen got M. Benac to offer, so as to avoid the difficulties on the
qualities, and this opinion served to examine the loss this proposition
would bring to the country in the general receipt.

I have no other interest than the Prince's service, and to please
these gentlemen I should like to know, heartily, of some expedient,
because it is absolutely necessary to find one to satisfy the indian ; M.
the Earl of Frontenac is under a delusion : I may say it, they will give
us the goby, and after that all shall be lost, I am not sure even, if they
would not repeat the Sicilian Vespers, to show their good will, and
that they never want to make it up.   I am so isolated that I do not
say anything about it, as I am afraid for myself, but I know well that
it is indian's nature to betray, and that our affairs are not at all good
in the upper country.

To a great evil great remedy.   I had said to M. de Frontenac
that the 25 per cent could be abolished and make it up on something
else, as it is a question of saving the country, but he did not deem fit
of anything being said about it.

I also told him and M. de Champigny that we might treat with a
Dutchman to bring on a clearance English and Dutch goods which are
much thought of by our indians for their good quality and their price,
that this vessel would not go up the river but stay below at a stated
place, where we could go for his goods, and give him beaver for his
rightful lading.

The company should have the control of these merchandise, so as
to sell them to the indians on the base of a tariff, so as to prevent the
greediness of the *voyageurs* which contributes very much to the discontent of the natives, because at first the French only went to the Hurons
and since to Michilimakinac where they sold to the indians of the locality,
who then went to exchange with other indians in distant woods, lands
and rivers, but now the said Frenchmen holding permits to have a
larger gain pass over all the Ottawas and indians of Michilimakinac to
go themselves and find the most distant tribes which displeased the
former very much.

APPENDIX

This has led to fine discoveries and four or five hundred young men of Canada's best men are employed at this business.

Through them we have become acquainted with several indian's names we knew not, and 4 and 500 leagues farther away, there are other indians unknown to us.

Down the Gulf in French Acadia, we have always known the Abenakis and Micmacs.

On the north shore of the River, from Seven islands up we have always known the Papinachois, Montagnais, Poissons Blancs, (White Fish), (these being in what is called limits of Tadoussac), Mistassinis, Algonquins.

At Quebec

There are Hurons, remains of the ancient Hurons, defeated by the Iroquois, in Lake Huron.

There is also south of the Chaudiere (River), five leagues from Quebec, a large village of christian Abenakis.

The Hurons & Abenakis are under the Jesuit Fathers.

These Hurons have staid at Quebec so as to pray God more conveniently and without fear of the Iroquois.

The Abenakis pray God with more fervor than any indians of these countries. I have seen and been twice with them when warring ; they must have faith to believe as they do and their exactitude to live well according to principles of our religion. Blessed be God ! They are very good men at war and those who have give and still give so much trouble to the Bostoners.

At Three-Rivers

Wolves and Algonquins both sides of the river.

At Montroyal or Ville-Marie

There are Iroquois of the five nations who have left their home to pray (everyone is free to believe) but it is certain that threefourths have no other motive nor interest to stay with us than to pray.

There are, then, Senecas, Mohawks, Cayugas, Wyandotts, Oneida partly on the mountain of Mont-Royal under the direction of Messrs of St Sulpice, and partly at the Sault (Recollet) south side, that is to say, above the rapids; under the R. F. Jesuits, whose mission is larger than St Sulpice's.

150 leagues from Mont Royal the Grand River leading to the Ottawas; to the north are the Temiscamingues, Abitiby, Outanloubys, who speak Algonquin.

At lake Nepissing, the Nipissiniens, Algonquin language, always going up the Grand River.

In lake Huron, 200 leagues from Montreal, the Mississagues and Amikoués : Algonquins.

At Michilimackinac, the Negoaschendaching or people of the Sable, Ottawas, Linago Kikacons or Cut Tail, the men from Forked Lake Onnasaccoctois, the Hurons, in all 1000 men or thereabouts half Huron and half Algonquin language.

In the Michigan or lake Illinois, north side, the Noquets, Algonquins, Malomini (Menomeenee), or men of the Folle-Avoine : different language.

South of Puants (Green) Bay

The Wanebagoes otherwise Puans, because of the name of the Bay; language different from the two others.

The Sakis, 3 leagues from the Bay, and Pottewatamis, about 200 warriors.

Towards lake Illinois, on River St Joseph, the Miamis or men of the Crane who have three different languages, though they live together. United they would form about 600 men.

Above the Bay, on Fox river, the Ottagamis, the Mascoutins and the Kicapoos : all together 1200 men.

At Maramegue river where is situated Nicholas Perrot's post, are some more Miamis numbering five to six hundred; always the same language.

The Illinois midway on the Illinois river making 5 to 6 different villages, making in all 2000 men.

We traffic with all these nations who are all at war with the Iroquois.

In the lower Missipy there are several other nations very numerous with whom we have no commerce and who are trading yet with nobody.

Above Missoury river which is of the Mississippi below the river Illinois, to the south, there are the Mascoutins Nadoessioux, with whom we trade, and who are numerous.

Sixty leagues above the missisipi and St Anthony of Padua Fall, there is lake Issaquy otherwise lake of Buade, where there are 23 villages of Sioux Nadoessioux who are called Issaquy, and beyond lake Oettatous, lower down the auctoustous, who are Sioux, and could muster together 4000 warriors. Because of their remoteness they only know the Iroquois from what they heard the French say.

In lake Superior, south side are the saulteurs who are called Ouchijoé (objibway), Macomili, Ouxcinacomigo, Mixmac and living at Chagoumigon, it is the name of the country, the Malanas or men of the Cat-fish; 60 men; always the Algonquin language.

Michipicoten, name of the land; the Machacoutiby and Opendachiliny, otherwise Dung-heads; lands' men; algonquin language.

The Picy is the name of a land of men, way inland, who come to trade.

Bagoasche, also name of a place of men of same nation who come also to trade 200 and 300 men.

Osepisagny river being discharge of lake Asémipigon; sometimes the indians of the lake come to trade; they are called Kristinos and the nation of the Great Rat. These men are Algonquins, numbering more than 2000, and also go to trade with the English of the north.

There are too the Chichigoe who come sometimes to us, sometimes north to the English.

Towards West-Northwest, it is nations called Fir-trees; numerous; all their traffic is with the English.

All those north nations are rovers, as was said, living on fish and game or wild-oats which is abundant on the shores of their lakes and rivers.

In lake Ontario, south side, the five Iroquois nations ; our enemies ; about 1200 warriors live on indian corn and by hunting.

We can say, that, of all the indians they are the most cruel during war, as during peace, they are the most humane, hospitable, and sociable; they are sensible at their meetings, and their behaviour resembles much to the manners of republics of Europe.

Lake Ontario has 200 leagues in circumference.

Lake Erie above Niagara 250 leagues ; lakes Huron and Michigan joined 552 leagues : to have access to these three lakes by boat, there is only the portage of Niagara, of two leagues, above the said lake Ontario.

All those who have been through those lakes say they are terrestrial paradises for abundance of venison, game, fishing, and good quality of the land.

From the said lakes to go to lake Superior there is only one portage of 15 (?) The said lake is 500 leagues long in a straight line, from point to point, without going around coves nor the bays of Michipicoten and Kaministiquia.

To go from lake Superior to lake Asemipigon there is only 15 leagues to travel, in which happen seven portages averaging 3 good leagues ; the said lake has a circumference of 280 leagues.

From lake Huron to lake Nipissing there is the river called French River, 25 leagues long ; there are 3 portages ; the said lake has 60 to 80 leagues of circumference.

Lake Assiniboel is larger than lake Superior, and an infinity of others, lesser and greater have to be discovered, for which I approve of M. the Marquis of Denonville's saying, often repeated : — that the King of France, our monarch was not high lord enough to open up such a vast country, as we are only beginning to enter on the confines of the immensity of such a great country.

The road to enter it is by the Grand River and lake Ontario by Niagara, which should be easy in peaceful times in establishing families at Niagara for the portage, and building boats on Lake Erie. I did not find that a difficult thing, and I want to do it under M. the Marquis of Denonville, who did not care, so soon as he perceived that his war expedition had not succeeded.

I have given you in this memorandum the names of the natives known to us and with whom our wood rovers (coureurs de bois) have traded; my information comes from some of the most experienced.

The surplus of the memorandum will serve to inform you that prior to M. de Tracy, de Courcelle and Talon's arrival, nothing was regulated but by the governor's will, although there was a Board; as they were his appointments and that by appearances, only his creatures got in, he was the absolute master of it and which was the cause that the Colony and the inhabitants suffered very much at the beginning.

M. de Tracy on his arrival by virtue of his commission dismissed the Board and the Councillors, to appoint another one with members chosen by himself and the Bishop, which existed until the 2nd and 3rd year of M. de Frontenac's reign, who had them granted at Court, provisions by a decree for the establishment of the Council.

It is only from that time that the King having given the country over to the gentlemen of the Co'y of West Indies, the tax of one fourth and the Tadoussac trade were looked upon as belonging to the Company, and since to the King, because M. Talon, who crippled as much as he could, this company dare not touch to these two items of the Domain, of which the enjoyment remained to them until cessation of their lease.

So, it was in favor of this company that all the regulations were granted in reference to the limits and working out of Tadoussac as well as to prevent cheating on the beaver tax.

Tadoussac is leased to six gentlemen for the sum of   yearly; I took shares for one fourth, as it was an occasion to dispose of some goods and a profit to everyone of at most 20   yearly.

About beavers there is no fraud to be feared, everybody preferring to get letters of exchange to avoid the great difficulties on going out, the entry and sale in France, and of large premiums for the risks; in a word, no one defrauds nor thinks of it. The office is not large enough to receive all the beaver.

The ships came in very late ; I could not get M. Dumenu the secretary to the Board to send you the regulations you ask for the beaver trade ; you shall have them, next year, if it pleases God. They contain prohibition to embark from France under a penalty of 3000 livres' fine, confiscation of the goods, even of the ships ; however, under the treaty of Normandy, I had a Dieppe captain seized for about 200 crowns worth of beaver, and the Council here confiscated the vessel, and imposed a fine of 1500 livres, on which the captain appealed to France, and he obtained at the King's Council, replevin on his ship and the fine was reduced to 30 livres.

As prior to M. Talon nobody sent traders in the woods as explained in this memorandum there was not to my knowledge any regulation as to the said woods before the decree of 1675. On the contrary I remember that those two individuals under M. de Lauzon's government who brought in each for 14. or 15,000 livres applied to me to be exempted from the tax of one fourth, because, they said we were obliged to them for having brought down a fleet which enriched the country.

(Not signed.)

INDEX

A

Abenaki Indians, the, 363.

Abitiby Indians, the, 364.

Acadia, Indian tribes located in, 363.

Albanel, Charles, Jesuit missionary, 141; overland trip of, to Hudson Bay, 143–146; at King Charles Fort, 147.

Albany (Orange), 32 ; Iroquois freebooting expedition against, 36–38 ; Radisson's escape to, 39–41.

Algonquin Indian, murder of Mohawk hunters by a, 20.

Algonquin Indians, Radisson and Groseillers travel to the West with, 73–79 ; territory of the, 359 ; wars with the Iroquois, 359–360 ; tribes of, on Lake Huron, 364.

Allemand, Pierre, companion of Radisson, 154.

Allouez, Père Claude, 142.

Amsterdam, Radisson's early visit to, 42.

Arctic Ocean, Hearne's overland trip to, 257–265 ; arrival at, 265–266 ; Mackenzie's trip of exploration to, 281–286.

Arms, supplied to Mohawks by Dutch, 9 n.; desire for, cause of Sioux' friendliness to Radisson, 120, 122.

Assiniboine Indians, origin of name, 10 n., 85 ; Radisson learns of, from prairie tribes, 85 ; defence of the younger Groseillers by, 184 ; De la Vérendrye meets the, 218–221 ; ac-

company De la Vérendrye to the Mandans, 223–227 ; Saint-Pierre's encounter with, 237.

Assiniboine River, 218, 219, 221–222.

Athabasca country, Hearne explores the, 268–269.

Athabasca Lake, Hearne's arrival at, 268–269.

Athabasca River, 277.

Athabascan tribes, Matonabbee and the, 249.

Aulneau, Father, 210, 211 ; killed by Indians, 214.

B

Baptism of Indian children by Radisson and Groseillers, 92.

Barren lands, region of "Little Sticks," 253–254, 259–260.

Bath of purification, Indian, 14, 268.

Bay of the North. *See* Hudson Bay.

Bayly, Charles, governor of Hudson's Bay Company, 140; in Canada, 140–142 ; encounter with the Jesuit Albanel, 141–142, 147 ; accusations against Radisson and Groseillers, 147–148.

Bear, Lewis's experience with a, 318.

Beauharnois, Charles de, governor of New France, 201, 203, 235.

Beaux Hommes, Crow Indians, 232.

Beckworth, prisoner among Missouri Indians, 33.

Belmont, Abbé, cited, 5 n., 98 n.

Bering, Vitus, 195.

Bigot, intendant of New France, 236.

Bird, prisoner of the Blackfeet, 33.
Bird's egg moon, the (June), 279.
Blackbird, Omaha chief, grave of, 311.
Bochart, governor of Three Rivers.
See Duplessis-Kerbodot.
Boësme, Louis, 70.
Boissons, drinking matches, 280.
Boston, Radisson and Groseillers in, 136.
Bourassa, *voyageur*, 213.
Bourdon, Jean, explorations by, 102, 134 n.
Bow Indians, the, 232–233.
Bridgar, John, governor of Hudson's Bay Company, 166, 169, 171, 173, 174, 175, 180.
Brower, J. V., cited, 88 n.
Bryce, Dr. George, 6 n., 88 n., 187 n.
Buffalo-hunts, Sioux, 92 n., 124.
Button, Sir Thomas, explorations of, 134 n.

C

Cadieux, exploit and death of, 197–198.
Cameahwait, Snake Indian chief, 324–326.
Cannibalism among Indians, 24, 77.
Cannibals of the Barren Lands, 255.
Cape Breton, discovery and fortification of, 350.
Caribou, Radisson's remarks on, 127.
Caribou herds in Barren Lands, 255; Indian method of hunting, 259.
Carr, George, letter from, to Lord Darlington, 136 n.
Carr, Sir Robert, urges Radisson to renounce France, 136.
Cartier, Jacques, 71, 193, 350–351.
Cartwright, Sir George, Radisson and Groseillers sail with, 136–137; shareholder in Hudson's Bay Company, 140.
Catlin, cited, 14 n., 226.
Cayuga Indians, the, 34, 55, 364.

Chaboneau, guide to Lewis and Clark, 312, 326, 332.
Chame, M., commissioner of Company of Normandy, 355, 357.
Champlain, governor in Canada, 351–353.
Charlevoix, mission of, 202.
Chichigoe tribe of Indians, the, 365.
Chinook Indians, Lewis and Clark friends with, 328.
Chipewyans, bath of purification practised by, 14 n.; Hearne's journey with, 257–263; massacre of Eskimo by, 263–265.
Chouart, M., letters of, 335–337. *See* Groseillers, Jean Baptiste.
Chouart, Médard. *See* Groseillers, Médard Chouart.
Chronique Trifluvienne, Sulte's, 4 n.
Clark, William, companion of Meriwether Lewis, 308–309; exploration of Yellowstone River by, 329; hero-qualities of, 332–333. *See* Lewis.
Clatsop Indians, Lewis and Clark among the, 328.
Clearwater River, Lewis and Clark on the, 327.
Coal, use of, by Indians, 89.
Colbert, Radisson pardoned and commissioned by, 148; withholds advancement from Radisson, 152; summons Radisson and Groseillers to France, 176–177; death of, 177.
Colleton, Sir Peter, shareholder in Hudson's Bay Company, 140.
Colter, frontiersman with Lewis and Clark, 332.
Columbia River, Lewis and Clark travel down the, 327.
Company of Miscou, the, 352.
Company of Normandy, the, 354–357.
Company of the North, the, 151, 154, 175, 176.

Company of One Hundred Associates, the, 133, 352, 353.
Company of Tadoussac, the, 352.
Company of the West Indies, the, 133, 153; account of formation of, 357.
Comporté, M., letter to, from M. Chouart, 335–336.
Coppermine River ("Far-Off-Metal River"), 245, 249, 252, 262, 267.
Copper mines, Radisson receives reports of, 112, 124; discovery of, by Hearne, 267.
Council Bluffs, origin of name, 311.
Council pipe, smoking the, 16, 29.
Couture, explorations of, 103, 129–130.
Couture (the younger), 143.
Cree Indians, first reports of, 69, 85; Radisson's second visit to, 112–113, 116; wintering in a settlement of, 117; a famine among, 118–119; De la Vérendrye assisted by, 206–208.
Crow Indians, De la Vérendrye's sons among, 232–233.

D

Dablon, Claude, Jesuit missionary, 103, 134 n., 142.
D'Ailleboust, M., governor of Company of Normandy, 354.
Dakota, Radisson's explorations in, 89.
D'Argenson, Viscomte, governor of New France, 99, 129–130, 356–357, 360.
D'Avaugour, governor, 104, 105, 107, 133, 143, 357, 360.
Death-song, Huron, 24, 54.
De Casson, Dollier, cited, 5 n., 96 n., 98 n.
De la Galissonnière, governor, 235.
De la Jonquière, governor, 236.
De Lanoue, fur-trade pioneer, 204.

De la Vérendrye, François, 215, 222, 229, 230, 233.
De la Vérendrye, Jean Baptiste, 197, 205, 208–209, 210, 212; murder of, by Sioux, 214.
De la Vérendrye, Louis, 215, 229.
De la Vérendrye, Pierre, 215, 222, 229, 230, 235, 315.
De la Vérendrye, Pierre Gaultier de Varennes, leaves Montreal on search for Western Sea (1731), 194–197; at Nepigon, 201; previous career, 201–203; traverses Lake Superior to Kaministiquia, 204; Fort St. Pierre named for, 206; among the Cree Indians, 206–208; return to Quebec to raise supplies, 210; loss of eldest son in Sioux massacre, 214; explores Minnesota and Manitoba to Lake Winnipeg, 215–216; at Fort Maurepas, 217; return to Montreal with furs, 218; explores valley of the Assiniboine, 219–221; visits the Mandan Indians, 224–225; takes possession for France of the Upper Missouri, 225; superseded by De Noyelles (1746), 235; decorated with Order of Cross of St. Louis, 235; death at Montreal, 236.
De Niverville, lieutenant of Saint-Pierre, 236–237.
Denonville, Marquis of, 336, 366, 367.
De Noyelles, supersession of De la Vérendrye by, 235.
De Noyon, explorations of, 204.
Dieppe, merchants of, interested in Canada trade, 352, 353.
Dionne, Dr. N. E., cited, 76 n., 88 n., 106 n., 139 n.
Dog Rib Indians, Mackenzie among, 283–284.
Dollard, fight of, against the Iroquois, 96–98, 198.

Dreuillettes, Gabriel, discoveries by, 70–71, 103, 134 n.

Drewyer, companion of Meriwether Lewis, 331.

Drugging of Indians, 63–64.

Duchesnau, M. Jacques, 149 n., 358.

Dufrost, Christopher, Sieur de la Jemmeraie, 197, 203, 205, 209, 210, 211.

Du Péron, François, 47.

Duplessis-Kerbodot, murder of, by Iroquois, 5 n., 19, 45.

Dupuis, Major, at Onondaga, 46, 55–66.

Dutch, arms supplied to Mohawk Indians by, 9 n.; war of, with the English, 137–138.

E

England, arrival of Radisson and Groseillers in, 137; effect of war between Holland and, on exploring propositions, 137–138; Hudson's Bay Company organized in, 139–140; fur-trading expeditions from, 140–149. *See* Hudson's Bay Company *and* Radisson.

Erie Indians, the, 34.

Eskimo, massacre of, by Chipewyans, 263–265.

F

"Far-Off-Metal River," the, 245, 249, 252; Hearne reaches the, 262.

Feasts, Indian, 60, 62–63, 67 n.

Festins à tout manger, 60, 67 n.

Fields, companion of Meriwether Lewis, 330–331.

Flathead Indians, assistance given Lewis and Clark by, 327, 328.

Floyd, Sergeant, of Lewis and Clark's expedition, 332.

Forked River, term applied to Mississippi and Missouri rivers, 86, 100; Radisson's account of people on the, 86–87.

Fort, Dollard's so-called, at the Long Sault, 97; Radisson and Groseillers', in the Northwest, 114–115.

Fort Bourbon (Port Royal), on Hayes River, 161–175, 182–186.

Fort Bourbon, on Saskatchewan, 229.

Fort Chipewyan, 277.

Fort Clatsop, Lewis and Clark's winter quarters, 327–328.

Fort Dauphin, 229.

Fort King Charles, 139, 146.

Fort Lajonquière, 237.

Fort Mandan, stars and stripes hoisted at, 312.

Fort Maurepas, construction, 209; description, 216–217; De la Vérendrye at, 217.

Fort Orange, Radisson and the Iroquois at, 36–38; Radisson's escape to, 39–41.

Fort Poskoyac, 229, 235.

Fort Prince of Wales, building of, 243; description, 244–245; Hearne becomes governor of, 270; surrender and destruction of, 271–272.

Fort de la Reine, construction of, 222; De la Vérendrye returns to, after visiting Mandans, 228; abandonment of, 237.

Fort Rouge, 221.

Fort St. Charles, 208–209, 210, 215.

Fort St. Louis, of Quebec, first fortification on site of, 351.

Fort St. Pierre, 206.

Fort William, 280, 283, 287.

Fraser River, Mackenzie's explorations on, 294–302.

Frog moon, the (May), 279.

Frontenac, governor of New France, 154, 358, 360, 361, 362, 367.

Fur companies of New France, 130, 133, 151, 153, 175–176, 352–358.

Fur company, Hudson's Bay. *See* Hudson's Bay Company.

Fur trade, the French, 101–102, 104; regulations governing the, 104, 153 n.; effect of, on development of West, 113.

G

Gantlet, running the, 15–16.

Gareau, Leonard, journey and death of, 70.

Garneau, cited, 5 n., 87 n.

Gillam, Ben, encounters with Radisson, 163–164, 168–175.

Gillam, Zechariah, Radisson's first transactions with, 135–136 ; Groseillers' voyage to Hudson Bay with, 138–139 ; at Rupert River with Hudson's Bay Company ship, 148 ; active enmity of, toward Radisson, 165–167, 168–169, 171, 176, 180.

Godefroy, Jean, companion of Radisson, 154.

Godefroy family, the, 154 n.

Goose month (April), 253–254.

Gorst, Thomas, 140 n., 147 n.

Grand River of the North. *See* Mackenzie River.

Gray, Captain, 308.

Great Falls of the Missouri, Lewis discovers the, 317.

Great Rat, nation of the, 131, 365.

Green Bay, western limit of French explorations until Radisson, 69 ; Radisson's winter quarters at, 79–80, 99–100.

Groseillers, nephew of explorer, title of nobility ordered granted to, 142.

Groseillers, Jean Baptiste, accompanies Radisson to Hudson Bay (1682), 154 ; trip up Hayes River, 158, 161 ; left in charge of Fort Bourbon, 175 ; troubles with Indians and with English, 182–183 ; surrenders fort to Radisson, acting for Hudson's Bay Company, 184 ;

letters to mother, 184, 335–337; carried to England by force, 186 ; offer from Hudson's Bay Company, 187.

Groseillers, Médard Chouart, birth, birthplace, and marriage, 45 ; journey to Lake Nipissing, 71 ; engages with Radisson in voyage of exploration to the West (1658), 71–79 ; winter quarters at Green Bay, 79–80 ; explorations in West and Northwest, 80–90 ; return to Quebec, 99 ; second trip to Northwest (1661), 103–129 ; imprisoned and fined on return to Quebec (1663), 130 ; goes to France to seek reparation, 133 ; meets with neglect and indifference, 133–134; deceived into returning to Three Rivers and going to Isle Percée, 135 ; goes to Port Royal, N.S., becomes involved with Boston sea-captain, and reaches England *via* Boston and Spain (1666), 135–137 ; backed by Prince Rupert, fits out ship for Hudson Bay, and spends year in trading expedition (1668–1669), 138–139 ; on return to London, created a *Knight de la Jarretière*, 139 ; second voyage from England (1670), 140 ; involved with Radisson in suspicions of double-dealing, 147–148 ; in meeting of fur traders at Quebec, 149 ; retires to family at Three Rivers, 151 ; summoned by Radisson to join expedition in private French interests to Hayes River (1681–1682), 153–158 ; successful trade in furs, 158, 167 ; jealousy and lawsuits on return to Quebec, 175–176 ; summoned to France by Colbert (1684), 176–177 ; petition for redress of wrongs ignored by French court, 179 ; gives up struggle and retires to Three Rivers, 179.

H

Hayes, Sir James, 180, 181.

Hayes River, Radisson's canoe trip up the, 158–160; Fort Bourbon established on, 161; Radisson's second visit to, 182–186.

Hayet, Marguerite, Radisson's sister, 6 n., 43; death of first husband, 19, 45; marriage with Groseillers, 45; letters from son, 184, 335–337.

Hayet, Sébastien, 6 n., 43 n.

Hearne, Samuel, cited, 14 n.; departure from Fort Prince of Wales on exploring trip, 249–252; in the Barren Lands, 253–255, 259–260; crosses the Arctic Circle, 261; discovers the Coppermine River, 262–263; massacre of Eskimo by Indians accompanying, 264–265; arrival at Arctic Ocean, 265; takes possession of Arctic regions for Hudson's Bay Company, 266–267; returns up the Coppermine River and discovers copper mines, 267; travels in Athabasca region, 268–269; returns to Fort Prince of Wales, 269; becomes governor of post, 270; surrenders fort to the French, 271–272.

Hénault, Madeline, Radisson's mother, 6 n., 43.

Hudson Bay, overland routes to, 71; Radisson's early discoveries regarding, 90–91, 127–128.

Hudson Bay, Robson's, cited, 139 n., 140 n., 147 n., 161 n., 166 n.

Hudson's Bay Company, origin of, 139–140; early expeditions, 140–149; distrust of Radisson by, 150; contract between Radisson and, 181–182; final treaty of peace made between Indians and, 185; poor treatment of Radisson by, 188;

quietly prosperous career of, 241–242; encroachments of French traders, 242–243; demand for activity, 243–244; possession taken of Arctic regions for, by Hearne, 266–267.

Huron Indians, death songs of, 24, 54; massacre of Christian, by Iroquois, 50–54; band of, with Dollard, against the Iroquois, 97–98; territory of, 359; tribes of, at Michilimackinac, 364.

Husky dogs, 277.

I

Icebergs, Labradorian, 155.

Iroquois Confederacy, the five tribes composing the, 34; characteristics of, 366.

Iroquois Indians, murder of inhabitants of Three Rivers by, 5 n., 19, 45; treatment of prisoners by, 15–16, 25–28, 54; Radisson's life with, 16–39; Frenchmen at Montreal scalped by, 48; hostages of, held at Quebec, 48, 55–56; siege of Onondaga by, 55–67; encounters between Algonquins and Radisson and, 76–78, 79–80; Radisson's fight with, on the Grand Sault, 94–96; Dollard's battle with, 97–98; Radisson's fights with, on second Western trip, 107–108, 109–111; wars between Algonquins and, 359.

Isle of Massacres, 50–54.

Issaguy tribe of Indians, 131 n.

J

Jemmeraie, Sieur de la, De la Vérendrye's lieutenant, 197, 203, 205, 209, 210; death of, 211.

Jesuit Relations, cited, 57 n., 69 n., 71 n., 73 n., 80 n., 81 n., 82 n., 91 n., 92 n., 96 n., 141 n.; quoted, 88.

Jesuits, in Onondaga expedition, 44–67; lives of Iroquois saved by, 65; start with Radisson and Groseillers on first Western expedition, 73; turn back to Montreal, 77.
Jogues, Father, 4, 56, 68, 69.
Jolliet, 84 n., 149, 151.

K

Kaministiquia, fur post at, 204.
Kickapoo Indians, location of, 364.
King Charles Fort. See Fort King Charles.
Kirke, Mary, marriage with Radisson, 138; becomes a Catholic, 152.
Kirke, Sir John, shareholder in Hudson's Bay Company, 140; claims of, against New France, 152; forbids daughter's going to France, 152; friendly influence used for Radisson, 180.
Knight de la Jarretière, Groseillers created a, 139.

L

La Barre, governor of New France, 176.
La Chesnaye, cited, 115 n., 131 n.; backs Radisson in Northern expedition, 152–153; outcome of Radisson's dealings with, 175–176.
Lake Assiniboel, 366.
"Lake of the Castors," the (Lake Nipissing), 76 n., 106 n., 364.
Lake Ontario, tribes about, 366.
Lake Superior, exploration of, by Radisson, 89; explorer's second visit to, 111–112.
Lamoignon, M. de, president of Company of Normandy, 355, 356, 357.
La Perouse, French admiral, 271.
Larivière, companion of Radisson and Groseillers, 105, 106–107.
La Salle, 84 n., 85, 149, 151, 194.

Lauzon, M. de, governor of Company of Normandy, 355–356, 368.
La Vallière, 103.
La Vérendrye. See De la Vérendrye.
Ledyard, John, 308.
Letters of Marie de l'Incarnation, cited, 46 n., 58 n., 60 n., 63 n., 81 n., 90 n., 96 n., 98 n., 139 n.
Lewis, Meriwether, starts on expedition to explore Missouri and Columbia rivers, 308–309; reaches villages of Mandan Indians, 311–313; first views the Rocky Mountains, 314–315; discovers the Great Falls of the Missouri, 317; narrowly escapes death from a bear, 318–319; enters the Gates of the Rockies, 321; reaches sources of the Missouri, 322–323; makes friends with Snake Indians, 323–327; crosses Divide to the Clearwater River and travels down the Columbia, 327; arrival on Pacific Ocean, 327; winters at Fort Clatsop (1805–1806), 327–328; return trip by main stream of the Missouri, 329; adventures with Minnetaree Indians, 329–331; arrival at St. Louis, 332; tribute to character and qualities of, 332–333.
Liberte, traitor in Lewis and Clark's expedition, 311.
Little Missouri, Lewis and Clark pass the, 313.
"Little Sticks," region of, 253–254, 259–260.
London, Radisson's first visit to, 137–138.
Long Sault, Rapids of, Dollard's battle at, 96–98, 198.
Lord Preston, English envoy in France, 177, 180, 181.
Low, A. P., quoted, 128 n., 146 n., 149 n.

M

Mackay, Alexander, Mackenzie's lieutenant, 288, 291, 292, 293, 296, 299.

Mackenzie, Sir Alexander, early career of, 276; stationed at Fort Chipewyan, 276–277; exploration of Mackenzie River by, 280–285; crosses the Arctic Circle, 285; reaches Arctic Ocean, 285–286; returns up the Mackenzie to Fort Chipewyan, 286; exploration of Peace River by, 288–294; discovers source of Peace River, 294; crosses the Divide and reaches head waters of Fraser River, 294; travels down the Fraser, 294–298; adventures with Indians, 298–300; reaches the Pacific Ocean, 302–303; return to Fort Chipewyan *via* Peace River, 304–305; later life, 306.

Mackenzie, Charles, 311.

Mackenzie, Roderick, 278, 279.

Mackenzie River, exploration of, 280–287, 296–302.

Mandan Indians, bath of purification practised by, 14 n.; Radisson discovers the, 86, 88; De la Vérendrye's visit to, 222, 225–227; the younger De la Vérendryes' second visit to, 230–231; Lewis and Clark at villages of, 311–313, 332.

Manitoba, Radisson's explorations in, 113–128.

Marquette, Père, 84 n.

Martin, Abraham, Plains of Abraham named for, 45 n.

Martin, Helen, Groseillers' first wife, 45 n.

Martinière, plan of, to capture Radisson for French, 188.

Mascoutins, "people of the fire," 80, 131 n., 364, 365; location of the, 86; Radisson among the, 100.

Matonabbee, chief of Chipewyans, 248–249; aid afforded Hearne by, 256–263; massacre of Eskimo directed by, 264–265; suicide of, 272.

Ménard, Father, 105, 112.

Messaiger, Father, 204, 205, 209.

Miami Indians, location of the, 364.

Michigan, Indian tribes in, 364.

Michilimackinac, Island of, Radisson passes, 112; early headquarters of fur trade, 201; Indian tribes at, 364.

Micmac Indians, the, 363.

Minnesota, dispute as to discovery of eastern, 71 n.; Radisson's explorations in, 89; Radisson may have wintered in, on second trip, 113.

Minnetaree Indians, Lewis and the, 329–331.

Mississippi, Radisson discovers the Upper, 80–81.

Mississippi Valley, Radisson first to explore the, 85–89.

Missouri, tribes of the, 86; De la Vérendrye takes possession of the Upper, 225; Lewis and Clark explore the, 313–323.

Mistassini, Lake, Father Albanel at, 146.

Mistassini Indians, the, 363.

Mohawk Indians, murder of French of Three Rivers by, 5 n., 19, 45; adoption of Radisson by a family of, 17; murder of three, by Radisson and an Algonquin, 20; jealous as to French settlement among Onondagas, 47–48; siege of Onondaga by, 55–59; outwitted by Radisson at Onondaga, 59–67; location of the, 364.

Montagnais Indians, the, 363.

Montana, punishment of Indians by scouts in, 25 n.

Montmagny, M. de, governor in Canada, 353–354.

Montreal, expedition for Onondaga leaves, 47; Iroquois scalp Frenchmen at, 48; return of Onondaga party, 66; De la Vérendrye's departure from, 194–197; Indian tribes located in vicinity of, 363–364.
Munck, explorations of, 134 n.

N

"Nation of the Grand Rat," 131, 365.
Nelson River, Radisson on the, 140, 161, 164–167, 170–174, 179 n.
Nemisco River, called the Rupert, 139.
Nepigon, De la Vérendrye at, 201, 202.
New York in 1653, 41–42.
New York Colonial Documents, 9 n.
Nez Perces Indians, help given to Lewis and Clark by, 328.
Nicolet, Jean, 68, 69.
Nicolls, Colonel Richard, quoted, 136 n.
Nipissing, Lake, 76 n., 106 n., 364.
Nipissinien Indians, the, 364.
Northwest, the Great, discovery of, by Radisson, 80–85.
Northwest Fur Company, the, 279, 280, 287.
Northwest Passage, reward of £20,000 offered for discovery of, 278.
Norton, Marie, 247, 270, 271–272.
Norton, Moses, governor of Fort Prince of Wales, 244; character of, 246–247; death of, 269–270.

O

Ochagach, Indian hunter, 202.
Octbaton tribe of Indians, 131 n.
Ojibway Indians, 115, 365.
Oldmixon, John, cited, 92 n., 114 n., 130 n., 147 n.
Omaha Indians, Radisson's possible visit to, 86, 88.
Omtou tribe of Indians, 131 n.
Oneida Indians, the, 34, 364.

Onondaga, settlement at, 46; Iroquois conspiracy against, 46–48; garrison besieged at, 55–63; escape of French from, 64–67.
Onondaga tribe, the, 34; Jesuit mission among (1656), 46–47; treacherous conduct of, toward Christian Hurons, 50–54.
Orange. *See* Albany.
Orimha, Radisson's Mohawk name, 16.
Oudiette, Jean, 154 n.
"Ouinipeg," Lake, 69, 71.
Outanlouby Indians, the, 364.

P

Pacific Ocean, Mackenzie's expedition reaches the, 302–303; Lewis and Clark's expedition reaches, 327.
Papinachois Indians, the, 363.
Parkman, Francis, cited, 5 n., 19 n., 46 n., 87 n., 96 n.
Pays d'en Haut, "Up-Country," defined, 201 n.
Peace River, the, 281; exploration of, 287; Mackenzie reaches the source of the, 294.
Pemmican, defined, 223.
"People of the Fire," the, Mascoutin Indians, 80 n., 86 n., 100, 131 n.
Pictured Rocks of Lake Superior, the, 112.
Piescaret, Algonquin chief, 4.
Pipe of peace, smoking the, 121–123.
Plains of Abraham, named for Abraham Martin, 45 n.
Poinsy, M. de, commander at St. Christopher, 353.
Poissons Blancs (White Fish) Indians, the, 363.
Poncet, Père, 41.
Port Nelson, 140, 161–175, 182–186.
Port Royal, Nova Scotia, Radisson and Groseillers at, 135.
Prince Maximilian, 226.

Prince Rupert, patron of French explorers, 138–139, 180; first governor of Hudson's Bay Company, 140.

Prisoners, treatment of, by Iroquois, 15–16, 25–28, 54.

Prudhomme, Mr. Justice, 88 n.

Purification, bath of, Indian rite, 14, 268.

Q

Quebec, Iroquois hostages for safety of Onondaga held at, 48, 55–56; celebration at, on return of Radisson and Groseillers, 99; meeting of fur traders at (1676), 149; Indian tribes located about, 363.

R

Radisson, Pierre Esprit (the elder), 6 n., 43 n.

Radisson, Pierre Esprit, uncle of the explorer, 43 n.

Radisson, Pierre Esprit, date and place of birth, 6; genealogy of, 6 n., 43 n.; captured by Iroquois Indians, 9; adopted into Mohawk tribe, 17; escape to Fort Orange (1653), 39–41; proof of Catholicism of, 41 n.; visits Europe and returns to Three Rivers (1654), 42–44; joins expedition to Onondaga (1657), 47; besieged by Iroquois throughout winter, 55–64; saves the garrison and returns to Montreal, 65–67; goes on trapping and exploring trip to the West (1658), 73–74; reaches Lake Nipissing and Lake Huron, 78; in winter quarters at Green Bay, 79–80; crosses present state of Wisconsin and discovers Upper Mississippi, 80–85; explorations to the west and south, 86–89; in Minnesota and Manitoba, 89–91; en-

counter with Iroquois at Long Sault of the Ottawa, 94–96; at scene of Dollard's fight of a week before, 96–98; arrival at Quebec (1660), 99; sets forth on voyage of discovery toward Hudson Bay (1661), 105; traverses Lake Superior, 111–112; builds fort and winters west of present Duluth, 113–116; visits the Sioux, 123–124; reaches Lake Winnipeg, 127; returns to Quebec (1663), 129; bad treatment by French officials, 130; goes to France to gain his rights, 133–134; ill-treatment, deception by Rochelle merchant, dealings with Captain Gillam of Boston, and visit to Boston (1665), 134–136; goes to England, 137–138; marriage with Mary Kirke, 138; formation of Hudson's Bay Company (1670), 139–140; trading voyage to Port Nelson (1671), 140–141; recalled to England and poorly treated (1674–1675), 148; receives commission in French navy (1675–1676), 148; complications between wife's father and French government, 152; backed by La Chesnaye, engages in new expedition to Hudson Bay, 152–153; returns to Quebec (1681) and sails to Hayes River (1682), 153–158; troubles with English and Boston ships, 161–175; jealousy and lawsuits on return to Quebec, 175–177; unsuccessfully presses claims in France, 179–180; commissioned by Hudson's Bay Company, 181–182; sails to Hayes River and takes possession of Fort Bourbon and French furs (1684), 182–185; return to England, 186–187; annual voyages to Hudson Bay for five years, 188; distrusted on breaking out of war with France, and neglect in old age, 188–189: consideration of character and career, 189–190.

Radisson's Relation, cited, 9 n., 46 n., 63 n., 80 n., 81 n., 98 n., 99 n., 122, 127, 163 n., 179; language used in, 82; time of writing, 138.

Ragueneau, Father Paul, 46 n., 47, 48, 50, 51, 52, 53, 59 n., 63 n.

Rascal Village, Indian camp, 305.

Red River, first white men on, 219.

Rhythm as an Indian characteristic, 160 n.

Ricaree Indians, insolence of, to Lewis and Clark, 311–312.

Robson, cited, 139, 140, 147, 161, 166.

Rochelle, Radisson's visit to, in 1654, 43.

Rocky Mountains, Radisson's nearest approach to the, 89; Pierre de la Vérendrye reaches the, 233; Lewis's first view of the, 314–315; Lewis and Clark enter Gates of the, 321.

Rouen, merchants of, interested in Canada trade, 352, 353, 357.

Roy, J. Edmond, cited, 102 n.

Roy, R., translations of documents, 335.

Rupert River, the Nemisco renamed the, 139.

S

Sacajawea, squaw guide to Lewis and Clark, 312, 321, 326, 332.

St. Louis, departure of Lewis and Clark's expedition from, 308–309 ; return to, 332.

Saint-Lusson, Sieur de, 142.

Saint-Pierre, Legardeur de, 236–237.

Saskatchewan River, exploration of, 229.

Sautaux Indians, the, 89–90, 92 n., 131 n., 365.

Scalp dance, the, 12, 14.

Seneca Indians, the, 34, 55, 364.

Sioux Indians, the, 69; Radisson and the, 85, 88, 120–124 ; desire of, for firearms, 120, 122 ; location of the, 365.

Skull-crackers, Indian, defined, 25, 121.

Slave Lake, Mackenzie on, 282.

Slave Lake Indians, the, 280, 282, 290.

Smith, Donald (Lord Strathcoma), 275–276.

Snake Indians, Lewis and Clark make friends with, 323–326.

Society of One Hundred. *See* Company of One Hundred Associates.

Songs, Indian, 159, 160.

Sturgeons, Radisson's river of, 112.

Sulte, Benjamin, cited, 4, 5 n., 6 n., 7 n., 19 n., 43 n., 68 n., 76 n., 86 n., 99 n., 102 n., 139 n., 54 n.

T

Tadoussac (Quebec), Company of, 352.

Talon, intendant of New France, 7 n., 142–143, 357–358, 360, 367, 368.

Tanguay, Abbé, 5 n., 19 n. 88 n.

Tar bed, Mackenzie's discovery of a, in the Arctic, 286.

Temiscamingue Indians, the, 364.

Thousand Islands, massacre of Huron captives by Iroquois at, 53–54.

Three Forks of the Missouri, Lewis and Clark arrive at, 321.

Three Rivers, population of, 7 n.; in 1654, 44–45; De la Vérendrye born at, 201 ; Indians of, 363.

Touret, Eli Godefroy, French spy, 137.

Torture, Indian methods of, 15–16, 25–28, 54.

Travaille, defined, 224.

Tripe de roches, defined, 78.

V

Vérendrye. *See* De la Vérendrye.
Ville-Marie (Montreal), Indian tribes about, 363–364.
Voorhis, Mrs. Julia Clark, Clark letters owned by, 312 n.

W

Wampum, significance to Indians, 17.
War-cry, Indian, sounds representing the, 11 n.
Waste, viewed by Indians as crime, 60.
West Indies Company. *See* Company of the West Indies.
Windsor, member of Lewis and Clark's expedition, 315–316.

Winnipeg, Lake, first reports of, 69, 71; Radisson arrives at, 127; rumours of a tide on, 216; De la Vérendrye on, 216–218.
Wisconsin, Radisson's travels in, 80–81, 89.
Wolf Indians located at Three Rivers, 363.
Wyandotte Indians, the, 364.

Y

Yellowstone River, exploration of, by Lewis and Clark, 313, 329.
York (Port Nelson), 140, 161–175, 182–186.
Young, Sir William, champions Radisson's cause, 180, 181, 188.